'[G]overnments and regulators often appear to me to forget that the volume and complexity of laws and regulations, or the level of tax, should not be such as to deter commercial activity and stifle entrepreneurism. … As the authors of this book show, Hong Kong is not in danger of falling into this particular trap: the Region is unusual in the extent to which it leaves people in the financial and commercial worlds free to carry on their businesses as they see fit without extensive legislative or regulatory interference or excessive taxation.'

The Right Honourable the Lord Neuberger of Abbotsbury
Hong Kong Court of Final Appeal

'[T]he present volume makes an original and unique contribution to both the international and domestic understanding of the essence of the "Hong Kong system" that constitutes one of the "Two Systems" under "One Country, Two Systems". The authors point out that from the legal and constitutional point of view, the Hong Kong system is one of "free market constitutionalism".'

Professor Albert HY Chen
The University of Hong Kong

THE FREEST MARKET IN THE WORLD

On the 25th anniversary of the establishment of the Hong Kong Special Administrative Region of the People's Republic of China, this book presents the first monographic study of the Hong Kong Basic Law as an economic document. The Basic Law codifies what Gonzalo Villalta Puig and Eric C Ip call *free market constitutionalism*, the logic of Hong Kong's economic liberty as the freest market economy in the world.

This book, which is the outcome of several years of study with the financial support of the General Research Fund of Hong Kong's Research Grants Council, evaluates the public choice rationale of the Basic Law and its projection on the Hong Kong economy, with a focus on the policy development of economic liberty both internally and externally. In the academic tradition of James M Buchanan's constitutional political economy, the book opens with a conceptualisation of free market constitutionalism in Hong Kong. It studies the origins of this concept in the 19th-century classically liberal common law and how it developed into a Hayekian laissez-faire convention under British colonial rule, was codified into the Basic Law and is interpreted and applied by the branches of the Government of the Region. The book closes with remarks on the future of Hong Kong's free market constitutionalism in face of recent challenges as the year 2047 approaches and the 50 years of 'unchanged' capitalist system under the Basic Law pass.

This book will appeal to students, scholars and practitioners of law, economics, political science and public administration. It will especially appeal to those with an interest in Hong Kong law, international economic law or comparative constitutional law.

Gonzalo Villalta Puig holds the Chair in Public International Law at the University of Navarra. He previously held the established Chair in the Law of Economic Integration at The University of Hull, where he headed the School of Law and Politics. Until then, he was Professor of Law and Outstanding Fellow of the Faculty of Law at The Chinese University of Hong Kong, which he served as Associate Dean (Research).

Eric C Ip is Associate Professor of Law at The University of Hong Kong, where he is the Director of the Government and Laws Programme and a Fellow of the Asian Institute of International Financial Law. He earlier taught at University College London and The Chinese University of Hong Kong, where he served as Assistant Dean (Undergraduate Studies) of the Faculty of Law.

ROUTLEDGE RESEARCH IN INTERNATIONAL ECONOMIC LAW

The Legality of Economic Activities in Occupied Territories
International, EU Law and Business and Human Rights Perspectives
Antoine Duval and Eva Kassoti

International Investment Protection within Europe
The EU's Assertion of Control
Julien Berger

Trade, Migration and Law
Free Movement of Persons in the South African Development Community
Victor Amadi

The Americanization of the World Trade Order
Asif H Qureshi

Reform and Regulation of Economic Institutions in Afghanistan
Haroun Rahimi

The Freest Market in the World
The Constitutional Logic of Economic Liberty in China's Hong Kong
Gonzalo Villalta Puig and Eric C Ip

International Trade Regulation
Evolving Dynamics and Shifting Foundations
Zhiqiong June Wang and Jianfu Chen

For more information about this series, please visit https://www.routledge.com/Routledge-Research-in-International-Economic-Law/book-series/INTECONLAW

THE FREEST MARKET IN THE WORLD

The Constitutional Logic of Economic Liberty in China's Hong Kong

Gonzalo Villalta Puig and Eric C Ip

Routledge
Taylor & Francis Group
LONDON AND NEW YORK

Designed cover image: © Getty Images

First published 2023
by Routledge
4 Park Square, Milton Park, Abingdon, Oxon OX14 4RN

and by Routledge
605 Third Avenue, New York, NY 10158

Routledge is an imprint of the Taylor & Francis Group, an informa business

British Library Cataloguing-in-Publication Data
A catalogue record for this book is available from the British Library

Library of Congress Cataloging-in-Publication Data
A catalog record has been requested for this book

ISBN: 978-0-367-35707-8 (hbk)
ISBN: 978-1-032-41971-8 (pbk)
ISBN: 978-0-429-34122-9 (ebk)

DOI: 10.4324/9780429341229

Typeset in Bembo
by Taylor & Francis Books

For my daughter, Blanca.
GVP

For my wife, Giselle.
ECI

CONTENTS

ABOUT THE AUTHORS

Professor Gonzalo Villalta Puig holds the Chair in Public International Law at the University of Navarra.

Professor Villalta Puig studies the law of international and regional economic integration with a particular research interest in the constitutionalisation of free trade in the European Union, Australia and other non-unitary market jurisdictions. He previously held the established Chair in the Law of Economic Integration at The University of Hull, where he headed the School of Law and Politics. In that role, he served on the University Council and was an executive member of The Committee of Heads of United Kingdom Law Schools. Until then, he was Professor of Law and Outstanding Fellow of the Faculty of Law at The Chinese University of Hong Kong, which he served as Associate Dean (Research) and as Associate Dean (Development and External Affairs). He has held academic appointments at La Trobe University and other universities in Australia.

Professor Villalta Puig has authored over one hundred publications, mainly on matters of constitutional economics and legal issues of economic integration with a focus on the economic constitution of his two home jurisdictions, the European Union and Australia. His books include *Economic Relations between Australia and the European Union: Law and Policy* with a foreword by former Director-General of the World Trade Organization, The Rt Hon Mike Moore ONZ, and *The High Court of Australia and Section 92 of the Australian Constitution* with a foreword by then Justice of the High Court of Australia, The Hon Michael Kirby AC CMG, and *Boundaries of Commercial and Trade Law* with Prof Christian Twigg-Flesner, Chair in International Commercial Law at The University of Warwick. He has published in the World Trade Organization's *World Trade Review, Journal of World Trade, The Journal of World Investment & Trade, Legal Issues of Economic Integration, European Law Journal, European Law Review, European Foreign Affairs Review, Australian Journal of International Affairs, Australian Law Journal, Public Law Review* and in periodicals as diverse as *The International Lawyer, Journal of Corporate Law Studies, Company and Securities Law Journal, Lloyd's Maritime and Commercial Law Quarterly, Chicago Journal of International Law, Indiana Journal of Global Legal Studies, The George Washington International Law Review, Chinese Journal of International Law, Hong Kong Law Journal, Arab Law Quarterly, Australian Quarterly, Law Society Journal*, the Parliament of Australia's *Papers on Parliament* and the Parliament of Spain's *Revista de las Cortes Generales, Anuario Español de Derecho Internacional*, the American Bar Association's *Public Contract Law Journal* and *Law in Context*. He has written with The Hon Chief Justice Susan Kiefel AC of the High Court of Australia for the *Global Journal of Comparative Law*. His research work has won awards for excellence and high impact; the High Court of Australia and other courts and institutions have cited it.

Professor Villalta Puig has presented papers at national and international conferences and congresses, including the World Congress of the International Association of Constitutional Law, the Global Conference of the Society of International Economic Law, the Annual Conference of The International Society of Public Law, the Conference of the University Association for Contemporary European Studies, the Conference of The Society of Legal Scholars and the Conference of The Australasian Law Teachers Association. He has also presented seminars and workshops, such as at the Europa Institute (Leiden University), the Menzies Australia Institute (King's College London) or the Government of Spain's Centre for Political and Constitutional Studies. He has spoken at the Department of Justice (International Law Division) – The Government of the Hong Kong Special Administrative Region of the People's Republic of China, the inaugural European Union – Australia Senior Leaders' Forum, the Kiel Institute for the World Economy's Global Economic Symposium and other notable fora. He has served as advisor to the European Commission's Directorate-General for Trade and the National Assembly for Wales. He has visited, among others, Utrecht University, Bocconi University, The University of Auckland, Waseda University, Foreign Trade University and had a residence as Visiting Fellow at the Australian National University's Centre for European Studies. He teaches for The University of Lincoln. He has appeared in Australian Broadcasting Corporation and Radio Television Hong Kong productions and written for the *South China Morning Post* (Hong Kong), *China Daily* (Hong Kong), *The Age* (Melbourne), *Okaz* (Riyadh) and Spain's oldest newspaper of record *ABC* (Madrid).

Professor Villalta Puig is an Overseas Fellow of the Australian Academy of Law, a Fellow of the European Law Institute and an Associate Member of the International Academy of Comparative Law. He chairs the International Association of Constitutional Law's Research Group for Constitutional Studies of Free Trade and Political Economy and has been a member of several International Law Association committees and study groups, including the Committee on the Procedure of International Courts and Tribunals, the Committee on International Trade Law and the Study Group on Preferential Trade Agreements. He has served on the Full Council of the International Law Association. He served on the Members Consultative Committee for The American Law Institute and European Law Institute joint project on Principles for a

Data Economy: Data Transactions and Data Rights as well as for the European Law Institute project on Freedom of Expression as a Common Constitutional Tradition in Europe. He serves on the Members Consultative Committee for the European Law Institute project on Fundamental Constitutional Principles. He has an affiliation with the Club of Rome, Spanish Chapter. He is Associate Editor of the *Global Journal of Comparative Law* (Brill Nijhoff). He has served as a peer reviewer for The Higher Education Academy, the British Academy, Austrian Science Fund, Research Foundation – Flanders, Luxembourg National Research Fund, the Government of Portugal's Foundation for Science and Technology and the Government of South Africa's National Research Foundation and as external examiner and assessor for numerous universities around the world, including the University of Melbourne, Monash University, University of Macau, The University of Exeter and the Solicitors Regulation Authority, the independent regulatory body of The Law Society of England and Wales. He is a Senior Fellow of The Higher Education Academy. He holds a Graduate Certificate in Higher Education and has written on pedagogical research for such periodicals as *The Law Teacher: The International Journal of Legal Education* and the *Journal of Commonwealth Law and Legal Education*.

Formerly a Justice of the Peace of the Australian Capital Territory, Professor Villalta Puig is enrolled as a Barrister and Solicitor of the High Court of Australia, a Barrister and Solicitor of the High Court of New Zealand and a Solicitor of the Senior Courts of England and Wales. He practised law with Clayton Utz, a leading Australian law firm. He was a Scholar of the International Bar Association.

Professor Villalta Puig is a Doctor of Juridical Science and read law at the Australian National University.

Dr Eric C Ip is Associate Professor of Law, Director of the Government and Laws Programme, Deputy Director of the Centre for Medical Ethics and Law and Fellow of the Asian Institute of International Financial Law at The University of Hong Kong.

Dr Ip is an expert in comparative public law. His award-winning research on comparative administrative and constitutional law has been published in peer-reviewed periodicals such as *The American Journal of Comparative Law, Oxford Journal of Legal Studies, International & Comparative Law Quarterly* and *International Journal of Constitutional Law*. He is the prize-winning author of *Hybrid Constitutionalism: The Politics of Constitutional Review in the Chinese Special Administrative Regions* (Cambridge University Press 2019), *Judging Regulators: The Political Economy of Anglo-American Administrative Law* (Edward Elgar 2020) and *Behavioral Public Choice Economics and the Law* (Springer, 2022), and a co-editor of *The Oxford Handbook of Comparative Administrative Law* (Oxford University Press 2021) from the prestigious Oxford Handbook series.

Dr Ip is additionally a specialist in public health law and ethics. His work has appeared in *The Lancet Public Health, The Lancet Planetary Health, American Journal of Public Health, Medical Law Review, Journal of Law and the Biosciences, Health Economics, Policy and Law* and *Public Health Ethics*. He is pioneering a new paradigm of planetary health law, which helps to develop a more coherent legal regime that addresses, among other things, the implications of the climate crisis on health and human rights. He teaches global health law for the Li Ka Shing Faculty of Medicine at The University of Hong Kong.

Prior to joining The University of Hong Kong, he taught at University College London and The Chinese University of Hong Kong, where he served as Assistant Dean (Undergraduate Studies) of the Faculty of Law. He was the founding convenor of the constitutional law examination of the Hong Kong Overseas Lawyers Qualification Examination. He served as a member of the Constitutional and Human Rights Committee of the Law Society of Hong Kong.

Dr Ip earned his DPhil degree from the Faculty of Law, University of Oxford. He also holds an advanced degree from the Faculty of Medicine and Health at The University of Sydney, specialising in bioethics.

FOREWORDS

THE RIGHT HONOURABLE THE LORD NEUBERGER OF ABBOTSBURY

Non-Permanent Judge of the Hong Kong Court of Final Appeal

Former President of The Supreme Court of the United Kingdom

As a Non-Permanent Overseas Judge of the Hong Kong Court of Final Appeal, I can speak with some authority and experience about the rule of law in Hong Kong, and I can also speak as a visitor, worker and consumer about social and economic life in Hong Kong. And, as a practising lawyer for over 20 years and as a judge in various jurisdictions across the world for over 25 years, I can say how vital an enlightened commercial legal system and a competent, effective, independent and trusted legal profession and judiciary are to a successful and thriving economy. (Other aspects of law also play a part but, as a serving Hong Kong judge, it is not appropriate for me to discuss laws that I may have to consider judicially.)

Without a legal system staffed by competent, independent, reliable lawyers and courts presided over by independent, competent, reliable judges whose orders are enforced, there will be no rule of law. People will not be able to know of their rights and obligations and they will not be able to enforce their rights or defend claims against them. The strong and the dishonest will prevail against the vulnerable and the honourable. Society will be unjust and unhappy and any faith in government will dissipate. Even more directly to the point, people will be reluctant to commit money and effort into building premises and businesses, making other investments, employing people and committing themselves to contracts.

But, in order to have a thriving economy, it is not enough to have the rule of law. Without a significant degree of freedom of contract, and some respect for market forces, investment and commerce will be disheartened and will shrivel. Of course, particularly in today's complex and global world, it is necessary to have rules and regulations to curb anti-competitive and other unfair activities such as monopolistic price fixing and, even more, dishonest activities, such as issuing false prospectuses. And a sensible level of taxation and some consumer protection are both requisite. But governments and regulators often appear to me to forget that the volume and complexity of laws and regulations, or the level of tax, should not be such as to deter commercial activity and stifle entrepreneurism. Legislation, regulation and taxation can have downsides as well as upsides and sometimes the undoubted benefits of some laws, rules and taxes may be outweighed by the disadvantages they also bring.

As the authors of this book show, Hong Kong is not in danger of falling into this particular trap: the Region is unusual in the extent to which it leaves people in the financial and commercial worlds free to carry on their businesses as they see fit without extensive legislative or regulatory interference or excessive taxation. This is one of the major factors that explains the remarkable success and international reputation of Hong Kong as a financial and commercial centre: it is a place in which the rule of law is respected and upheld and where legislators and regulators seek to ensure that regulation and taxation are kept to a reasonable minimum.

David Neuberger
13 June 2022

PROFESSOR ALBERT HY CHEN

Cheng Chan Lan Yue Professor of Constitutional Law at The University of Hong Kong

Member of the Committee for the Basic Law of the Hong Kong Special Administrative Region under the Standing Committee of the National People's Congress of the People's Republic of China

Hong Kong caught the world's attention during the 'Occupy Central' movement (also known as the 'Umbrella Movement') of fall 2014 and again during the massive demonstrations against a proposed extradition law that evolved into months of riots in the second half of 2019. In order to restore law and order and political stability in its Hong Kong Special Administrative Region (HKSAR), the Chinese government enacted a national security law for Hong Kong in 2020 and introduced political reforms in the city in 2021. The reaction of Western governments to the measures by the People's Republic of China (PRC) has generally been negative. In particular, the United States (US) government imposed economic sanctions on Hong Kong and on senior PRC and Hong Kong officials.

Nevertheless, the society and economy of Hong Kong have proved to be resilient even after the turmoil of 2019 and in spite of the onslaught of COVID-19 in 2020. Hong Kong today remains the world's third largest financial centre, its third most popular destination for foreign direct investment, its sixth largest merchandise trading centre, its seventh largest stock market, its busiest air cargo hub, its fourth largest ship registry and, what is more, its largest offshore renminbi (RMB) hub. In 2021, the number of overseas and mainland Chinese companies that have business operations in Hong Kong rose to a record high of 9,000. The HKSAR, using the name 'Hong Kong, China', has signed more than 600 bilateral agreements with foreign countries on matters of trade and investment and in other domains. Since Britain returned Hong Kong to China and the HKSAR was established in 1997, Hong Kong's gross domestic product (GDP) has risen from US$176 billion to 368 billion in 2021, with an average annual growth rate of 3.1 per cent. Hong Kong's per capita GDP has increased from US$27,300 in 1997 to 46,300 in 2020, representing a 70 per cent increase.

These facts suggest that the 'mainstream' view of Hong Kong held by Western governments and media since 2019 is one-sided and unfair. In spite of some political turmoil generated by the aspirations of some of the Hong Kong population for Western-style democracy based on universal suffrage and multiparty competition, the project of 'One Country, Two Systems' has not been without its achievements and is actually alive and well. As originally conceived in the early 1980s, the 'Two Systems' refer to the 'socialist system' in mainland China and the 'capitalist system' in Hong Kong. It was never intended that the 'Two Systems' would mean the 'socialist system' in mainland China and a 'Western-style democracy' in the HKSAR.

In my view, the present volume makes an original and unique contribution to both the international and domestic understanding of the essence of the 'Hong Kong system' that constitutes one of the 'Two Systems' under 'One Country, Two Systems'. The authors point out that from the legal and constitutional point of view, the Hong Kong system is one of 'free market constitutionalism'. This is a concept developed by the authors, drawing on economic thought, classical liberalism, public choice theory and constitutional political economy or constitutional economics, as developed by a lineage of great thinkers from Adam Smith to Friedrich Hayek, Milton Friedman and James Buchanan.

In the authors' opinion, constitutionalism constrains 'government action to certain areas' and restricts 'the means government can employ in the production of public goods'. Free market constitutionalism is a concept developed by merging this idea of constitutionalism with that of the free market – including free markets for labour, land and capital – as the main mechanism for the coordination of economic activities.

In this system, the government has obligations such as the maintenance of law and order, protection of private property rights, enforcement of contracts, promotion of fair competition, provision of essential public goods and 'minimal welfare for dignity in life', etc. But the government should refrain from 'too close a management of' citizens' lives and their economic activities and from over-proactive interventions in the market.

Free market constitutionalism promotes economic liberty, which the authors define as a joint freedom of ownership of private property and freedom of contract. 'Economic liberty facilitates individual happiness in the common good', which means 'the full development of human personality' and 'integral and sustainable fulfilment for both the individual and the community'.

In this volume, the authors point out that the origins of free market constitutionalism in Hong Kong can be traced back to its colonial era, when Hong Kong was a free port and allowed a free flow of capital in the absence of foreign exchange controls. There was a relatively small state, a relatively limited government, practising an economic policy of 'positive non-intervention'. At the same time, the common law system provided for the rule of law, judicial independence, protection of property rights and effective enforcement of contracts. The authors explain that it was this tradition or convention of free market constitutionalism that was codified when the Basic Law of the HKSAR was drafted by the PRC in the late 1980s. Thus the Basic Law contains important principles of constitutional economics such as fiscal transparency, a balanced budget instead of deficit spending, a low tax rate and the maintenance of Hong Kong as a free port with a free trade policy and an international financial centre with a free flow of capital.

These provisions were implemented after the Basic Law came into effect in Hong Kong in 1997. As pointed out by the authors, post-handover Hong Kong has consistently been assessed as the freest economy in the world; it is also one of the world's most competitive cities for international business. The HKSAR is

China's window to the world and Asia's most global city. It also has a strong reputation for its rule of law, judicial independence and absence of corruption.

In this volume, the authors have considered the post-1997 practice of free market constitutionalism in Hong Kong at both the constitutional and the sub-constitutional levels. The relevant jurisprudence developed by the Hong Kong courts, the economic philosophy of successive Chief Executives of the HKSAR government and the practice of external economic policy have all been meticulously examined in this volume. In the concluding chapter, the authors discuss the challenges that lie ahead for Hong Kong and the role that it can play in the context of China's national economic development plans and strategies.

Interestingly and insightfully, the authors identify two paradoxes of Hong Kong under 'One Country, Two Systems'. The first paradox is that with the existence of Hong Kong's free markets and their positive economic functions in connecting China with global markets, mainland China can afford to keep its economy partially closed. The second paradox is that Hong Kong's economic liberty actually works in the interest of mainland China's relatively conservative policies in maintaining its financial sustainability and its socialist political institutions. Most importantly, the authors also rightly point out that Hong Kong's future depends on the mainland's perception of its utility to China's overall economic development.

The authors' conclusion in this regard is reinforced by President Xi Jinping's important speech in Hong Kong on 1 July 2022 at the ceremony to celebrate the 25th anniversary of the establishment of the HKSAR. In this speech, Xi praised Hong Kong's economic success in the past 25 years as an international financial, transportation and trading centre with a first-class business environment, a top-ranking free and open economy and a common law-based legal system. He pointed out that the world marvels at Hong Kong's vitality as a cosmopolitan city.

As for the future, Xi declared that China's policy is to maintain Hong Kong's unique status and advantages, which are based on the fact that Hong Kong has the support of the motherland, on the one hand, and connects to the world, on the other. The central government would support the maintenance of Hong Kong's status as an international financial, transportation and trading centre, with a business environment that is free, open and well regulated and a common law-based legal system. Xi stressed that Hong Kong can make a major contribution to the construction of a modernised socialist state in China and the realisation of the project of the rejuvenation of the Chinese nation.

In his speech, Xi reiterated the central government's firm and unwavering commitment to the 'One Country, Two Systems' policy. He pointed out that the 'One Country, Two Systems' policy as implemented in Hong Kong and Macau has been well tested and validated by practice, and is in the interest of and supported by all parties concerned: 'There is no reason why such a good system should be changed. It should be maintained in the long term.'

The authors' closing statement at the end of this book is as follows: 'In the final analysis, the free market constitutionalism of the Hong Kong Special Administrative Region of the People's Republic of China stands or falls on the mainland's perception of its utility. The Region has its work cut out to reinforce just that perception. We believe that there is cause for hope.' The hope in Hong Kong's future expressed by the authors converges with Beijing's vision of Hong Kong's future. The contribution of this book is that it enables us to understand better why such hope is justified. It is justified because under the 'One Country, Two Systems' policy as codified in the Basic Law of the HKSAR, Hong Kong has practised, and will continue to practise, what the authors call 'free market constitutionalism', which well complements mainland China's socialist system and is conducive to China's development as a whole.

Albert HY Chen
4 July 2022

PREFACE

'[T]he most efficient means of organizing … activities is that of leaving … voluntary solutions full freedom to emerge', wrote James M Buchanan and Gordon Tullock in *The Calculus of Consent*,[1] the work that brought forth public choice theory and established the study of constitutional economics as a vibrant research programme in the social sciences. Anyone who has lived in or even just passed through Hong Kong, China, would notice that voluntary solutions are everywhere in what is the world's freest market economy. From the elderly toilet attendant in an overflowing shopping centre in Tsim Sha Tsui, to the middle-aged couple selling curry fishballs from a stall off Temple Street, to the young estate agent handing out brochures for the latest property development in Shatin, to the pawn shop in Sham Shui Po that has remained in the same family for generations, to the mainland-born cinema industry magnate with studios in Clearwater Bay, to the Hakka woman taking weekenders on her boat to Hap Mun Bay Beach, to the Filipina domestic helper working at a residence in The Peak, to the Mandarin-Cantonese-English-speaking Ivy League graduate Beijinger working at a magic circle law firm in Central, to the British expat investment banker with The Hongkong and Shanghai Banking Corporation … Hong Kong gives its residents a large measure of freedom to organise their talents and resources. It is a dynamic and diverse, creative and innovative, entrepreneurial and secure marketplace, where self-interested, self-directed, self-reliant and self-respecting citizens – individually and collectively – can act out their economic agency in economic liberty. Red tape is minimal, taxes are low, streets remain safe by day and by night, trains and buses run like clockwork, parks and facilities stay tidy, bridges and tunnels marvel with engineering wonder, cash reserves boast months of riches, colleges and universities

1 *The Collected Works of James M Buchanan*, Volume 3, James M Buchanan and Gordon Tullock, *The Calculus of Consent: Logical Foundations of Constitutional Democracy* (Indianapolis: Liberty Fund 1999) 58.

rank top and world-class medical care is available to all for all at little more than HK $180 (US$20).

The publication of this book coincides with the 25th anniversary of the entry into effect of the Basic Law of the Hong Kong Special Administrative Region of the People's Republic of China. We argue in this book that the world's freest market economy became what it is, in large part, due to what we call its *free market constitutionalism*, namely, Hayekian constitutional principles of economic liberty, which evolved over the course of one and a half centuries of British colonial rule and were meritoriously codified into the Hong Kong Basic Law by China's National People's Congress. The Basic Law is, therefore, a rarity in the universe of constitutional instruments, being the model expression of classical liberalism and laissez-faire economics against the tide of interventionist welfarism in the late 20th and early 21st-centuries. The economic provisions of this landmark economic document read out like a charter of market opportunities: the right to property; the freedom of choice of occupation; independent finances; fiscal prudence under a balanced budget; an independent, low tax system; maintenance of the status as an international financial centre; the free operation of financial business and markets; the free flow of capital; maintenance of the status of a free port; the policy of free trade and the free movement of goods; a separate customs territory with its own certificates of origin; access for ships to the ports; maintenance of the status as a centre of international and regional aviation; and freedom of movement.

The surest way to rise up to the challenges that have faced Hong Kong over the past few years — be it the 2019 turmoil, the coronavirus disease 2019 (COVID-19) pandemic or renewed tensions between East and West – is to foster an ever stronger commitment to the fundamental principles of the Basic Law, namely 'one country, two systems', 'Hong Kong governed by the people of Hong Kong' and 'high degree of autonomy',[2] on which economic liberty, the rule of law and judicial independence flourish. From its seat at the mouth of the Pearl River Delta – the world's factory floor – Hong Kong presents East and West with an open gateway into and out of the entire Chinese market, the world's second largest economy; and the other markets of East Asia, collectively, the world's fastest growing economic region. Prosperous and stable, Hong Kong — the Fragrant Harbour, the Pearl of the Orient, Asia's World City — this book salutes you.

The book states the law as it was on 1 July 2022, the 25th anniversary of the establishment of the Hong Kong Special Administrative Region of the People's Republic of China.

Gonzalo Villalta Puig
University of Navarra
Eric C Ip
The University of Hong Kong

2 The State Council Information Office of the People's Republic of China, *Hong Kong Democratic Progress Under the Framework of One Country, Two Systems* (Beijing: Foreign Languages Press 2021) 46.

ACKNOWLEDGMENTS

The idea for this book came up spontaneously in conversation one sunny spring afternoon in the academic rooms of the Faculty Law at The Chinese University of Hong Kong in Shatin, Hong Kong. It was 2016; we were colleagues, our rooms standing next to one another and we shared walls as we shared a commitment to the study of constitutional economics, the classical principles of economic liberty and the prosperity and stability of Hong Kong, the only common law jurisdiction of China and of East Asia more widely. Although our rooms are now a great distance apart, our commitment could not be closer to our hearts and minds. And so, our first acknowledgment must be to our friendship, without which this book would not have been possible.

We acknowledge the enthusiastic interest in our manuscript of our publisher, Routledge, which, back in 1944, first published Friedrich Hayek's *The Road to Serfdom*, and, then, in the 1970s, *Law, Legislation and Liberty*, books to which this book owes so much. We acknowledge our research assistant, Trevor Wan, for his outstandingly resourceful support. He has our praise and admiration. We acknowledge, too, the financial support of the General Research Fund of the Research Grants Council – University Grants Committee of the Hong Kong Special Administrative Region of the People's Republic of China, which allowed us to translate an idea into words.

We acknowledge, with sincere and respectful gratitude, the many colleagues whose books, articles and papers have inspired so many aspects of this work, especially Douglas Arner, Johannes Chan, Albert HY Chen, Anton Cooray, Richard Cullen, Yash Ghai, Evan Gibson, Danny Gittings, Stuart Hargreaves, Oliver Jones, Priscilla Leung Mei-fun, CL Lim, Bryan Mercurio, Malcolm Merry, Michael Ramsden, Stephen Thomson, Firew Kebede Tiba, Raymond Wacks, Simon NM Young and others too numerous to mention. Our thanks go also to The Right Honourable the Lord Neuberger of Abbotsbury, a Non-Permanent Judge of the Hong Kong Court of Final Appeal and a former President of The Supreme Court of the United Kingdom and to

Professor Albert HY Chen, Cheng Chan Lan Yue Professor of Constitutional Law at The University of Hong Kong and a member of the Committee for the Basic Law of the Hong Kong Special Administrative Region under the Standing Committee of the National People's Congress of the People's Republic of China, for their invaluable forewords. They humble us with their kindness. All errors are, of course, our own.

We acknowledge our university employers, past and present, for their encouragement: The Chinese University of Hong Kong, The University of Hong Kong, The University of Hull and the University of Navarra. And we are grateful to our families who have patiently, lovingly, accompanied us in this journey through ups and downs, births, deaths, moves and pandemics. Our book is theirs also.

> 'Liberty not only means that the individual has both the opportunity and the burden of choice; it also means that he must bear the consequences of his actions and will receive praise or blame for them. Liberty and responsibility are inseparable.'

FA Hayek, *The Constitution of Liberty: The Definitive Edition* in Ronald Hamowy (ed.), *The Collected Works of FA Hayek*, Volume XVII (Abingdon: Routledge 2011) 133.

1

THE CONCEPT OF FREE MARKET CONSTITUTIONALISM IN HONG KONG UNDER CHINESE SOVEREIGNTY

China's Hong Kong as the World's Freest Market Economy

The Hong Kong Special Administrative Region of the People's Republic of China, a world-leading international financial centre, the world's largest free port and long the world's freest market economy,[1] owes much of its success to a unique tradition of constitutional economic liberty now codified in the Hong Kong Basic Law.[2] The Region presents a definitive case study in constitutional economics,[3] which, inexplicably, has yet to receive the scholarly attention that it so deserves.

Hong Kong is an inalienable part of China that comes directly under the sovereign jurisdiction of the Central People's Government.[4] The Chinese Constitution and the

1 James Gwartney et al., *Economic Freedom of the World 2022: Annual Report* (Vancouver: Fraser Institute 2022) vi; see Kui–wai Li, *Economic Freedom: Lessons of Hong Kong* (Singapore: World Scientific 2012). See The Government of the Hong Kong Special Administrative Region of the People's Republic of China, Press Release: Hong Kong Once Again Ranked as the World's Freest Economy (8 September 2022), https://www.info.gov.hk/gia/general/202209/08/P2022090800841.htmt, accessed 9 September 2022.

2 The Basic Law of the Hong Kong Special Administrative Region of the People's Republic of China (Adopted at the Third Session of the Seventh National People's Congress on 4 April 1990; Promulgated by Order No 26 of the President of the People's Republic of China on 4 April 1990; Effective as of 1 July 1997).

3 James M Buchanan, 'Constitutional Economics' in John Eatwell, Murray Milgate and Peter Newman (eds), *The World of Economics* (London: Palgrave Macmillan 1991) 134–142, 134: '[C]onstitutional economic analysis attempts to explain the working properties of alternative sets of legal-institutional-constitutional rules that constrain the choices and activities of economic and political agents, the rules that define the framework within which the ordinary choices of economic and political agents are made.'

4 The Law of the People's Republic of China on Safeguarding National Security in the Hong Kong Special Administrative Region (Adopted at the 20th session of the Standing Committee of the 13th National People's Congress on 30 June 2020), Article 2; Decision of the National People's Congress on Establishing and Improving the Legal

DOI: 10.4324/9780429341229-1

Hong Kong Basic Law, in that order,[5] 'jointly form the constitutional basis' of the Region.[6] In accordance with the principle of 'one country, two systems',[7] 'the people of Hong Kong administer Hong Kong with a high degree of autonomy'.[8] Further to Article 31 of the Constitution, Article 11(1) of the Basic Law makes provision for the Region's systems and policies, including 'the social and economic systems, the system for safeguarding the fundamental rights and freedoms of its residents, the executive, legislative and judicial systems, and the relevant policies'. The Basic Law, in turn, expressly provides that '[t]he socialist system and policies shall not be practised';[9] that 'the previous capitalist system and way of life shall remain unchanged for 50 years';[10] and, that the Region shall 'safeguard the rights and freedoms of [its] residents',[11] especially 'the right of private ownership of property'.[12]

Consequently, for Hong Kong's High Court, between the Region and mainland China, there exist 'materially different legal systems and different economic models',[13] indeed, 'two markets, two monetary systems and two responsible

System and Enforcement Mechanisms for the Hong Kong Special Administrative Region to Safeguard National Security (Adopted at the Third Session of the Thirteenth National People's Congress on 28 May 2020).

5 State Council Information Office of the People's Republic of China, *Hong Kong Democratic Progress Under the Framework of One Country, Two Systems* (Beijing: Foreign Language Press 2021) 12.

6 Decision of the National People's Congress on Improving the Electoral System of the Hong Kong Special Administrative Region (Adopted at the Fourth Session of the Thirteenth National People's Congress on 11 March 2021), Preamble.

7 See, generally, Basic Law of the Hong Kong Special Administrative Region of the People's Republic of China, Preamble; Decision of the National People's Congress on Establishing and Improving the Legal System and Enforcement Mechanisms for the Hong Kong Special Administrative Region to Safeguard National Security (Adopted at the Third Session of the Thirteenth National People's Congress on 28 May 2020), Article 1; The Law of the People's Republic of China on Safeguarding National Security in the Hong Kong Special Administrative Region (Adopted at the 20th session of the Standing Committee of the 13th National People's Congress on 30 June 2020), Article 1; Decision of the National People's Congress On Improving the Electoral System of the Hong Kong Special Administrative Region (Adopted at the Fourth Session of the Thirteenth National People's Congress on 11 March 2021), Preamble.

8 The Law of the People's Republic of China on Safeguarding National Security in the Hong Kong Special Administrative Region (Adopted at the 20th session of the Standing Committee of the 13th National People's Congress on 30 June 2020), Article 1; Decision of the National People's Congress on Improving the Electoral System of the Hong Kong Special Administrative Region (Adopted at the Fourth Session of the Thirteenth National People's Congress on 11 March 2021), Article 1.

9 Basic Law of the Hong Kong Special Administrative Region of the People's Republic of China, Article 5.

10 Basic Law of the Hong Kong Special Administrative Region of the People's Republic of China, Article 5.

11 Basic Law of the Hong Kong Special Administrative Region of the People's Republic of China, Article 4.

12 Basic Law of the Hong Kong Special Administrative Region of the People's Republic of China, Article 6.

13 *Nuoxi Capital Ltd v Peking University Founder Group Co Ltd* [2021] HKCFI 3817, [65] (Harris J).

monetary authorities'.[14] This unusual constitutional arrangement must be understood in the light of Hong Kong's achievement as one of a handful of economies that transitioned from the Third World to the First World over the course of the Cold War, 'without exploiting petroleum or achieving independence from colonial rule'.[15] In *Kwok Cheuk Kin v Director of Lands*, the Hong Kong Court of Final Appeal succinctly summarised the 19th-century establishment of this jurisdiction, thus:

> As is well-known, the British colony of Hong Kong comprised three blocks of territory occupied at different times. The island of Hong Kong was ceded to Great Britain by the Treaty of Nanking in 1842 and the southern part of the Kowloon peninsula by the Convention of Peking in 1860. Under the Second Convention of Peking, in 1898, the Qing Government leased part of the administrative district of San On to Great Britain for 99 years with effect from 1 July 1898, and the district thereafter became known as the New Territories.[16]

Hong Kong turned out to be the last major and most economically successful British dependency in a transition quite incomparable with the constitutional development of other Asian colonies of the Crown such as India or Malaysia.[17] The establishment of the Hong Kong Special Administrative Region on 1 July 1997 was an unprecedentedly peaceful transfer of a global city from one permanent, veto-wielding member of the United Nations Security Council to another.[18] In the 1950s, the territory – still in recovery from the shocks of the Second World War – was in the midst of a migrant crisis, with a major influx of arrivals from mainland China; yet, by the 1990s, it had morphed into 'a glittering forest of skyscrapers with a gross domestic product per capita higher than that of its erstwhile colonial overlord'.[19]

Milton Friedman once cited Hong Kong as 'the best example' of all the contemporary economies that 'rely primarily on voluntary exchange through the market to organize their economic activity in which government is limited'.[20] His grandson later recounted how Friedman, on the eve of China's resumption of the exercise of sovereignty over Hong Kong, expressed his admiration for the fragrant harbour:

14 Douglas W Arner, 'Hong Kong: Evolution and Future as a Leading International Financial Centre' in Jiaxiang Hu, Matthias Vanhullebusch and Andrew Harding (eds), *Finance, Rule of Law and Development in Asia Perspectives from Singapore, Hong Kong and Mainland China* (Leiden: Brill Nijhoff 2016) 49–75, 57.

15 Peter E Hamilton, *Made in Hong Kong: Transpacific Networks and a New History of Globalization* (New York: Columbia University Press 2021) 1.

16 *Kwok Cheuk Kin v Director of Lands* (2021) 24 HKCFAR 349, [4].

17 John M Carroll, *A Concise History of Hong Kong* (Hong Kong: Hong Kong University Press 2007) 215.

18 David R Meyer, *Hong Kong: China's Global City* (New York: Routledge 2019) 414.

19 Peter E Hamilton, *Made in Hong Kong: Transpacific Networks and a New History of Globalization* (New York: Columbia University Press 2021) 1.

20 Milton Friedman and Rose Friedman, *Free to Choose: A Personal Statement* (Orlando: Harcourt 1980) 34.

> In short, from 1960 to 1996, Hong Kong's per capita income rose from about one-quarter of Britain's to more than a third larger than Britain's. It's easy to state these figures. It is more difficult to realize their significance. Compare Britain – the birthplace of the Industrial Revolution, the nineteenth-century economic superpower on whose empire the sun never set – with Hong Kong, a spit of land, overcrowded, with no resources except for a great harbor. Yet within four decades, the residents of this spit of overcrowded land had achieved a level of income one-third higher than that enjoyed by the residents of its former mother country.[21]

Beginning in 1995, Hong Kong was rated as the 'freest economy in the world' for 25 consecutive years on the Index of Economic Freedom, published annually by The Heritage Foundation. The Region lost this title to Singapore in 2020 and then only for non-economic considerations; indeed, a year later, it was removed from the Index altogether.[22] As at September 2022, however, Canada's Fraser Institute continued to rank Hong Kong as the world's freest economy.[23] At the centre of the freest economy of the world is none other than that constitutional document commonly known as the Hong Kong Basic Law, the Region's insignia of economic liberty, whose provisions ratify the fidelity of its constitutional order to the principles of the free market 'on an unprecedented scale by historical and contemporary standards'.[24] Today, *the* free port is a premier centre for all banking and finance, from hedge funds, asset management, private equity and wealth management to corporate and investment banking.[25] The Region's value to China consists not in its economic size but, rather, in its function as the country's 'most important window' onto the world through which large state-owned enterprises and private firms can raise capital, refine their corporate governance and perform manifold, essential commercial operations in fully liberalised markets.[26] In sum, Hong Kong's value to China is as 'Asia's world city', as the Region proudly calls itself.

21 Joe Quirk and Patri Friedman, *Seasteading: How Floating Nations Will Restore the Environment, Enrich the Poor, Cure the Sick, and Liberate Humanity from Politicians* (New York: Free Press 2017) 190.

22 Jamie Peck, Rachel Bok and Jun Zhang, 'Hong Kong – A Model on the Rocks?' *Territory, Politics, Governance* (2020) 2.

23 James Gwartney et al., *Economic Freedom of the World 2022: Annual Report* (Vancouver: Fraser Institute 2022) vi.

24 Miron Mushkat and Roda Mushkat, 'The Economic Dimension of Hong Kong's Basic Law: An Analytical Overview' (2009) 7(2) *New Zealand Journal of Public and International Law* 273–315, 309.

25 David R Meyer, *Hong Kong: China's Global City* (New York: Routledge 2019) 417.

26 Ho-fung Hung, 'Chinese State Capitalism in Hong Kong' Tai-lok Lui, Stephen WK Chiu and Ray Yep (eds), *Routledge Handbook of Contemporary Hong Kong* (New York: Routledge 2019) 430–447, 430.

Theory and Thought of Free Market Constitutionalism

Throughout this book, we understand economic liberty in negative terms.[27] Economic liberty is, in these terms, freedom *from* state coercive intervention in the economic lives of citizens, or, more practically, the use of their talents and resources. In its ideal expression, economic liberty translates into the institutionalisation of capitalism[28] by a largely non-interventionist[29] state economic system, a facilitation of laissez-faire in other words. For us, then, economic liberty is the ability of the individual citizen to act as an economic agent with inherent freedoms and rights[30] to work, to venture, to transact, to hold property and to use property:

1. Liberties of working (of the person as laborer): liberties to employ one's body, time, and mind in productive activities of one's choice and according to the terms one has freely consented to (such as to donate, sell, trade, and buy labor).
2. Liberties of transacting (of the person as entrepreneur): liberties to engage in economic activities, liberties to manage one's own affairs, to buy and sell goods, to save and invest, to start, run, and close a commercial enterprise such as a business or farm, and to engage in the activities of running such an enterprise: to hire workers, buy and use land, display, advertise, and sell one's products or services.
3. Liberties of owning/holding property (of the person as owner): liberties of acquisition, holding, and transfer of property (whether personal or productive), of using and developing one's property for commercial and productive purposes, to sell, trade, invest and bequest one's property.
4. Liberties of using property (of the person as consumer): liberties to buy, use, consume, destroy, or otherwise do as one pleases with one's goods, resources, and services.[31]

27 Gavin Kerr, 'Neo-Classical Liberalism, "Market Freedom," and the Right to Private Property' (2020) *Critical Review of International Social and Political Philosophy* 2–3.
28 Gavin Kerr, 'Neo-Classical Liberalism, "Market Freedom," and the Right to Private Property' (2020) *Critical Review of International Social and Political Philosophy* 2–3.
29 Legrend to Jean-Baptiste Colbert (First Minister of State in the government of Louis XIV, King of France): '*laissez-nous faire*' ('leave us alone'); George H Smith, *The System of Liberty: Themes in the History of Classical Liberalism* (Cambridge: Cambridge University Press 2013) 15.
30 Wesley Newcomb Hohfeld, 'Fundamental Legal Conceptions as Applied in Judicial Reasoning' (1917) 26(8) *The Yale Law Journal* 710–770. See John Tomasi, 'Democratic Legitimacy and Economic Liberty' (2012) 29(1) *Social Philosophy and Policy* 50–80, 53.
31 Jeppe von Platz and John Tomasi, 'Liberalism and Economic Liberty' in Steven Wall (ed.), *The Cambridge Companion to Liberalism* (Cambridge: Cambridge University Press 2015) 261–281, 264. See also Jeppe von Platz, 'Are Economic Liberties Basic Rights?' (2014) 13(1) *Politics, Philosophy & Economics* 23–44, 25–26. See, originally, James Nickel, 'Economic Liberties' in Victoria Davion and Clark Wolf (eds) *The Idea of a Political Liberalism: Essays on Rawls* (Lanham: Rowman & Littlefield Publishers 2000) 155–176, 156–157.

On our definition, economic liberty presupposes state recognition of civic rights to autonomous economic activity and to personal and productive property, both guarantors of the freedom to produce and distribute goods and services.[32] Collectively, private property rights enable individual citizens to use and manage that which they own.[33] Private property rights, more fundamentally, empower individual citizens to act as creators, making reasoned choices and laying plans accordingly. To infringe private property rights is to interfere with acts of creation and, thus, to destroy the fruits of those labours.[34] The institution of private property rights plays a pivotal role in the protection of citizens against abuses of economic power by elites, such as the deprivation of property without just compensation and due process of law.[35]

Ultimately, we define economic liberty as a joint freedom of private ownership[36] and of contract or, to put it differently, a freedom of choice[37] in both property[38] and contract.[39] We exclude from this definition the positive determinants of the opportunities and capacities as well as the innate abilities and acquired means for individual citizens to exercise economic liberty.[40] On this interpretation, we believe that the state, through and under the rule of law, ought to actuate economic liberty but not the exercise by citizens, individually and collectively, of their economic capabilities.[41]

32 Bernard H Siegan, *The Supreme Court's Constitution: An Inquiry into Judicial Review and Its Impact on Society* (New Brunswick: Transaction Publishers 1987) 41. See also John Harrison, 'The Constitution of Economic Liberty' (2008) 45(3) *San Diego Law Review* 709–728, 709.

33 Adam J MacLeod, *Property and Practical Reason* (Cambridge: Cambridge University Press 2015) 2.

34 Adam J MacLeod, *Property and Practical Reason* (Cambridge: Cambridge University Press 2015) 3.

35 Daron Acemoglu and Simon Johnson, 'Unbundling Institutions' (2005) 113(5) *Journal of Political Economy* 949–995, 955.

36 James Nickel, 'Economic Liberties' in Victoria Davion and Clark Wolf (eds), *The Idea of a Political Liberalism: Essays on Rawls* (Lanham: Rowman & Littlefield Publishers 2000) 155–176, 156–57. See also John Tomasi, 'Democratic Legitimacy and Economic Liberty' (2012) 29(1) *Social Philosophy and Policy* 50–80, 54.

37 Milton Friedman and Rose Friedman, *Free to Choose: A Personal Statement* (Orlando: Harcourt 1980) 65: 'An essential part of economic freedom is freedom to choose how to use our income: how much to spend on ourselves and on what items; how much to save and in what form; how much to give away and to whom.'

38 Anthony Honoré, 'Ownership' in AG Guest (ed.), *Oxford Essays in Jurisprudence: A Collaborative Work* (Oxford: Oxford University Press 1961) 107–147.

39 Barry R Weingast, 'Capitalism, Democracy, and Countermajoritarian Institutions' (2015) 23 *Supreme Court Economic Review* 255–278, 256–257; Randy E Barnett, 'Does the Constitution Protect Economic Liberty?' (2012) 35(1) *Harvard Journal of Law & Public Policy* 5–12, 5; James W Ely Jr, 'The Constitution and Economic Liberty' (2012) 35(1) *Harvard Journal of Law & Public Policy* 27–36, 35.

40 Jeppe von Platz and John Tomasi, 'Liberalism and Economic Liberty' in Steven Wall (ed.), *The Cambridge Companion to Liberalism* (Cambridge: Cambridge University Press 2015) 261–281, 275.

41 Jeppe von Platz and John Tomasi, 'Liberalism and Economic Liberty' in Steven Wall (ed.), *The Cambridge Companion to Liberalism* (Cambridge: Cambridge University Press 2015) 261–281, 276.

Our belief is a verbalisation of classical liberal, specifically Anglo-British, economic thought and the idea of spontaneous order of John Locke, Bernard Mandeville, David Hume, Josiah Tucker, Adam Smith, Adam Ferguson, David Ricardo, Richard Cobden, John Stuart Mill, John Bright, Herbert Spencer, and Friedrich Hayek. We believe that the spontaneous and voluntary interaction of economic agents – self-interested, self-directed, self-reliant and self-respecting[42] – minimises waste, maximises production, effects the optimal, efficient distribution of resources, promotes creative innovation[43] and facilitates sociopolitical interdependence.[44] Our concept of 'the market' adheres to that of Hayek:

> The market is the only known method of providing information enabling individuals to judge comparative advantages of different uses of resources of which they have immediate knowledge and through whose use, whether they so intend or not, they serve the needs of distant unknown individuals. This dispersed knowledge is essentially dispersed, and cannot possibly be gathered together and conveyed to an authority charged with the task of deliberately creating order.[45]

We further believe that free economic agency in the market leads to prosperity,[46] and, through prosperity, to social peace – stable, secure, resilient[47] – because it not only enables 'good people to do good',[48] but also incentivises the bad to do the same. We recall Smith's famous edict:

> It is not from the benevolence of the butcher, the brewer, or the baker, that we expect our dinner, but from their regard to their own interest. We address ourselves, not to their humanity but to their self-love, and never talk to them of our own necessities but of their advantages.[49]

42 Charles Murray, *In Our Hands: A Plan to Replace the Welfare State* (Washington DC: The AEI Press 2006) 89. See John Tomasi, 'Democratic Legitimacy and Economic Liberty' (2012) 29(1) *Social Philosophy and Policy* 50–80, 70–71.
43 See Benjamin Chen and Robert Cooter, 'The New Economic Freedom' (2015) 23 *Supreme Court Economic Review* 59–76.
44 Jeppe von Platz and John Tomasi, 'Liberalism and Economic Liberty' in Steven Wall (ed.), *The Cambridge Companion to Liberalism* (Cambridge: Cambridge University Press 2015) 261–281, 269. See Eamonn Butler, *Classical Liberalism: A Primer* (London: The Institute of Economic Affairs 2015).
45 FA Hayek, *The Fatal Conceit* (London: Routledge 1988) 77.
46 Cephas Naanwaab, 'Does Economic Freedom Promote Human Development? New Evidence from a Cross–National Study' (2018) 52(3) *The Journal of Developing Areas* 183–198, 196.
47 Jeppe von Platz and John Tomasi, 'Liberalism and Economic Liberty' in Steven Wall (ed.), *The Cambridge Companion to Liberalism* (Cambridge: Cambridge University Press 2015) 261–281, 269.
48 Milton Friedman and Rose Friedman, *Free to Choose: A Personal Statement* (Orlando: Harcourt 1980) 4.
49 Adam Smith, *The Wealth of Nations* (Chichester: Capstone Publishing 2010) 27.

And we recall too Hayek's words:

> It is a social system which does not depend for its functioning on our finding good men for running it, or on all men becoming better than they now are, but which makes use of men in all their given variety and complexity, sometimes good and sometimes bad, sometimes intelligent and more often stupid.[50]

Economic liberty facilitates individual happiness in the common good (*bonum commune*) – a central and integrative principle of social ethics – which we, in turn, define to be the full development of human personality, that is, integral and sustainable fulfilment for both the individual and the community. True to the Aristotelian-Thomistic[51] ethical tradition, we believe that the ends of human existence are self-evident, hence the states and activities[52] behind them – for legal philosopher John Finnis, the 'basic forms of human good'[53] – call for the ever more perfect realisation of all that is virtuous – morally and intellectually, physically and spiritually – about the human person, and not merely the satisfaction of the passions.

For us as for Nobel Memorial Prize laureates in Economic Sciences Hayek and Friedman,[54] liberty is neither an absolute[55] nor a presumption, something that takes care of itself.[56] It is neither as thick as it is for libertarians nor as thin as it is for high liberals,[57]

50 FA Hayek, *Individualism and Economic Order* (Chicago: University of Chicago Press 1948) 12.

51 Thomas Aquinas, *Summa Theologica*; see Timothy McDermott, *Thomas Aquinas: Selected Philosophical Writings* (Oxford: Oxford University Press 1993); Aristotle, *The Politics* (London: Penguin 2000). See also Alasdair MacIntyre, *After Virtue: A Study in Moral Theory* (London: Bloomsbury Academic 2007).

52 John Finnis, *Natural Law and Natural Rights* (2nd edn.) (Oxford: Oxford University Press 2011) 85–90; John Finnis, *Fundamentals of Ethics* (Oxford: Clarendon Press 1983) 44.

53 John Finnis, *Natural Law and Natural Rights* (2nd edn.) (Oxford: Oxford University Press 2011). For Finnis, the basic values include life, knowledge, play, aesthetic experience, sociability (friendship), practical reasonableness and 'religion'.

54 FA Hayek, *The Constitution of Liberty: The Definitive Edition* (Chicago: The University of Chicago Press 2011); Milton Friedman, *Capitalism and Freedom* (Chicago: The University of Chicago Press 2020). See also David Hume, *Essays, Moral, Political, and Literary* in Tom L Beauchamp and Mark A Box (eds), *The Clarendon Edition of the Works of David Hume* (Oxford: Oxford University Press 2021); Adam Smith, *The Wealth of Nations* (Chichester: Capstone Publishing 2010) 27.

55 Milton Friedman and Rose Friedman, *Free to Choose: A Personal Statement* (Orlando: Harcourt 1980) 69: 'Freedom cannot be absolute. We do live in an interdependent society.' See Jeppe von Platz and John Tomasi, 'Liberalism and Economic Liberty' in Steven Wall (ed.), *The Cambridge Companion to Liberalism* (Cambridge: Cambridge University Press 2015) 261–281, 263.

56 Jeppe von Platz and John Tomasi, 'Liberalism and Economic Liberty' in Steven Wall (ed.), *The Cambridge Companion to Liberalism* (Cambridge: Cambridge University Press 2015) 261–281, 262.

57 Jeppe von Platz and John Tomasi, 'Liberalism and Economic Liberty' in Steven Wall (ed.), *The Cambridge Companion to Liberalism* (Cambridge: Cambridge University Press 2015) 261–281, 278.

but a moderate[58] yet an adequate[59] expression of free will to pursue the economic conditions for the moral life and, thereby, the pursuit of the commonweal that is civilisation. Economic liberty is, thus, a means to an end,[60] the sum of those conditions of social life like peace, justice, abundance, health and safety[61] that allow individuals and communities thorough and ready access to their own fulfilment.[62] Understood in this light, private property rights, so important to human dignity and development, are amenable to regulation by public authority in the interests of the commonwealth:[63] the state has a legitimate function in the administration of distributive justice schemes for fairness sake so far as they do not systematically revoke economic liberty. We believe, then, that the good of the political community legitimates regulation of economic activity to correct monopolies[64] and other market failures and frauds. And that it also legitimates taxation[65] not to finance income transfers but to finance cash grants[66] as well as to finance the compassionate provision of essential public goods[67] – education, health, housing[68] – to buttress basic human dignity, especially that of those who are, involuntarily, not able to act out their own economic agency.

58 Jeppe von Platz and John Tomasi, 'Liberalism and Economic Liberty' in Steven Wall (ed.), *The Cambridge Companion to Liberalism* (Cambridge: Cambridge University Press 2015) 261–281, 278.

59 Jeppe von Platz and John Tomasi, 'Liberalism and Economic Liberty' in Steven Wall (ed.), *The Cambridge Companion to Liberalism* (Cambridge: Cambridge University Press 2015) 261–281, 273.

60 Jeppe von Platz and John Tomasi, 'Liberalism and Economic Liberty' in Steven Wall (ed.), *The Cambridge Companion to Liberalism* (Cambridge: Cambridge University Press 2015) 261–281, 266–267.

61 Adrian Vermeule, *Common Good Constitutionalism* (Cambridge: Polity Press 2022) 7.

62 Richard A Epstein, *Principles for a Free Society: Reconciling Individual Liberty with the Common Good* (Cambridge: Perseus Publishing 1998) 4; John Finnis, *Human Rights and Common Good* (Oxford: Oxford University Press 2011) 89.

63 Adrian Vermeule, *Common Good Constitutionalism* (Cambridge: Polity Press 2022) 125.

64 FA Hayek, *The Constitution of Liberty: The Definitive Edition* (Chicago: The University of Chicago Press 2011) 264–66; Milton Friedman and Rose Friedman, *Free to Choose: A Personal Statement* (Orlando: Harcourt 1980) 27–30, 132–33; Jeppe von Platz and John Tomasi, 'Liberalism and Economic Liberty' in Steven Wall (ed.), *The Cambridge Companion to Liberalism* (Cambridge: Cambridge University Press 2015) 261–281, 270.

65 Daniel M Layman, 'The Fair Value of Economic Liberty' (2015) 21(4) *Res Publica* 413–428, 414.

66 Charles Murray, *In Our Hands: A Plan to Replace the Welfare State* (Washington DC: The AEI Press 2006).

67 Adam Smith, *Wealth of Nations* (Ware: Wordsworth Editions 2012) Book IV Chapter IX; Jeppe von Platz and John Tomasi, 'Liberalism and Economic Liberty' in Steven Wall (ed.), *The Cambridge Companion to Liberalism* (Cambridge: Cambridge University Press 2015) 261–281, 270.

68 FA Hayek, *The Constitution of Liberty: The Definitive Edition* (Chicago: The University of Chicago Press 2011) chapters 19, 24; Milton Friedman, *Capitalism and Freedom* (Chicago: The University of Chicago Press 2020) chapters 6, 11, 12. See further Jeppe von Platz and John Tomasi, 'Liberalism and Economic Liberty' in Steven Wall (ed.), *The Cambridge Companion to Liberalism* (Cambridge: Cambridge University Press 2015) 261–281, 270.

Our analytical framework rests on the research programme of constitutional political economy, also known as constitutional economics,[69] which distinguishes constitutional public choice from sub-constitutional public choice. In the second half of the 20th-century, economists began to theorise legal institutions that protect private property rights and freedoms of exchange as prerequisite to market prosperity and stability.[70] The constitutional code stands out as the most prominent of legal institutions.[71] James M Buchanan, winner of the Nobel Memorial Prize in Economic Sciences in 1986 and a founder of constitutional economics, and whose ideas of the fiscal constitution informed the drafters of the Basic Law,[72] stressed how important constitutional rules are. 'Changing the rules is … easier than changing the character of the players', he argued.[73] It is natural, from a game theory perspective, to view constitutions as the rules of the political game and public policies as outcomes of the equilibrium strategies of political players. Constitutional rules are instruments of opportunity and constraint.[74] Like Buchanan[75] before us, we believe that, if constitutions shape public policies and some public policies are better than others, then some constitutions must be better than others.[76] And, with Hong Kong's market economy as the world's freest for many commentators, we argue that there is no better economic constitution in design than the Basic Law.

69 See Viktor J Vanberg, 'Market and State: The Perspective of Constitutional Political Economy' (2005) 1(1) *Journal of Institutional Economics* 23–49, 24: 'Constitutional political economy can best be described as the economics of rules.'
70 See Randall G Holcombe, Robert A Lawson and James D Gwartney, 'Constitutions and Prosperity: The Impact of Legal and Economic Institutions on the Wealth of Nations' in Roger D Congleton and Birgitta Swedenborg (eds), *Democratic Constitutional Design and Public Policy: Analysis and Evidence* (Cambridge: MIT Press 2006) 289–318.
71 Pablo T Spiller, 'Regulatory Commitments and Utilities' Privatization: Implications for Future Comparative Research' in JS Banks and EA Hanushek (eds), *Modern Political Economy* (Cambridge: Cambridge University Press 1995) 63, 106; Torsten Persson and Guido Tabellini, 'Constitutions and Economic Policy' in Roger D Congleton and Birgitta Swedenborg (eds), *Democratic Constitutional Design and Public Policy: Analysis and Evidence* (Cambridge: MIT Press 2006) 104; Richard H Timberlake, *Constitutional Money: A Review of the Supreme Court's Monetary Decisions* (New York: Cambridge University Press 2013) 232.
72 See Shu–hung Tang, 'Fiscal Constitution, Income Distribution and the Basic Law of Hong Kong' (1991) 20(3) *Economy and Society* 283.
73 See James M Buchanan, 'Same Players, Different Game: How Better Rules Make Better Politics' (2008) 19 *Constitutional Political Economy* 171–179.
74 Georg Vanberg and Viktor Vanberg, 'Contractarian Perspectives in Law and Economics' in Francesco Parisi (ed.), *The Oxford Handbook of Law and Economics: Volume I: Methodology and Concepts* (Oxford University Press 2017) 246–267, 250.
75 James M Buchanan, *The Economics and the Ethics of Constitutional Order* (Ann Arbor: The University of Michigan Press 1991) 5; see also Geoffrey Brennan and James M Buchanan, *The Reason of Rules: Constitutional Political Economy* (Indianapolis: Liberty Fund 2000).
76 Roger Congleton and Birgitta Swedenborg, 'Introduction: Rational Choice Politics and Political Institutions' in Roger D Congleton and Birgitta Swedenborg (eds), *Democratic Constitutional Design and Public Policy: Analysis and Evidence* (Cambridge: MIT Press 2006) 1–36, 8.

We believe that constitutional design is important. More particularly, we believe that the importance of the economic design of constitutions is even greater. A constitution potentiates the production of non-rivalrous, non-excludable public goods, such as security and defence or the transport system,[77] which are systematically subject to undersupply by private actors. Government overreach can all too easily subvert economic liberty and harm the common good. The potential power of a constitution and its rules of the political game may uniquely tempt constitutional designers to tweak institutions to their future benefit in ways that may not conduce to economic liberty.[78] Additionally, constitutional ignorance – a notion traceable back to Hayek's work – warrants serious consideration: boundedly rational framers must be careful not to imbue into the constitutional order an interventionist or reconstructionist agenda that presumes foreknowledge that they do not and cannot possess.[79] Optimal constitutional arrangements permit state officials to make credible commitments to the protection of private property rights and freedoms of exchange, which, in turn, promote the success of free capital markets.[80] Constitutional provisions that promote fiscal transparency and check deficit spending can and do, empirically and demonstrably so, restrain yet enhance the effectiveness of government expenditure.[81] Conversely, constitutions with a suboptimal design aggravate rent-seeking and corruption and may imperil economic development.[82] Moreover, constitutions reinforce the principles of due process and natural justice and delimit a personal sphere into which legislation cannot encroach.[83] Our research method takes the analytic narrative approach, which best befits problem-driven, contextualized, single-jurisdiction case studies tracing processes specific to time and place with interesting political outcomes.[84] We do not concern ourselves with quantifying relative degrees of market openness, regulatory efficiency, government size or policy outcomes.[85] Our concern is the economics of the rules-making framework,[86] in short, constitutional economics.

77 Tom Ginsburg and Aziz Z Huq, *How to Save a Constitutional Democracy* (Chicago: University of Chicago Press 2018) 22.
78 See Tom Ginsburg, 'Public Choice and Constitutional Design' in Daniel A Farber and Anne Joseph O'Connell (eds), *Research Handbook on Public Choice and Public Law* (Cheltenham: Edward Elgar 2010) 261–282.
79 Stefan Voigt, *Institutional Economics: An Introduction* (Cambridge: Cambridge University Press 2019) 233.
80 Douglass C North and Barry R Weingast, 'Constitutions and Commitment: The Evolution of Institutions Governing Public Choice in Seventeenth-Century England' (1989) 49(4) *The Journal of Economic History* 803–832, 803.
81 Lorenz Blume and Stefan Voigt, 'The Economic Effects of Constitutional Budget Institutions' (2013) 29 *European Journal of Political Economy* 236–251, 245.
82 Tom Ginsburg and Aziz Z Huq, *How to Save a Constitutional Democracy* (Chicago: University of Chicago Press 2018) 21.
83 Eamonn Butler, *Classical Liberalism: A Primer* (London: The Institute of Economic Affairs 2015) 67.
84 See Robert H Bates et al., 'The Analytical Narrative Project' (2000) 94(3) *American Political Science Review* 696–702.
85 Terry Miller et al., *2021 Index of Economic Freedom* (Washington DC: The Heritage Foundation 2021) 13: 'The 12 aspects of economic freedom measured in the *Index* are grouped into four broad categories: – Rule of law (property rights, judicial effectiveness, and

We understand the free market economy as one in which the organisation of production, exchange and the operation of the price mechanism are the work of competitive markets – the factor markets of labour, land and capital – secure in the freedom of entry and movement, with the state in its legitimate economic roles as enforcer of contracts and protector of property.[87] Moreover, we understand constitutionalism as being about 'constraining government action to certain areas and restricting the means government can employ in the production of public goods'.[88] We merge these two concepts to form a new concept, which we call *free market constitutionalism*. We explain free market constitutionalism to entail, at the constitutional public choice stage, the establishment of a constitutional framework within which the state has fundamental obligations, which we identify to be the conservation of law and order, the protection of private property, the enforcement of contractual agreements, the promotion of fair competition, the integrity of money, the liberalisation of trade and the provision of minimal welfare for dignity in life, all we believe to be fundamental constitutional values for the preservation and promotion of economic liberty. Within that same constitutional framework, the state has a further equally fundamental obligation, that is, to refrain, as far as possible, from all too close a management of the lives of individual citizens as economic agents and from all too a proactive intervention in the market process through macroeconomic, industrial or income redistribution policies.[89] Free market constitutionalism coheres with what Hayek called 'the basic principle of a free society', which entails that 'the coercive powers of government are restricted to the enforcement of universal rules of just conduct'.[90] As proponents of free market constitutionalism, we believe, therefore, that there ought to exist, at the sub-constitutional public choice stage, checks and balances, such as independent judicial review, that foster compliance with these constitutional obligations. Sub-constitutional actions are important in their own right and not necessarily predetermined by constitutional design.

Structure of Argument

With this chapter, which introduces the concept that we call free market constitutionalism, the book comprises seven chapters. Chapter 2, concerned with

government integrity); – Government size (tax burden, government spending, and fiscal health); – Regulatory efficiency (business freedom, labor freedom, and monetary freedom); and – Market openness (trade freedom, investment freedom, and financial freedom).'

86 Tom Ginsburg, 'Public Choice and Constitutional Design' in Daniel A Farber and Anne Joseph O'Connell (eds), *Research Handbook on Public Choice and Public Law* (Cheltenham: Edward Elgar 2010) 261–282, 263.

87 Johan Graafland and Thomas R Wells, 'In Adam Smith's Own Words: The Role of Virtues in the Relationship Between Free Market Economies and Societal Flourishing, A Semantic Network Data-Mining Approach' (2021) 172 *Journal of Business Ethics* 31–42, 34.

88 Stefan Voigt, *Constitutional Economics: A Primer* (New York: Cambridge University Press 2020) 6.

89 FA Hayek, *Law, Legislation and Liberty: A New Statement of the Principles of Justice and Political Economy* (Vol. 3). (New York: Routledge 1979) 68.

90 FA Hayek, 'A Model Constitution' in Chiaki Nishiyama and Kurt R Leube (eds), *The Essence of Hayek* (Stanford: Hoover Institution Press 1984) 382–406, 401.

constitutional public choice, argues that the economic provisions of the Basic Law, set on a 'principle of continuity',[91] have their early origins in the uncodified Victorian constitution of Hong Kong under British colonial rule. True to the common law tradition at the time, it was an expression of classical economic liberalism. Under the Victorian constitution, the state was small and heavily dependent on merchants and private organisations to govern its population of majority ethnic Chinese.[92] It had no desire to 'redeem' or regiment the lives of its residents.[93] Its economy was 'adamantly capitalist' and its Governors 'content to let market forces prevail'.[94] By the latter half of the 20th-century, successive Governors imagined themselves – through that inimitable Hong Kong aphorism, 'positive non-interventionism' – as playing a modest role in the political game;[95] assisted by a civil service whose credo was 'system-maintenance, limited government and the preservation of the bureaucracy as the only major political institution in the colony'.[96] Free market constitutionalism became an unwritten but entrenched tradition, redolent of what Hayek had to say over a century later. By the time China resumed the exercise of sovereignty over Hong Kong, the territory had developed a rule-of-law ideology providing both the rationality and predictability requisite to a free, competitive and efficient market through the enforcement of property and contract rights and the independent judicial scrutiny of a government accountable to the legislature. The practice of positive non-interventionism created a legal space for economic liberty to raise an international financial centre over an erstwhile fishing village; an economic environment, in brief, free of rent-seeking intervention, subjected only to private property rights, low taxes, balanced budgets, an absence of foreign exchange controls, the free movement of capital and goods, a free port and minimal, facilitative economic planning.

Chapter 3, equally concerned with constitutional public choice, is dedicated to the drafting process of the Basic Law under the auspices of Deng Xiaoping, then paramount leader of China. It argues that the economic element of the Basic Law was sensitive to the characteristics of Hong Kong's free market constitutionalism. At the prompt, in September 1981, of Ye Jianying, then Chairman of the Standing Committee of the National People's Congress, to establish a special administrative region with a high degree of autonomy for the Taiwan region that could accommodate its reunification with the mainland, Article 31 was incorporated into the

91 *Kwok Cheuk Kin v Director of Lands* (2021) 24 HKCFAR 349, [44].
92 David C Donald, *A Financial Centre for Two Empires: Hong Kong's Corporate, Securities and Tax Laws in its Transition from Britain to China* (Cambridge: Cambridge University Press 2014) 44.
93 David C Donald, *A Financial Centre for Two Empires: Hong Kong's Corporate, Securities and Tax Laws in its Transition from Britain to China* (Cambridge: Cambridge University Press 2014) 45.
94 Peter Wesley-Smith, *Legal Literature in Hong Kong* (Hong Kong: Centre of Asian Studies, University of Hong Kong 1979) 1.
95 Peter Harris, 'British Political Institutions in a Chinese Setting: The Case of the Crown Colony of Hong Kong' (1982) XXXV(2) *Parliamentary Affairs* 181–192, 187.
96 Siu-kai Lau, *Society and Politics in Hong Kong* (Hong Kong: The Chinese University Press 1982) 65.

Chinese Constitution to institute systems 'in the light of specific conditions'. With this provision – the 'one country, two systems' principle – China approached the resumption of the exercise of sovereignty over Hong Kong. The Basic Law gives effect, within the Region, to China's basic policies regarding Hong Kong further to the Sino-British Joint Declaration of 1984; thus, it conserves and codifies the continuity of the common law tradition and, thereby, divides Hong Kong's capitalist economic system from mainland China's mixed economic system. The Basic Law restates elements of that tradition in a code of principles and policies, which preserves personal, property and contractual rights instinct in the Victorian constitution and allows the market's invisible hand to freely allocate rents among competitive entry forces. The Drafting Committee codified, in Articles 107 and 108 of the Basic Law, a balanced budget principle and a low tax policy to avoid the economic crisis and currency depreciation consequent on deficit spending along with the rise in taxes, obtainment of foreign loans, issuances of government bonds and increase in money supply that inevitably come with it. Freedom of finance under Article 110(2) of the Basic Law, freedom of trade under Article 115 and free movement of capital under Article 112 bring up the rear.

Chapter 4 shifts our focus from constitutional public choice to sub-constitutional public choice. It outlines Hong Kong's economic constitution in the Basic Law, and its judicial interpretation and application. The Basic Law establishes a capitalist system, which it maintains apart from the officially socialist system of mainland China. The chapter then turns to the concessions that the Basic Law makes to economic coordination as a necessary moderation of the excesses of free market constitutionalism and how these have been construed by the common law courts. The unplanned spontaneity of Hong Kong's free market constitutionalism compelled the kind of discretionary toolkit that the Basic Law makes available for the sake of a proportionate public interest policy. The allowance of Basic Law provisions for economic coordination and social welfare is optimal in its restraint and only serves to enhance the economic liberty that it affords to Hong Kong. It concludes that the Basic Law gives Hong Kong's nearly bicentennial tradition of economic liberty a necessary policy safeguard. It enhances the economic liberty ideal with a triad of policy provisions – Articles 109, 118 and 119 – that allow the Government of the Region to fashion whatever legal and economic environment it deems right for Hong Kong. These provisions do not necessarily entail social welfare interventionism; instead, they allow the Region to stimulate and signpost the market's freedom as necessary. Economic freedom needs economic management, policy promotion and policy protection from time to time.

Chapter 5 remains committed to sub-constitutional public choice analysis. It studies the implementation of free market constitutionalism under the Basic Law with reference to the economic philosophies of the Region's first five Chief Executives and the economic jurisprudence of the Hong Kong courts. It argues that Hong Kong's internal economic policy remains within the broad contours of free market constitutionalism in spite of some deviation from the positive non-interventionist tradition. State intervention in the economy, especially through the implementation of industrial policies and the support of central banks, has been on the rise and the Government of the Region has, increasingly, adopted the rhetoric of proactive economic governance. Nevertheless, these interventions remain modest in comparison to those of other developed economies. Importantly, the Region has continued to abide by the Basic Law's imperatives on protection of private property rights, maintenance of low taxes and prudence in fiscal management. Moreover, Hong Kong's internationalised financial system has proved to be highly resilient having weathered the Asian financial crisis of 1997 and the global financial crisis of 2008. And the courts have consistently closed judicial review as a backdoor for the promotion of welfarism under the cover of constitutional interpretation. The economic achievements are many and undeniable, but the Region confronts the challenges that come with rising income inequality and real estate prices and that have, in recent years, precipitated a measure of social polarisation.

Chapter 6 extends our sub-constitutional public choice analysis to demonstrate that Hong Kong's external economic policy, further to the Basic Law, seeks to preserve and promote the free market. The Basic Law confers external economic personality and capacity on Hong Kong as a 'separate customs territory',[97] under Article 116, to pursue 'the policy of free trade',[98] under Article 115. The Region is the world's largest free port, a member of the World Trade Organization (WTO) since its establishment and a signatory to trade agreements and arrangements with many customs territories. These instruments and instrumentalities of trade have given Hong Kong's free market constitutionalism a global reach. The Region's external economic policy thus revolves around membership of the WTO[99] – with the twin objectives to support the multilateral trading system[100] and to make it freer and more open[101] – and a dynamic free trade agreement portfolio with a consistent concern for the liberalisation of trade in services. The free trade qualities of the Basic Law enable ever closer economic integration between Hong Kong and the rest of China through the Closer Economic Partnership Arrangement and participation in such economic development strategies as the Guangdong-Hong Kong-Macao Greater Bay Area plan and the Belt and Road Initiative.

97 Matthew Kennedy, 'Overseas Territories in the WTO' (2016) 65(3) *International and Comparative Law Quarterly* 741–762.

98 Zeng Huaqun, 'Unprecedented International Status: Theoretical and Practical Aspects of the HKSAR's External Autonomy' (2008) 9(3) *Journal of World Investment & Trade* 275–298; Roda Mushkat, 'Hong Kong's Exercise of External Autonomy: A Multi–Faceted Appraisal' (2006) 55(4) *International and Comparative Law Quarterly* 945–962; Eric C Ip, 'Comparative Subnational Foreign Relations Law in the Chinese Special Administrative Regions' (2016) 65(4) *International and Comparative Law Quarterly* 953–968; Sun Zhichao, 'International Legal Personality of the Hong Kong Special Administrative Region' (2008) 7(2) *Chinese Journal of International Law* 339–352.

99 World Trade Organization, *Trade Policy Review Report by the Secretariat: Hong Kong, China (Revision)* (30 January 2019) WT/TPR/S/380/Rev.1 [2.10].

100 World Trade Organization, *Trade Policy Review Report by the Secretariat: Hong Kong, China (Revision)* (28 January 2015) WT/TPR/S/306/Rev.1 [7].

101 World Trade Organization, *Trade Policy Review Report by the Secretariat: Hong Kong, China (Revision)* (30 January 2019) WT/TPR/S/380/Rev.1 [2.6].

In conclusion, Chapter 7 offers cautiously optimistic remarks on the various internal and external challenges that confront Hong Kong's free market constitutionalism as the year 2047 approaches and the 50 years of 'unchanged' capitalist system under the Basic Law pass. The chapter surveys Hong Kong's income inequality, social polarisation, the changes to the electoral and legal system, the COVID–19 pandemic and the economic future of the Region in an increasingly confident China.

2

THE VICTORIAN ORIGINS AND HAYEKIAN DEVELOPMENT OF HONG KONG'S FREE MARKET CONSTITUTIONALISM

Introduction

The Basic Law of the Hong Kong Special Administrative Region of the People's Republic of China conserves the uncodified constitution of the territory as it existed on the signature of the Sino-British Joint Declaration on 19 December 1984, towards the end of the United Kingdom's occupation of Hong Kong, first as a Crown Colony and then as a Dependent Territory (the Colony).[1] It is essential, given the hermeneutics of conservation that hold the Basic Law together,[2] to understand the original constitution, especially its inherent economic philosophy, if we are to make any sense of the arrangements governing the Region's economy since China's resumption of the exercise of sovereignty over Hong Kong. This chapter aims to achieve that.

1 Eric C Ip, *Law and Justice in Hong Kong: Principles of the Legal System* (4th edn) (Hong Kong: Sweet & Maxwell 2022) 25. In *Cheng Kar Shun v Li Fung Ying* [2011] 2 HKLRD 555, 569, Andrew Cheung J, as the Chief Justice of the Hong Kong Court of Final Appeal then was, compendiously summarised Hong Kong's legal status prior to the resumption of the exercise of Chinese sovereignty from the point of view of Hong Kong law: 'For over 150 years before 1 July 1997, Hong Kong was a British Crown Colony (reclassified as a British dependent territory in 1983). Its constitution took the form of a Royal Charter of 1843 which authorised, amongst other things, the establishment of the Legislative Council and empowered the Governor (for the time being) with the advice of the Legislative Council to make and enact all such laws and ordinances as may from time to time be required for the peace, order and good government of Hong Kong.' Contemporary Chinese constitutional theory denies the validity of the Treaty of Nanking that led to the establishment of the Crown Colony under Victorian British imperial law. See Kang-chung Ng, 'Debate Over Whether Hong Kong was Indeed British Colony Reflects Lack of Education on Chinese Constitution, Lawmakers Say' *South China Morning Post* (20 June 2022).

2 *Kwok Cheuk Kin v Director of Lands* (2021) 24 HKCFAR 349, 373.

DOI: 10.4324/9780429341229-2

Hong Kong's small-c constitution, understood, for comparative purposes, as the 'fundamental rules, norms, principles, conventions, and understandings'[3] that govern the Region could aptly be described as Victorian in character for it remained largely unchanged from the start of British occupation in 1841, under the reign of Queen Victoria, to the signature of the Sino-British Joint Declaration in 1984, several decades after her death.[4] Unlike the Basic Law, the British constitution for colonial Hong Kong enumerated no comprehensive checklist of provisions for the regulation of commercial affairs. Nevertheless, important principles of mercantile policy – with direct impact on economic freedoms and property and contractual rights – can be found in imperial legislation, the common law and constitutional conventions, which, together, made up the uncodified constitution of Hong Kong under British colonial rule. This constitution was undemocratic[5] although the constitutional traditions of limited and responsible government, the rule of law and what was later described as 'positive non-interventionism' all resulted in a legal system that, effectively, upheld economic liberty, maintained a free and competitive market, conserved fiscal prudence and secured reserve accumulation.[6] In Hayekian terms, the 'non-democratic government under the law' that this constitution established was, undoubtedly, a far lesser evil compared to an 'unlimited (and therefore entirely lawless) democratic government'.[7]

The organisation of this chapter is in sections. The first two sections study the origins of the Colony's constitution in the aftermath of the First Opium War and the earliest years of Queen Victoria's reign. The third examines Hong Kong's Hayekian convention of laissez-faire and how it was later understood as part of the doctrine of positive non-interventionism. It, in particular, exposes the myth of Hong Kong's 'myth of laissez-faire capitalism'.[8] The chapter closes with several remarks in conclusion.

3 Albert HY Chen, 'Constitutions and Constitutionalism: China' in David S Law (ed.) *Constitutionalism in Context* (New York: Cambridge University Press 2022) 61–86, 63.

4 Judith M Brown and Rosemary Foot, 'Introduction: Hong Kong's Transitions' in Judith M Brown and Rosemary Foot (eds), *Hong Kong's Transitions, 1842–1997* (London: Palgrave Macmillan) 1–32, 18.

5 Wai Fung Lam and Kwan Nok Chan, 'How Authoritarianism Intensifies Punctuated Equilibrium: The Dynamics of Policy Attention in Hong Kong' (2015) 28(4) *Governance* 549–570, 567. See State Council Information Office of the People's Republic of China, *Hong Kong Democratic Progress Under the Framework of One Country, Two Systems* (Beijing: Foreign Language Press 2021) 6.

6 See, generally, Gonzalo Villalta Puig, 'Fiscal Constitutionalism and Fiscal Culture: A Comparative Study of the Balanced-Budget Rule in the Spanish Constitution and the Hong Kong Basic Law' (2003) 43 *Hong Kong Law Journal* 5–53.

7 FA Hayek, 'Whither Democracy?' in Chiaki Nishiyama and Kurt R Leube (eds), *The Essence of Hayek* (Stanford: Hoover Institution Press 1984) 352–362, 354.

8 MK Chan, 'The Legacy of the British Administration of Hong Kong: A View from Hong Kong' (1997) 151 *The China Quarterly* 567–582, 577.

Hong Kong's Victorian Constitution

The northern littoral of the South China Sea long held attraction for the world's traders,[9] even if access was not always open by successive dynasties in Chinese history.[10] In this littoral is Hong Kong Island, one of over 260 islands historically under the jurisdiction of Xin'an County, sometimes called Bao'an County, of Guangdong Province, known to Europeans as Canton. Before British settlement, it was a nameless island populated by an estimated 5,650[11] fishermen, farmers and stonecutters living in little more than 20 villages scattered over its southern coast. Village elders, through the administration of custom and tradition, discharged all the duties and functions of local government[12] in the absence of a permanent Qing civil or military presence.[13]

British Hong Kong grew out of the trade disputes behind the Opium Wars of the 19th-century.[14] Sir James Matheson – a prominent Scottish trader, tai-pan and founder of the future Hong Kong-based British conglomerate, Jardines – had, as early as 1836, proposed the development of Hong Kong Island into a factory for the needs of British traders in the Far East.[15] Five years later, in February 1841, two proclamations of Sir Charles Elliot, Plenipotentiary and Chief Superintendent of British Trade in China, declared the island 'part of the dominions of the Queen of England'. In August 1842, by Article III of the unequal Treaty of Nanking, China's Daoguang Emperor formally ceded Hong Kong to the British Crown in perpetuity. Lord Stanley, the then Secretary of State for War and the Colonies, instructed the Island's first Governor, Sir Henry Pottinger, that the primary usage of the new Colony was, ironically, not for '[c]olonisation' but for 'diplomatic, commercial and military purposes'.[16] Thus, in 1842, Pottinger declared Hong Kong a free port, free of any meaningful tariffs, quotas or other restrictions on imports or exports.[17] In

9 Gordon Redding, Gilbert YY Wong and William KW Leung, 'Hong Kong: Hybrid Capitalism as Catalyst' in Michael A Witt and Gordon Redding (eds), *The Oxford Handbook of Asian Business System* (New York: Oxford University Press 2014) 33–54, 33.

10 Alvin Rabushka, 'Economic, Civil, and Political Freedoms: The Cases of Singapore and Hong Kong' in Michael A Walker (ed.), *Freedom, Democracy and Economic Welfare* (Vancouver: Fraser Institute 1988) 151–211, 166.

11 Richard J Garrett, *Royal Asiatic Society Hong Kong Studies Series – The Peak: An Illustrated History of Hong Kong's Top District* (Hong Kong: Blacksmith Books 2018) 1.

12 John M Carroll, *Edge of Empires: Chinese Elites and British Colonials in Hong Kong* (Hong Kong: Hong Kong University Press 2007) 19.

13 See James Hayes, 'Hong Kong Island Before 1841' (1984) 24 *Journal of the Royal Asiatic Society Hong Kong Branch* 105.

14 Eric Marcks, 'English law in Early Hong Kong: Colonial Law as Means for Control and Liberation' (2000) 35(2) *Texas International Law Journal* 265–288, 270.

15 Fu-Lai Tony Yu, 'The Architects of Two Asian Economic Miracles: Li Kuo-Ting of Taiwan and John Cowperthwaite of Hong Kong' (2011) 4(2) *Journal of Asian Public Policy* 131–148, 138.

16 John Darwin, 'Hong Kong in British Decolonisation' in Judith M Brown and Rosemary Foot (eds), *Hong Kong's Transitions, 1842–1997* (London: Palgrave Macmillan) 16–33, 21.

17 Neil Monnery, *A Tale of Two Economies: Hong Kong, Cuba and the Two Men Who Shaped Them* (London: Gulielmus Occamus & Co Ltd 2019) 151.

October 1843, a supplementary treaty gave Chinese subjects free access to the Colony for trade.[18] The Colony's geographical boundaries were then expanded twice. In October 1860, at the conclusion of the Second Opium War, the Xianfeng Emperor, further to the First Convention of Peking, ceded the Kowloon Peninsula and Stonecutters Island – both to the north of Hong Kong Island – to the British Crown, again in perpetuity. In June 1898, London had Peking lease it the entire landmass and surrounding islands to the south of the Sham Chun River – roughly 12 times the size of the original Colony – for a term of 99 years by what is known as the Second Convention of Peking.

The centrepiece of the written part of the Colony's constitution – the Hong Kong Letters Patent – was issued by Queen Victoria on 5 April 1843.[19] It made the Governor 'the single and supreme authority responsible to, and representative of, Her Majesty'.[20] Britain kept what might be termed the 'George III model' as its governance template for Hong Kong: a dominant executive government, a relatively weak legislature and an independent judiciary.[21] The Letters Patent conceptually divided political power into legislative, executive and judicial powers as witness the vice-regal deliberative body being named the 'Legislative Council',[22] the vice-regal advisory body, the 'Executive Council'[23] and the body administering justice for the Crown, the 'Court'.[24] The Letters Patent established a form of constitutional government in Hong Kong, the first of its kind in East Asia, almost five decades before Japan's promulgation of the Meiji Constitution. Other written constitutional sources include the Royal Instructions, the Colonial Regulations,[25] the Order in Council of 24 October 1860 annexing the Kowloon Peninsula and the Order in Council of 20 October 1898 annexing the so-called New Territories,[26] all of which were ordinances issued under the Crown's prerogative powers, residual powers of mediaeval kingship later defined by the common law and limited by parliamentary acts.

Rule of Law and Judicial Independence

British Hong Kong did not have an unblemished record of constitutionalism and rule of law. It was marred by 19th-century racist statutes, some so outrageous that Sir John

18 Alvin Rabushka, 'Economic, Civil, and Political Freedoms: The Cases of Singapore and Hong Kong' in Michael A Walker (ed.), *Freedom, Democracy and Economic Welfare* (Vancouver: Fraser Institute 1988) 151–211, 166.
19 Peter Harris, *Hong Kong: A Study in Bureaucratic Politics* (Hong Kong: Heinemann Asia 1978) 68.
20 Colonial Regulations, Pt. II, Cap. V.
21 Simon NM Young and Richard Cullen, *Electing Hong Kong's Chief Executive* (Hong Kong: Hong Kong University Press 2010) 34.
22 Hong Kong Letters Patent, Article III.
23 Hong Kong Letters Patent, Article IV.
24 Hong Kong Letters Patent, Article XI.
25 John Rear, 'The Law of the Constitution' in Keith Hopkins (ed.), *Hong Kong: The Industrial Colony* (Hong Kong: Oxford University Press 1971) 339–415, 341.
26 Norman J Miners, *The Government and Politics of Hong Kong* (4th edn) (Hong Kong: Oxford University Press 1986) 59.

Pope Hennessy, Governor from 1877 to 1883, called them 'monstrous'.[27] Magistrates indulged themselves in procedural shortcuts and relied on summary judgment in ways that compromised the integrity of the legal system.[28] Such officers, tightly controlled by the colonial Government, were responsible for law enforcement until 1862 and showed a 'scandalous tendency' to sentence practically any crime to corporal punishment.[29] Callous segregation, mass incarceration and summary justice, the colonial authorities all considered proper responses against violent criminals, pirates and even marginalised minorities such as the Hakka and Tanka.[30] Later, public order statutes, including the Emergency Regulations Ordinance of 1922,[31] aimed to suppress pro-China political forces in the territory, forces that, to the British authorities, had become existential threats to the colonial way of life.[32]

Nonetheless, the rule of law prevailed. Article VII of the Hong Kong Letters Patent obligated judges to dedicate themselves to 'the due and impartial administration of justice' and to 'putting the Laws into execution'. This provision implied a right on the part of residents to justice administered by an impartial judiciary; an inherent feature of the rule of law without which 'laws are liable to become a dead letter, the work done by Parliament may be rendered nugatory'.[33] The Supreme Court Ordinance of 1844, in Section 3, provided that the 'laws of England' until 5 April 1843 were to be 'in force in the Colony'. This enactment allowed foremost 'constitutional instruments'[34] such as Magna Carta to become the law of the new Colony. Of particular interest is that, since the 17th-century,[35] Magna Carta has been the primary source in English law of key principles of classical liberalism such as the rule of law and free trade. Thus, Clause 29 of Magna Carta, in its 1225 version, reads: 'No free man shall in future be arrested or imprisoned or disseised of his freehold, liberties or free customs, or outlawed or exiled or victimised in any other way, neither will we attack him or send anyone to attack him, except by the lawful judgment of his peers or by the law of the land. To no one will we sell, to no one will we refuse or delay right or justice.' And Clause 30 reads: 'All merchants … shall be able to go out of and come into England

27 Christopher Munn, *Anglo-China: Chinese People and British Rule in Hong Kong, 1841–1880* (Hong Kong: Hong Kong University Press 2009) 331.
28 Peter E Hamilton, *Made in Hong Kong: Transpacific Networks and a New History of Globalization* (New York: Columbia University Press 2021) 36.
29 Christopher Munn, 'The Rule of Law and Criminal Justice in the Nineteenth Century' in Steven Tsang (ed.), *Judicial Independence and the Rule of Law in Hong Kong* (Hong Kong: Hong Kong University Press 2001) 32.
30 Peter E Hamilton, *Made in Hong Kong: Transpacific Networks and a New History of Globalization* (New York: Columbia University Press 2021) 36.
31 See Michael Ng, Shengyue Zhang and Max Wong, 'Who but the Governor in Executive Council is the Judge? Historical Use of the Emergency Regulations Ordinance' (2020) 50(2) *Hong Kong Law Journal* 425–461.
32 Neil Monnery, *A Tale of Two Economies: Hong Kong, Cuba and the Two Men Who Shaped Them* (London: Gulielmus Occamus & Co Ltd 2019) 150.
33 *R (on the application of UNISON) v Lord Chancellor* [2017] UKSC 51 [68].
34 *R (HS2 Action Alliance Ltd) v Secretary of State for Transport* [2014] UKSC 3 [207].
35 See Jonathan Sumption, *Law in a Time of Crisis* (London: Profile Books 2021).

safely and securely and stay and travel throughout England, as well by land as by water, for buying and selling by the ancient and right customs free from all evil tolls.'

Throughout the Victorian era, these constitutional instruments guaranteed rights to equal justice under law, the due process of law, an independent judiciary as well as the principle of trial by jury for serious crimes and, most especially, economic liberty.[36] Again, further to Section 3 of the Supreme Court Ordinance, the common law – along with all its precedents in defence of economic liberty – became part of the law of Hong Kong. Historically, the English common law – perceived as 'a source of liberty and a champion of private property rights' – had curbed the ability of the Crown to abuse feudal privileges, grant monopolies and infringe property rights.[37] The common law, exported across the world through British imperialism, was thus, paradoxically, seen as a bastion of economic liberty;[38] in principle, protecting property rights and enforcing contracts.[39] Examples abound: *Hayward v Bettysworth*[40] and *Entick v Carrington*[41] affirmed that 'no man can set his foot upon his neighbour's close without his leave'; *Darcy v Allein*[42] ruled against monopolies because 'for every subject, by the law, has freedom and liberty to pit his cloth to be dressed by what clothworker he pleases, and cannot be restrained to certain persons, for that in effect would be a monopoly';[43] *Steel v Houghton*[44] defended the right to private property in that 'no person has, at common law, a right to glean in the harvest field'. Vibrant and secure rights of tenure – behind each of these landmark decisions – are presupposed for a level playing field of market competition that empowers participants to invest, innovate and carry on voluntary exchange, all essential to sustained economic development.[45]

In case after case, the colonial courts affirmed the rule of law principles of the common law tradition as part and parcel of the Hong Kong legal system. The Colony's legal system offered 'ample protection'[46] for private property and contract.

36 J Baker, *The Reinvention of Magna Carta 1216–1616* (Cambridge: Cambridge University Press 2017) 349.
37 Thorsten Beck, Asli Demirgüç–Kunt, and Ross Levine, 'Law and Finance: Why Does Legal Origin Matter?' (2003) 31 *Journal of Comparative Economics* 653–675, 657.
38 Eamonn Butler, *Classical Liberalism: A Primer* (London: The Institute of Economic Affairs 2015) 68.
39 Eamonn Butler, *Classical Liberalism: A Primer* (London: The Institute of Economic Affairs 2015) 67.
40 *Hayward v Bettysworth* (1591) Co NBk, BL MS Harley 6686A, fo 292.
41 *Entick v Carrington* (1765) 19 St Tr 1029, 95 ER 807.
42 *Darcy v Allein* (1603) 11 Co Rep 84b, 77 Eng Rep 1260. See, generally, Paul G Mahoney, 'The Common Law and Economic Growth: Hayek Might Be Right' (2001) 30(2) *The Journal of Legal Studies* 503–525, 508.
43 Timothy Sandefur, 'The Right to Earn a Living' (2003) 6 *Chapman Law Review* 207–277, 215.
44 *Steel v Houghton* (1788) 1 H Bl 51, 126 ER 32.
45 Eamonn Butler, *Classical Liberalism: A Primer* (London: The Institute of Economic Affairs 2015) 78.
46 Frank Welsh, *A Borrowed Place: The History of Hong Kong* (New York: Kodansha 1993) 138.

Indeed, by 1863, the Supreme Court of Hong Kong had, by virtue of its fierce independence, earned the title of 'the greatest nuisance in the East' in the eyes of colonialists, according to *The Times*.[47] In *Lugard v Chu Ping*,[48] Sir Francis Taylor Piggott, Chief Justice of Hong Kong, said, 'everything must be done regularly and in order; and if anything is done irregularly and out of order those officers who so act, the highest or the lowest, must take the consequences'.[49] These words, reportedly, deeply angered Governor Sir Frederick Lugard. The Court did not stop there. In *R v Ibrahim*,[50] it asserted for itself a constitutional power of judicial review in that any act of the Legislative Council 'which is not within the scope of the Letters Patent is made without jurisdiction, and the Courts would have no hesitation in pronouncing it bad'.[51] In *Attorney-General v Tsang Kwok Kuen*,[52] the Court faulted the colonial Government for stretching primary enabling legislation 'beyond all proper limits' contrary to 'the principle that subsidiary legislation must be confined within the scope of the enabling legislation', which is 'an essential part of the rule of law'.[53] And, in *Gregory Michael Hall v The Commissioner of the Independent Commission Against Corruption*,[54] the Court of Appeal affirmed the presumption of liberty; that 'everything is permitted except what is expressly forbidden', *not* 'everything is forbidden except what is expressly permitted'.[55] On this view, the acts of private individuals do not require justification for the law not unless they are inconsistent with a settled prohibitory rule.[56]

These principles doctrinally encoded a rule of law ideology that would, over the course of time, inspire numerous provisions of the Basic Law, distinguish 'Hong Kong as a modern civilized and open society from anarchy where the rule of might prevails' and guarantee that 'Hong Kong will continue to thrive as an international financial centre'.[57] *Free market constitutionalism*, a concept that we develop throughout this book, presupposes limits on the coercive discretion of public bodies, limits that enlarge the scope of individual liberty in economic and other voluntary exchanges in both the private sector and civil society.[58] Like the City of London

47 See Douglas Clark, *Gunboat Justice: British and American Law Courts in China and Japan (1842–1843) Volume 1: White Man, White Law, White Gun (1842–1990)* (Hong Kong: Earnshaw Books 2015), 46–47.
48 *Lugard v Chu Ping*, unreported 1909 judgment cited in Peter Wesley-Smith, 'Sir Francis Piggott: Chief Justice in His Own Cause' (1982) 12 *Hong Kong Law Journal* 260–292, 273.
49 *Lugard v Chu Ping*, unreported 1909 judgment cited in Peter Wesley-Smith, 'Sir Francis Piggott: Chief Justice in His Own Cause' (1982) 12 *Hong Kong Law Journal* 260–292, 273.
50 *R v Ibrahim* (1913) 8 HKLR 1.
51 *R v Ibrahim* (1913) 8 HKLR 1, 18.
52 *Attorney-General v Tsang Kwok Kuen* [1971] HKLR 266.
53 *Attorney-General v Tsang Kwok Kuen* [1971] HKLR 266, 290–291.
54 *Gregory Michael Hall v The Commissioner of the Independent Commission Against Corruption* [1987] HKLR 210.
55 *Gregory Michael Hall v The Commissioner of the Independent Commission Against Corruption* [1987] HKLR 210 [7].
56 John Laws, *The Constitutional Balance* (Oxford: Hart Publishing 2021) 80.
57 *Secretary for Justice v Wong Chi Fung (Criminal Contempt)* [2019] 2 HKLRD 1236, 1260 CA (Poon JA).
58 Todd J Zywicki, 'The Rule of Law, Freedom, and Prosperity' (2003) 10 *Supreme Court Economic Review* 1–26, 5.

and New York City, Hong Kong has benefitted from the common law tradition undergirding the efficiency and attractiveness of their respective financial markets.[59]

Constitutional Convention of Laissez-Faire

Article IX of the Hong Kong Letters Patent provided that '[t]he Governor, by and with the advice and consent of the Legislative Council, may make laws for the peace, order, and good government of the Colony', which, according to Lord Diplock in *Winfat Enterprise (HK) Co Ltd v Attorney-General of Hong Kong*, 'connote[s], in British constitutional language, the widest law making powers appropriate to a sovereign'.[60] Nevertheless, the colonial Government consistently preferred a very narrow interpretation of this mandate, eschewing social engineering and economic intervention. The laissez-faire philosophy that underpinned this interpretation can be summed up in a few short phrases: 'law and order, minimum interference in private affairs, and the creation of an environment conducive to profitable investment'.[61] Individuals were left to their own devices,[62] subject often to 'the harsh discipline of competitive market forces' within a 'spontaneous order', whose preservation was 'not without cost'.[63] The value of a spontaneous order, according to Friedrich Hayek, is its usefulness for the pursuit of 'a great many different, divergent and even conflicting individual purposes'.[64] The Governor delegated a substantial part of his sovereign-like[65] law-making powers 'for the peace, order, and good government of the Colony' to the general superintendence of his non-partisan Chief Secretary and, in turn, the civil service: politically neutral and meritocratic servants of the public interest. In this way, and with the acquiescence of its settler population, the Colony made laissez-faire its own: economic liberty under the rule of law in unison with Confucian filial piety and self-cultivation, both in conscious acceptance of minimal expenditure on welfare provision by government.

Before we explore what amounted to Hong Kong's Hayekian constitutional convention of laissez-faire, we must acknowledge that the territory's economic success cannot be entirely attributable to the economic liberty inherent in the common law. It can also be attributable to Hong Kong's strategic location and

59 Flora Huang and Horace Yeung, *Institutions and Economic Growth in Asia: The Case of Mainland China, Hong Kong, Singapore and Malaysia* (London: Routledge 2018) 103.

60 *Winfat Enterprise (HK) Co Ltd v Attorney-General of Hong Kong* [1985] AC 733, 747.

61 Alvin Rabushka, 'Economic, Civil, and Political Freedoms: The Cases of Singapore and Hong Kong' in Michael A Walker (ed.), *Freedom, Democracy and Economic Welfare* (Vancouver: Fraser Institute 1988) 151–211, 174.

62 GB Endacott, *Government and People in Hong Kong 1841–1962: A Constitutional History* (Hong Kong: Hong Kong University Press 1964) 73.

63 Yin-Ping Ho, *Trade, Industrial Restructuring and Development in Hong Kong* (London: The Macmillan Press 1992) 264.

64 FA Hayek, 'The Principles of a Liberal Social Order' in Chiaki Nishiyama and Kurt R Leube (eds), *The Essence of Hayek* (Stanford: Hoover Institution Press 1984) 363–381, 366.

65 *Winfat Enterprise (HK) Co Ltd v Attorney-General of Hong Kong* [1985] AC 733, 747.

close proximity to mainland China, the restoration of British colonial rule after the Second World War, the influx of migrants from the mainland and the commercial opportunities that came with the expansion of American influence in East Asia.[66] The establishment of The Hongkong and Shanghai Banking Corporation (HSBC) between 1865 and 1866 cemented the Colony's historical position as the linchpin of Asian finance and trade. In the 20th-century, financial firms from Europe, North America and Asia began increasingly to resort to the territory as a strategic centre for the management of their regional banking, private equity and hedge funds.[67] Migrants offered a large pool of labour that, between 1960 and 1980, made of Hong Kong a major industrial city, manufacturing light industrial and consumer goods for the world market. After mainland China became the world's factory, Hong Kong had to adapt, becoming a centre for the financial services needed to link the mainland with global markets.[68] Hong Kong's securities market burgeoned in the 1970s and its financial services sector was charged up by the relocation of manufacturing firms to the Pearl River Delta and the colonial Government's consequent efforts to attract their capital and investment.[69] Hong Kong's brand as a financial centre was little more than a government-driven publicity campaign to tout its locational advantages and favourable business climate for the provision of financial services.[70]

We must acknowledge also that Hong Kong's Hayekian constitutional convention of laissez-faire cannot be understood as an absolute. Consider the following policies, all of which would have failed in the face of non-interventionism. In 1954, the colonial Government passed new legislation establishing the Housing Authority to build small but safe and affordable accommodation in the aftermath of the Shek Kip Mei fire of Christmas Day 1953, which left over 50,000 people – mostly recent arrivals – helpless and homeless.[71] By the 1960s, the colonial authorities had housed one million people, with an average rent-to-income ratio at just 10 per cent.[72] With the 1967 Hong Kong riots in the backdrop, Governor Sir Murray MacLehose inaugurated a gamut of programmes in public housing, free comprehensive primary education, social security and public transport. Construction of industrial towns for low-cost labour to staff industrial plants, urbanisation of new

66 Peter E Hamilton, *Made in Hong Kong: Transpacific Networks and a New History of Globalization* (New York: Columbia University Press 2021) 287.
67 See David R Meyer, 'Hong Kong: China's Global City' in Tai-lok Lui, Stephen WK Chiu and Ray Yep (eds), *Routledge Handbook of Contemporary Hong Kong* (New York: Routledge 2018) 414–429.
68 Gordon Redding, Gilbert YY Wong and William KW Leung, 'Hong Kong: Hybrid Capitalism as Catalyst' in Michael A Witt and Gordon Redding (eds), *The Oxford Handbook of Asian Business System* (New York: Oxford University Press 2014) 33–54, 34.
69 JJ Woo, *The Evolution of the Asian Developmental State: Hong Kong and Singapore* (New York: Routledge 2019) 73.
70 Stephen W Chiu, KC Ho and Tai–Lok Lui, *City-States in the Global Economy* (Oxford: Westview Press 1998) 125.
71 Nicholas C Owen, 'Economic Policy in Hong Kong' in Keith Hopkins (ed.), *Hong Kong: The Industrial Colony* (Hong Kong: Oxford University Press 1971) 141–206, 167.
72 Nicholas C Owen, 'Economic Policy in Hong Kong' in Keith Hopkins (ed.), *Hong Kong: The Industrial Colony* (Hong Kong: Oxford University Press 1971) 141–206, 168.

towns to cater for a growing population, provision of public housing for low-income families, development of public infrastructure such as cross-harbour tunnels and underground railways, expansion of tertiary education and public health services were, for a hardworking, enterprising work force, considered better than cash handouts for promoting upward mobility.[73] The recession sparked by the 1973 oil crisis convinced the Governor in Council to intervene in the economy by way of four acts of emergency regulation, each empowering the colonial Government to steer the overall consumption and sale of oil, electricity and gas in the territory; they lasted for merely a month before being rescinded in 1974.[74] By 1983, a year before the signature of the Sino-British Joint Declaration, more than 40 per cent of the territory's population lived in public housing. The Colony's three major railways were managed by state-owned corporations. Education, charity and welfare programmes offered by civil society were financed by the colonial Government. Bus companies were franchised. Taxi fares were controlled.[75] And, to top it all off, the Black Monday stock market crash of 1987 triggered the colonial authorities to stage a rare intervention in the gigantic HK$4 billion bailout of the Guarantee Fund to conserve political stability and public order.[76]

That being said, laissez-faire in Hong Kong cannot be dismissed as a 'myth'.[77] The Colony was a free market in money: indeed, no barriers hindered the exchange of the Hong Kong dollar for other currencies.[78] Free entry into almost every line of production was not only permitted but encouraged. What is more, the colonial Government concentrated its policy initiatives almost exclusively on infrastructure and macro-development to the exclusion of industrial planning and government financing. In other words, market forces were allowed to determine which industries developed, not least the sizes of their constituent firms.[79] Possibly realising that the selective government subvention of business could provoke a level of unrest that might undermine the legitimacy of the colonial authorities,[80] successive Governors declined to pursue the kind of sectoral industrial policy that,

73 Ku-Wai Li, *Redefining Capitalism in Global Economic Development* (London: Academic Press 2017) 376.

74 See Michael Ng, Shengyue Zhang and Max Wong, 'Who but the Governor in Executive Council is the Judge? Historical Use of the Emergency Regulations Ordinance' (2020) 50(2) *Hong Kong Law Journal* 425–461.

75 David Mole, 'Introduction' in David Mole (ed.), *Managing the New Hong Kong Economy* (Hong Kong: Oxford University Press 1996) 1–17, 3.

76 Neil Gunningham, 'Moving the Goalposts: Financial Market Regulation in Hong Kong and the Crash of October 1987' (1990) 15(1) *Law and Social Inquiry* 1–48, 19.

77 See John D Wong and Michael HK Ng, 'Introduction: Negotiating the Legitimacy of Governance' in Michael HK Ng and John D Wong (eds), *Civil Unrest and Governance in Hong Kong: Law and Order from Historical and Cultural Perspectives* (New York: Routledge 2017) 1–7, 4.

78 The then-British Dependent Territory's currency, the Hong Kong dollar, has been linked to the United States dollar at a fixed rate of HK$7.80 to US$1 since October 1983.

79 See Nicholas C Owen, 'Economic Policy' in Keith Hopkins (ed.), *Hong Kong: The Industrial Colony* (Hong Kong: Oxford University Press 1971) 141–206.

80 See Leo F Goodstadt, 'Fiscal Freedom and the Making of Hong Kong's Capitalist Society' (2010) 24 *China Information* 273–294.

by default, grants priority to manufacturing in the allocation of resources. Indeed, total government expenditure on institutional support of industrial development amounted to only 0.39 per cent in 1987–1988, for example, far behind Singapore's 5.05 per cent in the same timeframe.[81] The Colony offered ample incentives for private capital accumulation but without intervening in the free flow and distribution of capital across sectors. That said, the cost of government remained consistently below 10 per cent of the gross domestic product (GDP).[82]

The Colony was released from London's Treasury control in 1870 and vested with more control over finances, culminating into the grant of financial autonomy in 1958. Hong Kong never gambled with Keynesian economics, neither with fiscal deficit financing nor with countercyclical fiscal policy.[83] Successive colonial Governments drew up highly prudent budgetary policies to impose discipline on total public expenditure.[84] Those policies sprang from an administrative culture that vowed to obtain value-for-money, maintain neutrality, avoid disruptive change and act rationally.[85] The Financial Secretary typically overestimated expenditure and underestimated revenue to the point that, in some years, underspending was as high as 10 per cent of budget estimates.[86] The metropole had no need to subsidise the periphery.

In fact, after the Second World War, London developed an increasingly big state that demanded high taxes, discouraging work and saving.[87] Whitehall had turned to industrial planning, deficit financing, economic interventionism and high levels of government spending and taxation to drive growth.[88] Predictably, London urged Hong Kong to set its tax rate at 25 per cent, still a notable concession from Prime Minister Clement Atlee's standard tax rate of 45 per cent with the highest at 92.5 per cent. The then Governor resisted, replying that 10 per cent was already a stretch. The Colony soon underwent rapid growth with tax revenue quickly recovering and the Treasury even running surpluses.[89] Only four kinds of direct tax were imposed: profits tax, salaries tax, property tax and estates tax. No broad-

81 Stephen W Chiu, KC Ho and Tai–Lok Lui, *City–States in the Global Economy* (Oxford: Westview Press 1998) 126.
82 Yasheng Huang, 'The Economic and Political Integration of Hong Kong: Implications for Government–Business relations' in Warren Cohen and Li Zhao (eds), *Hong Kong under Chinese Rule: The Economic and Political Implications of Reversion* (Cambridge: Cambridge University Press 1997) 96–113, 100.
83 Shu-hung Tang, 'Reforming Hong Kong's Fiscal System' in David Mole (ed.), *Managing the New Hong Kong Economy* (Hong Kong: Oxford University Press 1996) 35–53, 36.
84 Shu-hung Tang, 'Fiscal Constitution, Income Distribution and the Basic Law of Hong Kong' (1991) 20(3) *Economy and Society* 283–305, 288.
85 Ian Scott, *Public Administration in Hong Kong: Regime Change and its Impact on the Public Sector* (Singapore: Marshall Cavendish 2005) 36.
86 Shu-hung Tang, 'Reforming Hong Kong's Fiscal System' in David Mole (ed.), *Managing the New Hong Kong Economy* (Hong Kong: Oxford University Press 1996) 35–53, 36.
87 Eamonn Butler, *Classical Liberalism: A Primer* (London: The Institute of Economic Affairs 2015) 82.
88 Neil Monnery, *Architect of Prosperity: Sir John Cowperthwaite and the Making of Hong Kong* (London: London Publishing Partnership 2017) 1.
89 Nicholas C Owen, 'Economic Policy' in Keith Hopkins (ed.), *Hong Kong: The Industrial Colony* (Hong Kong: Oxford University Press 1971) 141–206, 160.

based consumption tax was levied.[90] Tax policy did not discriminate between residents and non-residents, effectively allowing foreign investors to fully own local factories. The territory's duty-free port enabled the free entry and exit of most raw materials, consumer goods and commodities with a mere registration charge. And the rejection of tariffs and exchange controls meant that manufacturers could supply domestic and foreign markets on the basis of least-cost production.[91]

One towering figure of Hong Kong's new 'positive non-interventionism', built on more than a century of laissez-faire constitutional convention and a concerted resistance against the welfare state, was Sir John Cowperthwaite, the Colony's Financial Secretary between 1961 and 1971. The subject of many an anecdote, a Member of the Legislative Council once demanded that the colonial Government should enact an industrial policy to encourage new industries and retire obsolete ones, to which Cowperthwaite replied that government should let the market choose the winner.[92] Real wages rose by 50 per cent during his tenure and the percentage of impoverished families dropped from 50 per cent to roughly 15 per cent.[93] Government spending was between 10 and 15 per cent of GDP up to 1997.[94] His contribution to Hong Kong's laissez-faire was so great that busts of him could be found in the newsrooms of *The Wall Street Journal* and even in the White House.[95]

This policy approach finally settled into a formula – *positive non-interventionism* – so named by one of Cowperthwaite's successor Financial Secretaries, Sir Philip Haddon-Cave. More than simply laissez-faire, positive non-interventionism implies an active role for the state in managing the economy, with 'positive' referring to a government's rightly active coordination role and 'non-interventionism' signalling favour to laissez-faire capitalism.[96] Haddon-Cave summed it up as follows: '[I]n the great majority of circumstances it is futile and damaging to the growth rate of the economy for attempts to be made to plan the allocation of resources available to the private sector.'[97] In a March 1981 letter to Li Ka-shing, Haddon-Cave reportedly vowed that:

90 Shu-hung Tang, 'Reforming Hong Kong's Fiscal System' in David Mole (ed.), *Managing the New Hong Kong Economy* (Hong Kong: Oxford University Press 1996) 35–53, 40.
91 Alvin Rabushka, 'Economic, Civil, and Political Freedoms: The Cases of Singapore and Hong Kong' in Michael A Walker (ed.), *Freedom, Democracy and Economic Welfare* (Vancouver: Fraser Institute 1988) 151–211, 172.
92 Fu-Lai Tony Yu, 'The Architects of Two Asian Economic Miracles: Li Kuo-Ting of Taiwan and John Cowperthwaite of Hong Kong' (2011) 4(2) *Journal of Asian Public Policy* 131–148, 140.
93 John M Carroll, *A Concise History of Hong Kong* (Hong Kong: Hong Kong University Press 2007) 160.
94 Neil Monnery, *Architect of Prosperity: Sir John Cowperthwaite and the Making of Hong Kong* (London: London Publishing Partnership 2017) 301.
95 Jamie Peck, Rachel Bok and Jun Zhang, 'Hong Kong – A Model on the Rocks?' (2020) *Territory, Politics, Governance*, DOI: 10.1080/21622671.2020.1837221.
96 JJ Woo, *The Evolution of the Asian Developmental State: Hong Kong and Singapore* (New York: Routledge 2019) 74.
97 Philip Haddon-Cave, 'Introduction: The Making of Some Aspects of Public Policy in Hong Kong' in David Lethbridge (ed.), *The Business Environment in Hong Kong* (Hong Kong: Oxford University Press 1980) xi–xviii, xii.

> I am determined, for as long as I am here, to keep the economy, and all the markets within it, free and that means free from unnecessary and clumsy Government intervention, free from fiscal discrimination, free from the stifling effects of excessive taxation and an over-large public sector and free from all other influences which inhibit competitive forces.[98]

Consistent with this minimalist philosophy, the colonial Government, until nearly the 1990s, regarded codification of social entitlements as alien to its constitutional tradition.[99] It believed that 'what is good for business is good for Hong Kong', subordinating the interests of workers, tenants and consumers to those of large firms, major banks, big developers and transport firms.[100] The doctrine of positive non-interventionism was a reflection of the political reality that the business community was influential, trade unions weak and consumer activism as yet undeveloped.[101] There was no legal protection from unemployment or minimum wage legislation. Indeed, until as late as mid-1995, anti-discrimination employment legislation was considered to be 'interventionist, costly to enforce, and unnecessary'.[102] The territory was 'probably the only advanced economy that ha[d] not enacted a competition law to confront possible abuse of marketing power'.[103]

It would be no exaggeration to say that classical liberal ideas of the Victorian age were constitutive of the Colony's economic identity. By the 1970s, residents had come to embrace a hybrid culture all their own; economic liberty and the rule of law coupled with Confucian moral and educational values.[104] The prevailing value system, with filial piety its cynosure, prized self-reliance and self-help over the welfare state.[105] The vast majority was content with a relatively powerless government confined to the minimal provision of public order and material enabling,[106] whose 'coercive functions', to borrow from Hayek's language, were

98 Catherine R Schenk, 'Hong Kong and Global Finance: The Limits to Free Market Foundations' (2018) 13 *Monde(s)* 67–88, 80.

99 See Frank Stock, 'Human Rights Litigation in the Hong Kong Special Administrative Region' (2001) 1 *Oxford University Commonwealth Law Journal* 147–170.

100 David Mole, 'Introduction' in David Mole (ed.), *Managing the New Hong Kong Economy* (Hong Kong: Oxford University Press 1996) 1–17, 4.

101 Nicholas C Owen, 'Economic Policy in Hong Kong' in Keith Hopkins (ed.), *Hong Kong: The Industrial Colony* (Hong Kong: Oxford University Press 1971) 141–206, 141.

102 Carole J Petersen, 'Hong Kong's First Anti–Discrimination Laws and Their Potential Impact on the Employment Market' (1997) 27(3) *Hong Kong Law Journal* 324–355, 325.

103 Pamela Chan, 'Protecting Hong Kong Consumers' in David Mole (ed.), *Managing the New Hong Kong Economy* (Hong Kong: Oxford University Press 1996) 95–107, 101.

104 See Kin Ming Kwong and Hong Yu, 'Identity Politics' in Yongnian Zheng and Chiew Ping Yew (eds), *Hong Kong under Chinese Rule: Economic Integration and Political Gridlock* (Singapore: World Scientific 2013) 125–149.

105 See Anthony BL Cheung, 'New Interventionism in the Making: Interpreting State Interventions in Hong Kong after the Change of Sovereignty' (2000) 9 *Journal of Contemporary China* 291–308.

106 See Henry N Geraedts, 'Hong Kong: The Economics of Political Dictates' in Jurgen Domes and Yu-ming Shaw (eds), *Hong Kong: A Chinese and International Concern* (Boulder: Westview Press 1988) 61–75.

'strictly limited to the enforcement of uniform rules of law, meaning uniform rules of just conduct towards one's fellows'.[107]

Conclusion

The uncodified Victorian constitution of Hong Kong under British colonial rule partially worked like the constitution of the United Kingdom in permitting 'an indeterminate mixture of substance and shadow'.[108] It set up a common law jurisdiction endowed with judicial independence and a rudimentary form of responsible government, which created a legal environment conducive to the development of an international financial centre, in particular, and economic liberty, in general, as witness private property rights, low taxes, balanced budgets, absence of foreign exchange controls, the free movement of capital and goods, a free port and negligible economic planning. Indeed, apart from taxation and land sales, the colonial Government did not possess other means of sustaining interventionist strategies.[109] It had fiscally prudent, reserve rich, value-for-money budgets free of deficit spending and countercyclical variables; a low tax regime free of consumption tax; competition free of consumer protection; labour free of unemployment protection and minimum wage but free to enter into almost every line of production and an economy free of government sectoral industrial development and resource allocation plans, state-owned enterprises and social entitlements. It seems that there was a strong correlation between the Victorian constitution and economic growth.[110] With its incentives for hard work and future investment, the territory's positive non-interventionism allowed private and social returns to produce a distribution of income with relatively little inequality. The preservation of economic liberty effected the eventual convergence of private and social returns, which resulted in Hong Kong's income distribution being comparable in equity to welfare state exemplars.[111] By 1997, the territory's GDP per capita was even higher than that of the United Kingdom, something unprecedented in the history of the British Empire.[112]

It has been argued that: 'The efforts of the judiciary, like those of the legislature and executive, did not, and were never intended to, serve the rule of law, at least

107 FA Hayek, 'The Principles of a Liberal Social Order' in Chiaki Nishiyama and Kurt R Leube (eds), *The Essence of Hayek* (Stanford: Hoover Institution Press 1984) 363–381, 368.

108 Peter Harris, 'British Political Institutions in a Chinese Setting: The Case of the Crown Colony of Hong Kong' (1982) XXXV *Parliamentary Affairs* 181–192, 191.

109 Stephen W Chiu, KC Ho and Tai-Lok Lui, *City-States in the Global Economy* (Oxford: Westview Press 1998) 126.

110 See Eric C Ip, 'The Constitution of Economic Liberty in Hong Kong' (2015) 26(3) *Constitutional Political Economy* 307–327.

111 See Yasheng Huang, 'The Economic and Political Integration of Hong Kong: Implications for Government-Business relations' in Warren Cohen and Li Zhao (eds), *Hong Kong under Chinese Rule: The Economic and Political Implications of Reversion* (Cambridge: Cambridge University Press 1997) 96–113, 100.

112 Mark Williams, *Competition Policy and Law in China, Hong Kong and Taiwan* (New York: Cambridge University Press 2005).

in its ideal form, but rather to maintain a colonial form of justice that served the Empire's objective to maintain and exert strong control over its colonies in the Far East.'[113] It is true that legislation was deployed during Hong Kong's British colonial era as an instrument of political control to 'camouflage the suppression of political activism'.[114] Then again, the common law tradition does not presume political officials and judges to be altruists who devotedly serve the rule of law. If this were so, then, its legal constraints on public power – one of the signatures of the common law – would be superfluous. The English common law that was imported into the Colony in the 1840s, clearly recognised, in the words of the Lord Chief Justice of England and Wales, Edward Law, in *R v Lambert and Perry*, that '[t]here have been errors in the administration of the most enlightened men'.[115]

Undeniably, British colonial rule brought the fundamental principles of the classical liberal, common law tradition to Hong Kong, namely, reason, fairness, toleration, the presumption of liberty,[116] perhaps, more ideal than real in expression. Nevertheless, whether or not one purpose of the English common law was to maintain colonial rule,[117] what is undeniable is that the same common law conferred important benefits on Hong Kong residents: '[T]he protection of their lives and property, the notion that the government was not above the law, and the raising of public consciousness of rights and the importance of fair government.'[118] By 1978, when Hayek celebrated his 80th birthday in Hong Kong at a meeting of The Mont Pelerin Society, which he co-founded with Milton Friedman, George Stigler and others three decades earlier, the then-Colony had become 'a model of nonmajoritarian market economy that limited popular sovereignty while maximizing capital sovereignty with a much-touted free-trade policy, a robust bank secrecy law, and a low corporate tax rate'.[119]

There is considerable 'legal, institutional and cultural continuity'[120] between the Special Administrative Region and the defunct Colony. Sir Anthony Mason, a former Chief Justice of Australia and Non-Permanent Judge of the Court of Final Appeal, said to this effect that '[t]he common law stands both as a symbol and as

113 Michael Ng, 'Rule of Law in Hong Kong History Demythologised: Student Umbrella Movement of 1919' (2016) 46(3) *Hong Kong Law Journal* 829–848, 847.

114 Michael HK Ng, 'Rule of Law in Hong Kong History Demythologised: Student Umbrella Movement of 1919' in Michael HK Ng and John D Wong (eds), *Civil Unrest and Governance in Hong Kong: Law and Order from Historical and Cultural Perspectives* (New York: Routledge 2017) 11–25, 24.

115 *R v Lambert and Perry* (1810) 2 Camp 405.

116 John Laws, *The Constitutional Balance* (Oxford: Hart Publishing 2021) 66.

117 Michael Ng, 'Rule of Law in Hong Kong History Demythologised: Student Umbrella Movement of 1919' (2016) 46(3) *Hong Kong Law Journal* 829–848, 847.

118 Eric Marcks, 'English Law in Early Hong Kong: Colonial Law as Means for Control and Liberation' (2000) 35(2) *Texas International Law Journal* 265–288, 269.

119 Quinn Slobodian, *Globalists: The End of Empire and the Birth of Neoliberalism* (Cambridge: Harvard University Press 2018) 235.

120 Stephen Thomson, *Administrative Law in Hong Kong* (Cambridge: Cambridge University Press 2018) 25.

link between Hong Kong's past, its present and its future'.[121] By the end of British colonial rule, he said, the territory 'had visible foundations of freedom, in the form of its economic success, its experience of the common law, ... an independent judiciary, a strong legal profession, a vibrant middle class, and an increasingly literate young population with firm roots in the soil'.[122] Economic liberty and the rule of law, the twin pillars of what we call free market constitutionalism, are generally considered the 'most important inheritances'[123] of the Hong Kong Special Administrative Region from the British colonial era, which transformed the territory from a clutch of fishing villages to an international financial centre and a great metropolis.[124]

121 Anthony Mason, 'The Role of the Common Law in Hong Kong' in Jessica Young and Rebecca Lee (eds), *The Common Law Lecture Series 2005* (Hong Kong: Faculty of Law, The University of Hong Kong 2005) 1–2.

122 Nihal Jayawickrama, 'The Bill of Rights' in Raymond Wacks (ed.), *Human Rights in Hong Kong* (Hong Kong: Oxford University Press 1992) 37–85, 64.

123 Steve Tsang, *A Modern History of Hong Kong* (Hong Kong: Hong Kong University Press 2004) 274.

124 Steve Tsang, *A Modern History of Hong Kong* (Hong Kong: Hong Kong University Press 2004) 273.

3

THE CODIFICATION OF FREE MARKET CONSTITUTIONALISM IN THE HONG KONG BASIC LAW

Introduction

On 19 December 1984, the People's Republic of China and the United Kingdom signed a Joint Declaration on the Question of Hong Kong, commonly known as the Sino-British Joint Declaration. China declares its decision to resume the exercise of sovereignty over Hong Kong with effect from 1 July 1997 to coincide with the expiry, under the Second Convention of Peking, of the British Crown's lease on the New Territories, the Colony's hinterland. China also declares that the 'social and economic systems in Hong Kong' and 'the lifestyle' 'will remain unchanged for 50 years'.

Several years later, on 4 April 1990, the National People's Congress of China adopted the Basic Law of the Hong Kong Special Administrative Region of the People's Republic of China, precisely to stipulate China's 'basic policies' regarding Hong Kong as declared in the Sino-British Joint Declaration. Most fundamentally, the Basic Law provides that Hong Kong's 'capitalist system and way of life' and mainland China's 'socialist system and policies' are to remain separate for 50 years under the principle of 'one country, two systems'.[1] Britain's restoration of Hong Kong to China was supposed to leave intact the Colony's successful constitution of economic liberty, hallowed by fiscal surplus, minimal welfare dependency, low taxes and a systematic eschewal of state subsidies and incentives.[2] Thus, with the Basic Law, China transcribed many of the constitutional traditions and conventions of Hong Kong that hailed back to its Victorian origins, affirming the economic

1 Basic Law of the Hong Kong Special Administrative Region of the People's Republic of China (Adopted at the Third Session of the Seventh National People's Congress on 4 April 1990), Article 5.
2 Eric C Ip, 'The Constitution of Economic Liberty in Hong Kong' (2015) 26(3) *Constitutional Political Economy* 307–327, 308.

DOI: 10.4324/9780429341229-3

rights and freedoms of its residents as enshrined in and protected by the common law. The principles of what we call *free market constitutionalism* were, thus, codified into the Region's constitutional instrument.

This chapter is organised into six sections, in addition to this Introduction. The first section explains the historical context and content of the Sino-British Joint Declaration. The second section provides an overview of the drafting and consultation processes that preceded the adoption of the Basic Law by the National People's Congress. The third section explains how the principle of 'one country, two systems' was embodied in various provisions of the Basic Law. The fourth section examines the extant legacy of the classical liberal Victorian constitution of colonial Hong Kong within the Basic Law. The fifth section reviews the Chinese Constitution as the ultimate legal foundation of the Hong Kong Basic Law. Finally, the sixth section closes the chapter with remarks on the various issues raised in the earlier sections.

Context and Content of the Sino-British Joint Declaration

In a burst of serendipity, Ye Jianying, then Chairman of the Standing Committee of the National People's Congress, proposed, in a speech delivered in September 1981, the establishment of a special administrative region for Taiwan – an inalienable part of China – that would enjoy a 'high degree of autonomy'.[3] With the adoption of Article 31 of the Chinese Constitution, which provides, precisely, for the establishment of 'special administrative regions' with systems 'in light of specific circumstances', Beijing announced its intention to resume the exercise of sovereignty over Hong Kong to coincide with the expiry, in 1997, of the British Crown's 99-year lease on the New Territories. The United Kingdom's victory at the time in the Falklands War left no impression on Beijing, which made it abundantly clear that London would have little option but to acquiesce. The Chinese further stipulated that Hong Kong's future would be decided exclusively between the two metropoles.

The Sino-British Joint Declaration set in motion the restoration of Hong Kong to China. With its statement of Chinese basic policy that Hong Kong's 'life-style shall remain unchanged for 50 years', the Joint Declaration affirmed the political status quo and undertook to have Hong Kong's 'social and economic systems' continue under a classically liberal, capitalist, common law framework. To begin, Article 3(1) of the Joint Declaration relates the establishment of a Hong Kong Special Administrative Region to Article 31 of the Constitution, with its purpose being to uphold 'national unity and territorial integrity' albeit in account of 'the history of Hong Kong and its realities'. Article 3(2) of the Joint Declaration provides that Hong Kong 'will be directly under the authority of the Central People's Government' – and, accordingly, not come under any provincial authority such as

3 Xiao Weiyun, *One Country, Two Systems: An Account of the Drafting of the Hong Kong Basic Law* (Beijing: Peking University Press 2001) 10. See also CL Lim, *Treaty for a Lost City: The Sino-British Joint Declaration* (Cambridge: Cambridge University Press 2022).

that of nearby Guangdong, to which Hong Kong had, historically, belonged – and, furthermore, that it 'will enjoy a high degree of autonomy, except in foreign and defence affairs'. Article 3(3) of the Joint Declaration provides that Hong Kong 'will be vested with executive, legislative and independent judicial power, including that of final adjudication' and that '[t]he laws currently in force in Hong Kong will remain basically unchanged'. Article 3(4) of the Joint Declaration details the principle that the Government of the Region will be 'composed of local inhabitants', although 'foreign nationals previously working in the public and police services in the government departments of Hong Kong may remain in employment' and 'British and other foreign nationals may also be employed to serve as advisers or hold certain public posts in government departments'.

Article 3(5) of the Joint Declaration guarantees that '[r]ights and freedoms, including those of the person, of speech, of the press, of assembly, of association, of travel, of movement, of correspondence, of strike, of choice of occupation, of academic research and of religious belief will be ensured by law', while '[p]rivate property, ownership of enterprises, legitimate right of inheritance and foreign investment will be protected by law'. Article 3(6) of the Joint Declaration conserves Hong Kong's 'status of a free port and a separate customs territory' just as 'the status of an international financial centre, and its markets for foreign exchange, gold, securities and futures' and 'free flow of capital' are preserved by Article 3(7) of the Joint Declaration. Hong Kong 'will have independent finances', assures Article 3(8) of the Joint Declaration, such that '[t]he Central People's Government will not levy taxes'. Hong Kong 'may establish mutually beneficial economic relations with the United Kingdom and other countries' further to Article 3(9) of the Joint Declaration, 'whose economic interests in Hong Kong will be given due regard'. Article 3(10) of the Joint Declaration allows, under the name of 'Hong Kong, China', the Region to 'maintain and develop economic and cultural relations and conclude relevant agreements with states, regions and relevant international organisations' and 'on its own issue travel documents for entry into and exit from Hong Kong'. Article 3(11) of the Joint Declaration reserves to the Government of the Region the 'maintenance of local public order'. In summation, Article 3(12) of the Joint Declaration, consequentially, declares: 'The above-stated basic policies of the People's Republic of China regarding Hong Kong and the elaboration of them in Annex I to this Joint Declaration will be stipulated, in a Basic Law of the Hong Kong Special Administrative Region of the People's Republic of China, by the National People's Congress of the People's Republic of China, and they will remain unchanged for 50 years.'

The content of these declarations is sufficiently explainable by China's incentive to integrate an advanced, Westernised economy that would further its own ambitious economic development plans with the provision of hard currency, access to trade and technology and fosterage of coastal South China's progress.[4] The

4 Alvin Rabushka, 'A Free–Market Constitution for Hong Kong: A Blueprint for China' (1989) 8 *Cato Journal* 641–652, 643.

rationale for codification of the status quo is easy to explain. The capacity of states to credibly commit to their promises is an invaluable international asset beneficial to stakeholders everywhere.[5] The articulation of promises in a master code serves to render such commitments as credible as they can be.[6]

Drafting and Consultation of the Basic Law

At the time of negotiations for the Sino-British Joint Declaration, the Chinese side was aware of the rising influence of Hong Kong's ethnic Chinese business elite, who were expanding their family dynasties and venturing major projects in the wake of the gradual exodus of British capital.[7] Against that background, the Chinese Communist Party's Hong Kong and Macau Work Committee compiled a list of candidates for membership of the Basic Law Drafting Committee. Candidates selected, the Standing Committee of the National People's Congress appointed the membership on 18 June 1985. Of the 59 seats, 23 (about 39 per cent) were filled by Hong Kong residents. Each draft provision required the approval of a two-thirds supermajority for adoption; failing which, the draft was to be revised until it crossed that threshold. This procedure meant that the Hong Kong drafters, even though a minority, could veto any proposal of their mainland peers if they voted as a bloc.[8]

Roughly 70 per cent of the Hong Kong members were preeminent businessmen and industrialists, several among the world's richest.[9] Li Ka-shing (Cheung Kong Holdings), David Li (Bank of East Asia), and Yue-Kong Pao (Worldwide Shipping Group and The Wharf) all joined the Basic Law Drafting Committee. According to Ambrose King,[10] a former Vice-Chancellor of The Chinese University of Hong Kong, the appointments reflected what he termed 'the political absorption of economics'; which is how China could signal to the Hong Kong business elite that their portfolios would have continuity after 1997. If not, however, for the century and a half of economic rights and

5 Stefan Voigt, 'Constitutional Political Economy: Analyzing Formal Institutions at the Most Elementary Level' in Eric Brousseau and Jean Michel–Glachant (eds), *New Institutional Economics: A Guidebook* (New York: Cambridge University Press 2008) 363–388, 368.

6 Michael Albertus and Victor Menaldo, 'The Political Economy of Autocratic Constitutions' in Tom Ginsburg and Alberto Simpser (eds), *Constitutions in Authoritarian Regime* (New York: Cambridge University Press 2014) 53–82, 59.

7 See Tai-lok Lui and Stephen Wing-kai Chiu, 'Governance Crisis and Changing State–Business Relations: A Political Economy Perspective' in Stephen Wing-kai Chiu and Siu-lun Wong (eds), *Repositioning the Hong Kong Government: Social Foundations and Political Challenges* (Hong Kong: Hong Kong University Press 2012) 91–122.

8 Xiao Weiyun, *One Country, Two Systems: An Account of the Drafting of the Hong Kong Basic Law* (Beijing: Peking University Press 2001) 39.

9 Christine Loh, *Functional Constituencies: A Unique Feature of the Hong Kong Legislative Council* (Hong Kong: Hong Kong University Press 2006) 33.

10 Ambrose YC King, 'The Hong Kong Talks and Hong Kong Politics' in Jurgen Domes and Yu-ming Shaw (eds), *Hong Kong: A Chinese and International Concern* (Boulder: Westview Press 1988), 42–60, 54.

freedoms in the British dependency, Hong Kong's business elite could not have assumed so prominent a role in drafting the Basic Law.[11]

Among the mainland members of the Basic Law Drafting Committee were several who had helped draft, back in 1982, the current Chinese Constitution. They included Zhang Youyu, then Deputy Director of the National People's Congress's Constitution and Law Committee, and academicians Hu Sheng, Xiao Weiyun and Xu Chongde. Other members, such as Deputy Foreign Minister Lu Ping and Shao Tianren, adviser to the National People's Congress Foreign Affairs Committee, had partaken in the highest level of negotiations that had yielded the Sino-British Joint Declaration.[12] Ji Pengfei, then Director of the State Council's Hong Kong and Macau Affairs Office, was made Chairman of the Basic Law Drafting Committee. In April 1986, during its second plenary session, the membership resolved to set up five subgroups, each to draft a different part of the Basic Law. The subgroups were responsible for the following domains: relationship between the central authorities and the Hong Kong Special Administrative Region; basic rights and duties of Hong Kong residents; political structure; economy; education, science, technology, culture, sports and religion. Each subgroup was chaired by two conveners, one from Hong Kong and one from the mainland. Chairman Ji and the conveners formed a presidium to superintend the Drafting Committee's overall progress.[13] The Subgroup on Economy was, logically, responsible for the Basic Law's Chapter on Economy. Every member of this Subgroup came from the business and industrial sector.[14] Not surprisingly, they spelled out in meticulous detail those provisions that now sustain the Region's economic liberty. After all, if Hong Kong were to maintain its capitalist system, several[15] in the drafting and consultation process[16] must have thought that the 'grand financial oligarchs',[17] necessarily, had to have a significant input.

The minimal economic role of the colonial state under its Victorian constitution had, as its guide, the conservatism of the politically neutral[18] civil service

11 See Eric C Ip, 'The Constitution of Economic Liberty in Hong Kong' (2015) 26(3) *Constitutional Political Economy* 307–327. See also Michael C Davis, 'Constitutionalism in Hong Kong: Politics versus Economics' (1997) 18(1) *University of Pennsylvania Journal of International Law* 157–193.

12 Emily Lau, 'The Early History of the Drafting Process' in Peter Wesley-Smith and Albert HY Chen (eds), *The Basic Law and Hong Kong's Future* (Hong Kong: Butterworths 1988) 90–104, 90–91.

13 Johannes Chan, 'From Colony to Special Administrative Region' in Johannes Chan and CL Lim (eds), *Law of the Hong Kong Constitution* (3rd edn) (Hong Kong: Sweet & Maxwell 2021) 3–37, 31.

14 Shu-hung Tang, 'Fiscal Constitution, Income Distribution and the Basic Law of Hong Kong' (1991) 20(3) *Economy and Society* 283–305, 296.

15 Xiao Weiyun, *One Country, Two Systems: An Account of the Drafting of the Hong Kong Basic Law* (Beijing: Peking University Press 2001) 6.

16 Byron Weng, 'Some Key Aspects of the 1982 Draft Constitution of the People's Republic of China' (1982) 91 *The China Quarterly* 492–506, 493.

17 Nai-keung Lau, *Qianggang zhenyan* [*Proverbs on Strengthening Hong Kong*] (Hong Kong: Chunghwa Publishing 2009) 58.

18 Wilson Wong, 'The Civil Service' in Wai-man Lam, Percy Luen-tim Lui and Wilson Wong (eds), *Contemporary Hong Kong Government and Politics* (2nd edn) (Hong Kong: Hong Kong University Press 2012) 87–110, 95.

establishment, whose mandate and authority came from outside the territory. There was no surety that the special interests embedded in the 'functional constituencies' of the Legislative Council and the similarly corporatist Election Committee, both located within Hong Kong and non-existent for much of the British colonial era, could perform the same role.[19] Thus, the drafters conceived the political system of the future Special Administrative Region as a division of labour between economic classes and even corporate blocs.[20] They specifically planned the Chief Executive to 'be selected by election or through consultations held locally and be appointed by the Central People's Government'.[21] To perform this selection, an Election Committee was provided for in Annex I of the Basic Law made up of either ex officio members such as Members of the Legislative Council or elected by 'functional' (socioeconomic) as distinct to popular (geographic) constituencies.

In the nearly five years of its existence, the Basic Law Drafting Committee held nine plenary sessions, 25 meetings of the Chairman and Vice-Chairmen, three meetings of the General Working Group, 73 meetings of the Special Groups and five meetings of the Committee for Selecting Designs for the Regional Flag and Regional Emblem.[22] The drafters were instructed by a Basic Law Consultative Committee whose 180 members all came from Hong Kong to represent the views of the general public.[23] They were drawn from 10 functional sectors: commerce; finance; both branches of the legal profession; other professionals; the media; labour and grassroots associations; organised religions; and expatriates. On 28 April 1988, the Basic Law Drafting Committee let out the Draft Basic Law for Solicitation of Opinions and, after a five-month consultation period, produced a second draft on 27 February 1989. The final version was adopted on 4 April 1990 at the Third Session of the Seventh National People's Congress and promulgated by Order No 26 of the President of China on the same day.[24]

19 See, generally, Anthony BL Cheung, 'New Interventionism in the Making: Interpreting State Interventions in Hong Kong after the Change of Sovereignty' (2000) 9(24) *Journal of Contemporary China* 291–308.

20 Christine Loh and Carine Lai, *Reflections of Leadership: Tung Chee Hwa and Donald Tsang 1997–2007* (Hong Kong: Civic Exchange 2007) 20.

21 Basic Law of the Hong Kong Special Administrative Region of the People's Republic of China, Article 45.

22 See Drafting Committee of the Basic Law of the Hong Kong Special Administrative Region of the People's Republic of China under the Standing Committee of the National People's Congress, Explanations on the Basic Law of the Hong Kong Special Administrative Region of the People's Republic of China (Draft) and its Related Documents (28 March 1990).

23 Johannes Chan, 'From Colony to Special Administrative Region' in Johannes Chan and CL Lim (eds), *Law of the Hong Kong Constitution* (3rd edn) (Hong Kong: Sweet & Maxwell 2021) 3–37, 31.

24 Shu-hung Tang, 'Fiscal Constitution, Income Distribution and the Basic Law of Hong Kong' (1991) 20(3) *Economy and Society* 283–305, 284

Codifying the 'One Country, Two Systems' Principle

Reflecting the terms of the Sino-British Joint Declaration, the Basic Law's overriding goal was to insulate the Region's laissez-faire economy from the mainland's 'socialist systems and policies'.[25] The two jurisdictions were, thus, strictly sequestered for the former Colony's sake, so it could survive the massive imbalance in size and power.[26] This insulation was accomplished with the affirmation of three fundamental constitutional principles. First, the principle of 'one country, two systems': 'The Hong Kong Special Administrative Region is an inalienable part of the People's Republic of China'[27] but '[t]he socialist system and policies shall not be practised … and the previous capitalist system and way of life shall remain unchanged for 50 years.'[28] Second, the principle of 'Hong Kong people administering Hong Kong': 'The executive authorities and legislature of the Hong Kong Special Administrative Region shall be composed of permanent residents of Hong Kong in accordance with the relevant provisions of this Law.'[29] Third, the principle of a 'high degree of autonomy': 'The National People's Congress authorizes the Hong Kong Special Administrative Region to exercise a high degree of autonomy and enjoy executive, legislative and independent judicial power, including that of final adjudication, in accordance with the provisions of this Law.'[30]

The Basic Law was, thus, a solemn promise by China to respect the 'way of life' and the pre-existing rights and freedoms of Hong Kong residents. By Article 159 (4) of the Basic Law – which provides '[n]o amendment to this Law shall contravene the established basic policies of the People's Republic of China regarding Hong Kong' – and its Preamble – which clarifies that these are as 'elaborated by the Chinese Government in the Sino-British Joint Declaration'[31] – the National People's Congress effectively forestalled any fundamental change to the 'one country, two systems' principle before 1 July 2047.[32] The Basic Law subjects the Region to the National People's Congress as its sovereign lawgiver, as it was once

25 See Miron Mushkat and Roda Mushkat, 'The Economic Dimension of Hong Kong's Basic Law: An Analytical Overview' (2009) 7 *New Zealand Journal of Public International Law* 273–315 (2009).

26 See Richard C Bush, *Hong Kong in the Shadow of China: Living with the Leviathan* (Washington, DC: Brookings Institution Press 2016).

27 Basic Law of the Hong Kong Special Administrative Region of the People's Republic of China, Article 1.

28 Basic Law of the Hong Kong Special Administrative Region of the People's Republic of China, Article 5.

29 Basic Law of the Hong Kong Special Administrative Region of the People's Republic of China, Article 3.

30 Basic Law of the Hong Kong Special Administrative Region of the People's Republic of China, Article 2.

31 Basic Law of the Hong Kong Special Administrative Region of the People's Republic of China, Preamble.

32 Eric C Ip, *Law and Justice in Hong Kong: Principles of the Legal System* (4th edn) (Hong Kong: Sweet & Maxwell 2022) 105.

subject to the Imperial Parliament of the United Kingdom, and likewise to the Standing Committee as supreme interpreter of its canonical text instead of the Judicial Committee of the Privy Council as it was in the colonial era. But equally, the Basic Law was deliberately drafted in such a way as to conserve the common law and its tradition.[33] Steeped in its terminology and principles, many of Hong Kong's practices and conventions have no equivalent in civil or socialist law.

The Basic Law, imbued with the 'principle of continuity',[34] cannot be grasped without reference to the history and ethos of the common law. Thus, Clause 29 of Magna Carta 1225, famously, provides: 'No free man shall in future be arrested or imprisoned or disseised of his freehold, liberties or free customs, or outlawed or exiled or victimised in any other way, neither will we attack him or send anyone to attack him, except by the lawful judgment of his peers or by the law of the land. To no one will we sell, to no one will we refuse or delay right or justice.' These words echo in Articles 28(2), 86, and 87 of the Basic Law. Similarly, the essence of the Habeas Corpus Act 1679 is distilled in Article 28(1) of the Basic Law. Clauses 1 and 3 of the Bill of Rights 1689, which prohibited the Crown to suspend laws or raise taxes without Parliament's consent, correspondingly, find their way into Articles 8 and 73(3) of the Basic Law. An elaborate version of Clause 12 of the Bill of Rights 1689, protecting private property, is found in Article 105 of the Basic Law; Article 77 of the Basic Law – 'Members of the Legislative Council of the Hong Kong Special Administrative Region shall be immune from legal action in respect of their statements at meetings of the Council' – mirrors Clause 9 of the Bill of Rights 1689 too, which provides 'that the freedom of speech and debates or proceedings in Parliament ought not to be impeached or questioned in any court or place out of Parliament'. *Entick v Carrington*[35] and its celebrated holding – 'no man can set his foot upon his neighbour's close without his leave' – is restated in the words of Article 29 of the Basic Law: 'The homes and other premises of Hong Kong residents shall be inviolable. Arbitrary or unlawful search of, or intrusion into, a resident's home or other premises shall be prohibited.'

Traditional common law principles of judicial independence exempt courts from electoral and other pressures by sheltering judges from the public mood so that they can give litigants full and fair hearings and apply the law to the facts dispassionately.[36] Hong Kong's economic success owes a great deal to the zealousness of its judiciary in the rigorous protection of property rights and economic freedoms against arbitrary state interference. Thus, Article 85 of the Basic Law provides, without qualification, that the courts 'shall exercise judicial power independently, free from any interference' and that '[m]embers of the judiciary shall be immune

33 Eric C Ip, *Law and Justice in Hong Kong: Principles of the Legal System* (4th edn) (Hong Kong: Sweet & Maxwell 2022) 83.

34 *Kwok Cheuk Kin v Director of Lands (No 2)* (2021) 24 HKCFAR 349, 373.

35 *Entick v Carrington* (1765) 19 St Tr 1029.

36 See Charles Gardner Geyh, *Who Is to Judge? The Perennial Debate over Whether to Elect or Appoint America's Judges* (Oxford: Oxford University Press 2019).

from legal action in the performance of their judicial functions'.[37] Similarly, Victorian constitutional conventions of responsible government subsist as Article 64 of the Basic Law evidences: 'The Government of the Hong Kong Special Administrative Region must abide by the law and be accountable to the Legislative Council of the Region: it shall implement laws passed by the Council and already in force; it shall present regular policy addresses to the Council; it shall answer questions raised by members of the Council; and it shall obtain approval from the Council for taxation and public expenditure.'[38] The protection of human rights in Hong Kong is constitutionally mandated to match high international standards, such that '[t]he rights and freedoms enjoyed by Hong Kong residents shall not be restricted unless as prescribed by law' although '[s]uch restrictions shall not contravene the provisions' of the International Covenant on Civil and Political Rights, the International Covenant on Economic, Social and Cultural Rights and international labour conventions as applied to Hong Kong, which 'shall remain in force and shall be implemented through the laws of the Hong Kong Special Administrative Region', provides Article 39 of the Basic Law.

To effectuate the above, the Basic Law erects a constitutional firewall to interdict the absorption of the legal system of Hong Kong into that of mainland China.[39] In particular, Article 22(1) of the Basic Law, which applies to the whole of the country, states that '[n]o department of the Central People's Government and no province, autonomous region, or municipality directly under the Central Government may interfere in the affairs which the Hong Kong Special Administrative Region administers on its own in accordance with this Law'. And '[a]ll offices set up in the Hong Kong Special Administrative Region by departments of the Central Government, or by provinces, autonomous regions, or municipalities directly under the Central Government, and the personnel of these offices', vows Article 22(3) of the Basic Law, 'shall abide by the laws of the Region'. On a literal interpretation of this provision, the common law in force in Hong Kong binds all governmental offices operating in the Region. These provisions mean that China commits to the exercise of its sovereignty over Hong Kong in accordance with the common law tradition, not its own socialist, civil law tradition. In a similar vein, what was left of the Victorian constitution as 'local affairs' is to be shielded from interference from '[m]ilitary forces stationed by the Central People's Government in the Hong Kong Special Administrative Region'.[40]

37 Basic Law of the Hong Kong Special Administrative Region of the People's Republic of China, Article 85.
38 Basic Law of the Hong Kong Special Administrative Region of the People's Republic of China, Article 64.
39 Yash Ghai, 'The Intersection of Chinese Law and the Common Law in the Hong Kong Special Administrative Region: Question of Technique or Politics?' (2007) 37 *Hong Kong Law Journal* 363–406, 367.
40 Basic Law of the Hong Kong Special Administrative Region of the People's Republic of China, Article 14(3).

Hong Kong's power of final adjudication was vested not in the Supreme People's Court in Beijing but in a Hong Kong Court of Final Appeal, 'which may as required invite judges from other common law jurisdictions to sit [there]on'[41] and is charged with responsibility to administer, under Chinese sovereignty, 'the common law, rules of equity, ordinances, subordinate legislation and customary law';[42] amid which it 'may refer to precedents of other common law jurisdictions'[43] the better to 'safeguard the rights and freedoms of the residents of the Hong Kong Special Administrative Region and of other persons in the Region'.[44] And, to make this arrangement credible, the Basic Law decrees the conservation of 'laws previously in force in Hong Kong';[45] '[t]he judicial system previously practised in Hong Kong';[46] and, 'the principles previously applied in [criminal or civil proceedings in] Hong Kong and the rights previously enjoyed by parties to proceedings'.[47] In principle, it is possible to construe the Basic Law in ways compatible with nearly all common law principles. Even the power of the Standing Committee of the National People's Congress to override the local jurisdiction of the Basic Law by legislative enactment through instruments labelled 'interpretations'[48] is not, prima facie, alien to the common law,[49] which is subordinate to a political body in the 'High Court of Parliament [that is] so high and so mighty in its nature that it might make law, and unmake that which was law'.[50]

Had the Basic Law intended the Region's status quo to end within 50 years of its entry into effect, at the stroke of midnight on 30 June 2047, the National People's Congress would, presumably, have made it clear in its provisions. However, no sunset article in the Basic Law provides for its cessation at any time. In fact, Deng Xiaoping himself issued a quite definitive sentence at the time of drafting: 'Our policy on Hong Kong will not change for 50 years after it is reunited with the motherland in 1997. That policy, along with the Basic Law you are now drafting, will remain in force for at least 50 years. And I want to add that

41 Basic Law of the Hong Kong Special Administrative Region of the People's Republic of China, Article 82.
42 Basic Law of the Hong Kong Special Administrative Region of the People's Republic of China, Article 8.
43 Basic Law of the Hong Kong Special Administrative Region of the People's Republic of China, Article 84.
44 Basic Law of the Hong Kong Special Administrative Region of the People's Republic of China, Article 4.
45 Basic Law of the Hong Kong Special Administrative Region of the People's Republic of China, Article 8.
46 Basic Law of the Hong Kong Special Administrative Region of the People's Republic of China, Article 81(2).
47 Basic Law of the Hong Kong Special Administrative Region of the People's Republic of China, Article 87(1).
48 Basic Law of the Hong Kong Special Administrative Region of the People's Republic of China, Article 158.
49 Eric C Ip, *Law and Justice in Hong Kong: Principles of the Legal System* (4th edn) (Hong Kong: Sweet & Maxwell 2022) 88.
50 (1453) Rot Parl Vol V, 239.

there will be even less need to change them after the 50-year period. Hong Kong's status will not change, nor will our policy towards Hong Kong.'[51] The drafters were apparently aware of such reality; indeed, they codified no termination for land leases renewed by the Government of the Region.[52]

The Classical Liberal Economic Constitution within the Basic Law

Given the significant input of the business elite into the drafting of the Basic Law, it is not at all a surprise that this instrument became in the 1980s 'unique among contemporary national constitutions in [that it] enshrines general principles and concrete policies to preserve individual economic freedom'.[53] Thus, insofar as it largely restricts state action to the maintenance of personal, property and contractual rights, the market is able to guarantee that rents, if any, are dissipated by competitive entry forces.[54] And in protecting property rights, enforcing contractual obligations and subjecting acts of the government to independent judicial scrutiny, the translation of the Victorian constitution into the Basic Law, buttressed by the common law's traditional presumption of economic liberty, cultivates the ideology of the rule of law and it offers the predictability and rationality requisite to a free and efficient market,[55] while entrenching incentives for hard work and future-oriented investment.[56] The Basic Law protects, in Article 6, 'the right of private ownership of property in accordance with law' and, in Article 105, 'the right of individuals and legal persons to the acquisition, use, disposal and inheritance of property and their right to compensation for lawful deprivation of their property'. 'Such compensation', it continues, 'shall correspond to the real value of the property concerned at the time and shall be freely convertible and paid without undue delay'.[57] The freedom of contract and other freedoms to engage in economic activities are made possible by the Basic Law through such principles as 'equal[ity]

51 X Deng, *Deng Xiaoping on 'One Country, Two Systems'* (Hong Kong: Joint Publishing 2004) 68.

52 Danny Gittings, *Introduction to the Hong Kong Basic Law* (2nd edn) (Hong Kong: Hong Kong University Press 2016) 316–317; Basic Law of the Hong Kong Special Administrative Region of the People's Republic of China, Article 122.

53 Alvin Rabushka, 'A Free-Market Constitution for Hong Kong: A Blueprint for China' (1989) 8 *Cato Journal* 641–652, 644.

54 See James M Buchanan, 'Rent Seeking and Profit Seeking' in James M Buchanan, Robert D Tollison and Gordon Tullock (eds), *Toward a Theory of the Rent-seeking Society* (College Station: Texas A&M University Press 1980) 3–15.

55 See Yash Ghai, *Hong Kong's New Constitutional Order: The Resumption of Chinese Sovereignty and the Basic Law* (2nd edn) (Hong Kong: Hong Kong University Press 1999); Jacques Delisle and Kevin P Lane, 'Cooking the Rice without Cooking the Goose: The Rule of Law, the Battle over Business, and the Quest for Prosperity in Hong Kong after 1997' in Warren I Cohen and Li Zhao (eds), *Hong Kong under Chinese Rule: The Economic and Political Implications of Reversion* (Cambridge: Cambridge University Press 2010) 31–70.

56 See Richard A Posner, 'The Constitution as an Economic Document' (1987) 56 *George Washington Law Review* 4–38.

57 Basic Law of the Hong Kong Special Administrative Region of the People's Republic of China, Article 105.

before the law';[58] the inviolability of the 'freedom of the person of Hong Kong residents';[59] freedom from 'arbitrary or unlawful arrest, detention or imprisonment';[60] 'the right to confidential legal advice, access to the courts, choice of lawyers for timely protection of … lawful rights and interests or for representation in the courts, and to judicial remedies';[61] and 'the right to institute legal proceedings in the courts against the acts of the executive authorities and their personnel'.[62]

For Friedrich Hayek, a model constitution should contain a 'basic clause' whose purpose is 'to define the limits of its coercive powers'.[63] This clause should provide that 'men could be restrained from doing what they wished, or coerced to do particular things, only in accordance with the recognized rules of just conduct designed to define and protect the individual domain of each; and that the accepted set of rules of this kind could be deliberately altered only by what we shall call the Legislative Assembly'.[64] The Basic Law contains exactly that clause:

> The rights and freedoms enjoyed by Hong Kong residents shall not be restricted unless as 'prescribed by law';[65] such restrictions 'shall not contravene' the provisions of 'the International Covenant on Civil and Political Rights, the International Covenant on Economic, Social and Cultural Rights, and international labour conventions as applied to Hong Kong'.[66] The Basic Law maintains that 'the common law, rules of equity, ordinances, subordinate legislation and customary law' are to be maintained, 'subject to any amendment by the legislature'.[67]

Hong Kong had a very consistent set of economic policies in the immediate post-war period that could be broadly labelled laissez-faire or 'positive non-interventionist'. And a great deal was built on classical liberal economics but there were, inevitably, policy divergences, as in housing, and there were areas where the Government wished it had diverged further than it did, as in

58 Basic Law of the Hong Kong Special Administrative Region of the People's Republic of China, Article 25.
59 Basic Law of the Hong Kong Special Administrative Region of the People's Republic of China, Article 28(1).
60 Basic Law of the Hong Kong Special Administrative Region of the People's Republic of China, Article 28(2).
61 Basic Law of the Hong Kong Special Administrative Region of the People's Republic of China, Article 35(1).
62 Basic Law of the Hong Kong Special Administrative Region of the People's Republic of China, Article 35(2).
63 FA Hayek, 'A Model Constitution' in Chiaki Nishiyama and Kurt R Leube (eds), *The Essence of Hayek* (Stanford: Hoover Institution Press 1984) 382–406, 386.
64 FA Hayek, 'A Model Constitution' in Chiaki Nishiyama and Kurt R Leube (eds), *The Essence of Hayek* (Stanford: Hoover Institution Press 1984) 382–406, 386.
65 Basic Law of the Hong Kong Special Administrative Region of the People's Republic of China, Article 39(2).
66 Basic Law of the Hong Kong Special Administrative Region of the People's Republic of China, Article 39(1).
67 Basic Law of the Hong Kong Special Administrative Region of the People's Republic of China, Article 8.

banking.[68] Indeed, government economic intervention through price-control schemes did still occur in fresh food supply, transport, power and subsidised healthcare and education; suffice to note that 30 per cent of people in Hong Kong live in public housing, with a further 17 per cent in subsidised home ownership.[69] Nevertheless, Hong Kong's stance as a small open economy, along with the influence of strong entrepreneurial activity driven by the institutional design of the colonial era, obviated any need for state-owned enterprises and capital, allowing the territory to rely on less-interventionist means of economic governance and development.[70] The low state regulation in the period before the return of Hong Kong to China let private citizens participate in almost any form of economic activity with few or no barriers to entry.[71]

The Basic Law Drafting Committee codified in the text many principles of economic liberty instinct in the Victorian constitution. Article 107 of the Basic Law, consistent with the tradition of positive non-interventionism, provides that the Government of the Region shall both 'follow the principle of keeping the expenditure within the limits of revenues in drawing up its budget' and 'strive to achieve a fiscal balance, avoid deficits and keep the budget commensurate with the growth rate of its gross domestic product'. Working documents of the Basic Law Drafting Committee indicate that, by 1987, some drafters opposed the inclusion of the balanced budget rule into the Basic Law on the premise that it would unduly restrict Hong Kong's discretion to manage its public finances, while other drafters went as far as to support the prescription of a timeframe of three to five years within which an approximate balance would have to be restored in case of a deficit.[72] Drafter Xiao Weiyun explained the rationale of this provision, which reflected 'a principle followed for many years by the [British] Hong Kong Government in drawing up its budget' so as 'to avoid economic turmoil and currency depreciation resulting from huge debts as has happened in some developed capitalist countries which indulged in deficit budgeting over a long period'.[73] Another drafter, Wang Shuwen, similarly explained that '[i]f expenditures are allowed to increase without regard to revenues, a deficit is bound to occur, or the [Hong Kong Special Administrative Region] will need to increase taxes, obtain foreign loans, issue government bonds in the Region or increase

68 Neil Monnery, *Architect of Prosperity: Sir John Cowperthwaite and the Making of Hong Kong* (London: London Publishing Partnership 2017) 296.

69 Gordon Redding, Gilbert YY Wong and William KW Leung, 'Hong Kong: Hybrid Capitalism as Catalyst' in Michael A Witt and Gordon Redding (eds), *The Oxford Handbook of Asian Business System* (New York: Oxford University Press 2014) 33–54, 37.

70 JJ Woo, *The Evolution of the Asian Developmental State: Hong Kong and Singapore* (New York: Routledge 2019) 74.

71 See YC Jao, 'Hong Kong's Future as a Free Market Economy' in Jurgen Domes and Yu-ming Shaw (eds), *Hong Kong: A Chinese and International Concern* (Boulder: Westview Press 1988) 205–230.

72 Michael Ramsden and Stuart Hargreaves, *Hong Kong Basic Law Handbook* (3rd edn) (Hong Kong: Sweet & Maxwell 2022) [107.2].

73 Xiao Weiyun, *One Country, Two Systems: An Account of the Drafting of the Hong Kong Basic Law* (Beijing: Peking University Press 2001) 398.

money supply to defray its expenditures', ultimately 'resulting in economic crisis'.[74] Article 108 of the Basic Law instructs laws on 'taxes, tax rates, tax reductions, allowances and exemptions, and other matters of taxation' to follow 'the low tax policy previously pursued'; the Basic Law's drafting history reveals that individual drafters resisted the admittedly vague notion of 'low tax' and its possible connotation that such a policy might prevent Hong Kong from restoring a balanced budget through an increase in taxes.[75]

Hong Kong as an international financial centre did not spring from any central economic plan but spontaneously, under the invisible hand of a market enabled by rule of law and limited government, plus being 'the right place and at the right time'.[76] Thus, in 1980, Sir Denys Roberts, Chief Justice of Hong Kong and a former Chief Secretary in the time of Sir Phillip Haddon-Cave as Financial Secretary,[77] praised the common law ideal of liberty in these words: 'By [a genuinely free society], I mean a society in which everyone is subject to the law, where nobody can be deprived of his property or personal freedom save in accordance with the law.' In these terms, the primacy of the individual prevalent in the Colony was reminiscent of what Hayek called 'an attitude of humility' and 'of tolerance to other opinions'.[78]

Article 109 of the Basic Law charges the Government of the Region to proactively 'provide an appropriate economic and legal environment for the maintenance of the status of Hong Kong as an international financial centre'. This provision, as drafter Xiao Weiyun maintained, admits of an interpretation compatible with the pre-existing constitutional tradition, as the phrase 'appropriate economic and legal environment' presumptively means 'effective economic policies previously in practice for a long time, implement and continuously improve previous laws on finance'.[79] Article 110(2) of the Basic Law mandates the Government of the Region to 'safeguard the free operation of business and financial markets'; Article 111(2) requires issuances of the Hong Kong dollar to be backed with 'a 100 per cent reserve fund', surely to resist the temptation to 'print money';[80] and, Article 112 prohibits the 'foreign exchange control' that would stop the Hong Kong dollar being a 'freely convertible' currency mediating 'the free flow of capital within, into and out of the Region'. Free movement of capital frees firms and individuals to reallocate assets and funds to wherever in the world they are at their safest and most productive; in effect, it means that persons are free to invest in that jurisdiction which they consider to best promote

74 Wang Shuwen et al., *Introduction to the Basic Law of the Hong Kong Special Administrative Region* (2nd edn) (Beijing: Law Press China 2009) 566.
75 Michael Ramsden and Stuart Hargreaves, *Hong Kong Basic Law Handbook* (3rd edn) (Hong Kong: Sweet & Maxwell 2022) [108.1].
76 Kam Hon Chu, 'Financial Development in Hong Kong and China: A Hayekian Perspective' (2021) 41(1) *Cato Journal* 25–44, 30.
77 See Paul Shieh, 'Speech of the Chairman of the Hong Kong Bar Association at the Opening of the Legal Year' (13 January 2014).
78 See FA Hayek, *The Road to Serfdom* (New York: Routledge 1994) 169–170.
79 Xiao Weiyun, *One Country, Two Systems: An Account of the Drafting of the Hong Kong Basic Law* (Beijing: Peking University Press 2001) 407.
80 Xiao Weiyun, *One Country, Two Systems: An Account of the Drafting of the Hong Kong Basic Law* (Beijing: Peking University Press 2001) 412.

opportunity.[81] Similarly, Article 115 of the Basic Law mandates the Government of the Region to 'pursue the policy of free trade and safeguard the free movement of goods, intangible assets and capital'. The financial infrastructure constitutionalised in the Basic Law implicitly acknowledges that smart macroeconomic policies delivered in a conducive legal and regulatory setting will not fail to attract private investment; that government efforts to lower the uncertainty of macroeconomic policy, develop the legal framework and enforce the rights of creditors and investors enhance financial and commodity markets.[82]

These provisions are countervailed by others evincing an intent to institute more state 'positive' interventionism when it comes to industrial planning,[83] seemingly contrary to the minimalist tradition of the Colony. Article 118 of the Basic Law directs the Government of the Region to 'provide an economic and legal environment for encouraging investments, technological progress and the development of new industries'. Article 119 of the Basic Law directs the Government of the Region to formulate sector-specific policies 'to promote and co-ordinate the development of various trades such as manufacturing, commerce, tourism, real estate, transport, public utilities, services, agriculture and fisheries, and pay regard to the protection of the environment'. According to drafter Xiao Weiyun, these two provisions were intended to impose on the Government of the Region a duty to 'draw up appropriate measures to facilitate continued development of each sector' as well as to 'coordinate the interests and divergences of all sectors, proceeding from Hong Kong's overall, long-term interests so that each sector will have a proper role to play, to develop harmoniously and together safeguard the social stability and economic prosperity of Hong Kong'.[84] Article 138 of the Basic Law even goes so far as to exact the duty to 'develop Western and traditional Chinese medicine and to improve medical and health services'. And, for the first time in Hong Kong's history, 'the right to social welfare' is conceived to be a legal entitlement as witnesses its citation in Article 36 of the Basic Law, precisely as part of the chapter on 'Fundamental Rights'. Article 145 of the Basic Law empowers the Government of the Region to 'formulate policies on the development and improvement of ["the previous social welfare system"] in the light of the economic conditions and social needs' without defining what these are. Article 147 of the Basic Law simply declares that the Government of the Region shall 'on its own [initiative] formulate laws and policies relating to labour'. These provisions certainly risk the adoption of top-down industrial policy, which is apt to proliferate inefficiency if it reallocates production to specific industries so as to stifle meaningful

81 See Kui-wai Li, *Economic Freedom: Lessons of Hong Kong* (Singapore: World Scientific 2012).
82 Yongfu Huang, *Determinants of Financial Development* (London: Palgrave Macmillan 2010).
83 Leo F Goodstadt, *Uneasy Partners: The Conflict Between Public Interest and Private Profit in Hong Kong* (Hong Kong: Hong Kong University Press 2005) 133.
84 Xiao Weiyun, *One Country, Two Systems: An Account of the Drafting of the Hong Kong Basic Law* (Beijing: Peking University Press 2001) 422.

competition.[85] However, a better interpretation is to understand them as consequentialist expressions of classical liberal economic thought. The good of society legitimates the regulation of economic activity to correct monopolies, frauds and other anti-competitive market failures and, through taxation, the compassionate provision of public goods – education, health and social welfare – to protect basic human dignity.

The Chinese Constitution as the Ultimate Legal Foundation of the Hong Kong Basic Law

The Preamble and Article 11(1) of the Basic Law refer to the Constitution as the legal basis on which it rests. No scholarly analysis of the economic constitution of the Hong Kong Special Administrative Region can be complete without a comparative assessment of the Hong Kong Basic Law and the Chinese Constitution, both adopted by the National People's Congress.[86] The Constitution, in Article 1, defines China to be 'a socialist state governed by a people's democratic dictatorship that is led by the working class and based on an alliance of workers and peasants' with the 'socialist system' as 'the fundamental system' of China. Indeed, Article 6 of the Constitution proclaims that 'socialist public ownership of the means of production' forms the basis of China's 'socialist economic system'. The Constitution sets no formal limit on the scope of economic intervention that the state might conduct.[87] For one, Article 2 of the Constitution states that the National People's Congress and the local people's congresses, on behalf of the people, manage 'state affairs, economic and cultural undertakings, and social affairs'. And Article 7 of the Constitution prescribes that '[t]he state sector of the economy, that is, the sector of the socialist economy under ownership by the whole people, shall be the leading force in the economy' and that 'the state shall ensure the consolidation and development of the state sector of the economy'. In that function, provides Article 14 of the Constitution, '[t]he state shall continually raise labor productivity and improve economic performance to develop productive forces by increasing working people's motivation and level of technical skill, promoting advanced science and technology, improving the systems of economic management and enterprise operation and management', which needs the state to 'appropriately handle accumulation and consumption'.

The difference between these particular provisions of the Constitution and the economic freedoms and property and contractual rights that the Basic Law codifies for the Hong Kong Special Administrative Region only reaffirms the constitutional

85 See John Weiss, 'Neoclassical Economic Perspectives on Industrial Policy' in Arkebe Oqubay, Christopher Cramer, Ha-Joon Chang and Richard Kozul-Wright (eds), *The Oxford Handbook of Industrial Policy* (Oxford: Oxford University Press 2020) 125–149.

86 See Eric C Ip, 'Comparative Constitutional Politics in the Chinese Special Administrative Regions of Hong Kong and Macau' in Ernst Hirsch Ballin et al. (eds), *European Yearbook of Constitutional Law 2020* (The Hague: Springer 2021) 101–133.

87 Roger Pilon, 'A Constitution of Liberty for China' in James A Dorn (ed.), *China in the New Millennium: Market Reforms and Social Development* (Washington: CATO Institute 1998) 333–353, 336.

status of the principle of 'one country, two systems'. Article 31 of the Constitution pertinently declares that '[t]he state may establish special administrative regions when necessary' and, moreover, that '[t]he systems instituted in special administrative regions shall, in light of specific circumstances, be prescribed by laws enacted by the National People's Congress'. The Basic Law is precisely that law of the National People's Congress for Hong Kong, which, in light of Hong Kong's 'specific circumstances', institutes for the Special Administrative Region its own system. Thus, under Article 5 of the Basic Law, '[t]he socialist system and policies shall not be practised in the Hong Kong Special Administrative Region, and the previous capitalist system and way of life shall remain unchanged for 50 years'. Indeed, on 4 April 1990, the National People's Congress, acting in its capacity as the highest organ of state power, issued a decision asserting that: 'The Basic Law of the Hong Kong Special Administrative Region is constitutional as it is enacted in accordance with the Constitution of the People's Republic of China and in the light of the specific conditions of Hong Kong.'[88] This decision reaffirms the validity of the Basic Law.

Conclusion

As Chapter 2 establishes, the spontaneous development of free market constitutionalism in Hong Kong under British colonial rule was made possible by the then government's longstanding commitment to laissez-faire and, since the 1960s, positive non-interventionism, the rise of the welfare, regulatory state in the United Kingdom itself notwithstanding. These constitutional values, which restrained public power in the economy, were themselves products of centuries of evolution in England, unplanned for the most part.[89] In the implementation of the Sino-British Joint Declaration, China drafted the Basic Law as an instrument to intentionally recreate for the Special Administrative Region 'a Chinese version of the British Crown Colony system of government that existed in Hong Kong in the 1980s'.[90] The Basic Law may be regarded as a 'well-designed' constitution in that it accommodates the spontaneously developed classical liberal economic values of the former Colony.[91] Many of the economic principles traceable back to the common law and instruments like Magna Carta have been written into the Basic Law. It is, then, no 'mere coincidence' that some 70 of the Basic Law's 160 provisions embody economic and financial principles considered indispensable to the continuation of Hong Kong's open, competitive, stable and capitalist economy.[92]

88 Decision of the National People's Congress on the Basic Law of the Hong Kong Special Administrative Region of the People's Republic of China (Adopted at the Third Session of the Seventh National People's Congress on 4 April 1990).

89 Scott A Boykin, 'Hayek on Spontaneous Order and Constitutional Design' (2010) 15 (1) *Independent Review* 19–34, 33.

90 Steve Tsang, *A Modern History of Hong Kong* (Hong Kong: Hong Kong University Press 2004) 244.

91 Scott A Boykin, 'Hayek on Spontaneous Order and Constitutional Design' (2010) 15 (1) *Independent Review* 19–34, 33.

92 Douglas W Arner et al., *Financial Markets in Hong Kong: Law and Practice* (2nd edn) (Oxford: Oxford University Press 2016) 47.

4

THE INTERPRETATION AND APPLICATION OF FREE MARKET CONSTITUTIONALISM IN THE HONG KONG BASIC LAW

Introduction

On the basis of Article 31 of the Constitution of the People's Republic of China,[1] China established the Hong Kong Special Administrative Region and put into effect its Basic Law on 1 July 1997 on resumption by China of the exercise of sovereignty over Hong Kong. Days later, Chief Judge of the High Court, Patrick Chan, said in *Hong Kong Special Administrative Region v Ma Wai Kwan David*[2] that the Hong Kong Basic Law 'is a unique document', unique because '[i]t deals with the relationship between the Sovereign and an autonomous region which practises a different system'.[3] Between the Chinese central authorities, as the national sovereign, and Hong Kong, as a special administrative region, that systematic difference is, most notably, economic. The Basic Law preserves that difference:[4] it institutes an economic system for

1 State Council Information Office of the People's Republic of China, *Hong Kong Democratic Progress Under the Framework of One Country, Two Systems* (Beijing: Foreign Language Press 2021) 12: 'The Constitution and the Basic Law together create the constitutional foundations underpinning the HKSAR. They grant the central authorities overall jurisdiction over the region, detail the powers directly exercised by the central authorities, empower the HKSAR to exercise a high degree of autonomy, and confirm the central authorities' right to supervise the exercise of this autonomy.'
2 *Hong Kong Special Administrative Region v Ma Wai Kwan David* [1997] HKCA 652.
3 See *Hong Kong Special Administrative Region v Ma Wai Kwan David* [1997] HKCA 652 [14] (Chan CJHC). The Basic Law of the Hong Kong Special Administrative Region ranks second to the Constitution of the People's Republic of China; see also Articles 78 and 79, Legislation Law of the People's Republic of China (Adopted at the Third Session of the Ninth National People's Congress on 15 March 2000).
4 Danny Gittings, *Introduction to the Hong Kong Basic Law* (2nd edn) (Hong Kong: Hong Kong University Press 2016) 2.

DOI: 10.4324/9780429341229-4

the Region that is different – divergent, more accurately – from that of mainland China.[5]

The Region is to maintain a capitalist system that is institutionally separate from the socialist system of mainland China.[6] To this end, the Basic Law must discharge its function as an economic constitution that codifies a plethora of capitalist principles, understood largely from the vantage point of classical economic liberalism,[7] buttressed by a complementary list of economic rights and freedoms.[8] Thus, the economic constitution of Hong Kong prioritises economic liberty and, to realise this ability, protects rights of private property and contract.[9] This economic constitution has been described as an 'unreconstructed[10] charter of capitalism',[11] one that is sensitive to its inherent economic[12] needs and wants,[13] albeit subject to a measure of textual elasticity for moderate – as in positive – state intervention and social welfare entitlement. The Basic Law

5 Yash Ghai, 'Litigating the Basic Law: Jurisdiction, Interpretation and Procedure' in Johannes MM Chan, HL Fu and Yash Ghai (eds) *Hong Kong's Constitutional Debate: Conflict over Interpretation* (Hong Kong: Hong Kong University Press 2000) 3–52, 49.

6 In *Kwok Cheuk Kin v Secretary for Justice* [2021] 3 HKLRD 140, 170, the Court of Appeal (Poon CJHC, Lam V-P and Barma JA) opined: 'The "one country, two systems" principle is underpinned by the imperative that the Mainland system and the Hong Kong system, though kept separate and distinct under the Basic Law, are within one country and one national constitutional order. There are interfaces where the two systems meet and interact within the constitutional framework set by the Constitution and the Basic Law. Accordingly, there are mechanisms in the Constitution and the Basic Law to regulate their interactions and to ensure that any subject matter lying at the interface conforms with both systems.' See also Yash Ghai, *Hong Kong's New Constitutional Order: The Resumption of Chinese Sovereignty and the Basic Law* (2nd edn) (Hong Kong: Hong Kong University Press 1999) 231.

7 Yash Ghai, *Hong Kong's New Constitutional Order: The Resumption of Chinese Sovereignty and the Basic Law* (2nd edn) (Hong Kong: Hong Kong University Press 1999) 233.

8 Yash Ghai, 'The Rule of Law and Capitalism: Reflections on the Basic Law' in Raymond Wacks (ed.), *Hong Kong, China and 1997: Essays in Legal Theory* (Hong Kong: Hong Kong University Press 1993) 343–365, 344.

9 Yash Ghai, *Hong Kong's New Constitutional Order: The Resumption of Chinese Sovereignty and the Basic Law* (2nd edn) (Hong Kong: Hong Kong University Press 1999) 232; Yash Ghai, 'The Rule of Law and Capitalism: Reflections on the Basic Law' in Raymond Wacks (ed.), *Hong Kong, China and 1997: Essays in Legal Theory* (Hong Kong: Hong Kong University Press 1993) 343–365, 346.

10 Yash Ghai, 'The Rule of Law and Capitalism: Reflections on the Basic Law' in Raymond Wacks (ed.), *Hong Kong, China and 1997: Essays in Legal Theory* (Hong Kong: Hong Kong University Press 1993) 343–365, 345.

11 Yash Ghai, 'The Rule of Law and Capitalism: Reflections on the Basic Law' in Raymond Wacks (ed.), *Hong Kong, China and 1997: Essays in Legal Theory* (Hong Kong: Hong Kong University Press 1993) 343–365, 345.

12 Yash Ghai, 'The Rule of Law and Capitalism: Reflections on the Basic Law' in Raymond Wacks (ed.), *Hong Kong, China and 1997: Essays in Legal Theory* (Hong Kong: Hong Kong University Press 1993) 343–365, 347.

13 Yash Ghai, 'The Rule of Law and Capitalism: Reflections on the Basic Law' in Raymond Wacks (ed.), *Hong Kong, China and 1997: Essays in Legal Theory* (Hong Kong: Hong Kong University Press 1993) 343–365, 349.

constitutes the Region into an economic unit[14] and institutes for it a public finance system in close alignment with Buchanian principles of fiscal conservativism.[15] It shields the operation of the market almost completely from disruptive government interference by way of a constitutional mandate for balanced budgets, low taxes and a sound and stable, backed currency.[16] Quite simply, the Basic Law permits the market to do its work. It amounts to an economic pact that embodies what we call *free market constitutionalism*.

The political structure assembled by the Basic Law exhibits the same free market commitment as its economic system. As Chapter 3 discusses, the Basic Law establishes an 'executive-led system'[17] of government, which facilitates better accountability to the central authorities[18] and allows greater effectiveness in governance both to maintain the prosperity and stability – the opportunity – of Hong Kong.[19] The free market commitment penetrates the legal structure – the legal system – of the Region as well.[20] The Basic Law manifests a near Weberian[21] concern for the functionality[22] of the rule of law[23] and law and

14 Albert HY Chen, 'A Comment on the Basic Law as the Constitutional Foundation of Hong Kong's Economic Future' in Say Goo, Douglas Arner and Zhongfei Zhou (eds), *International Financial Sector Reform: Standard Setting and Infrastructure Development* (London: Kluwer Law International 2002) 251–256, 254.
15 Yash Ghai, 'The Rule of Law and Capitalism: Reflections on the Basic Law' in Raymond Wacks (ed.), *Hong Kong, China and 1997: Essays in Legal Theory* (Hong Kong: Hong Kong University Press 1993) 343–365, 344–345.
16 Yash Ghai, 'The Rule of Law and Capitalism: Reflections on the Basic Law' in Raymond Wacks (ed.), *Hong Kong, China and 1997: Essays in Legal Theory* (Hong Kong: Hong Kong University Press 1993) 343–365, 347, 348.
17 Decision of the Standing Committee of the National People's Congress on Issues Relating to the Methods for Selecting the Chief Executive of the Hong Kong Special Administrative Region in the Year 2007 and for Forming the Legislative Council of the Hong Kong Special Administrative Region in the Year 2008 (Adopted at the Ninth Session of the Standing Committee of the Tenth National People's Congress on 26 April 2004).
18 Yash Ghai, 'The Rule of Law and Capitalism: Reflections on the Basic Law' in Raymond Wacks (ed.), *Hong Kong, China and 1997: Essays in Legal Theory* (Hong Kong: Hong Kong University Press 1993) 343–365, 344.
19 State Council Information Office of the People's Republic of China, *Hong Kong Democratic Progress Under the Framework of One Country, Two Systems* (Beijing: Foreign Language Press 2021) 13: 'Hong Kong practices an executive-led system with the Chief Executive at its core. Under this system, there are checks and balances, and the judiciary exercises its power independently.'
20 Yash Ghai, *Hong Kong's New Constitutional Order: The Resumption of Chinese Sovereignty and the Basic Law* (2nd edn) (Hong Kong: Hong Kong University Press 1999) 239.
21 Max Weber and Keith Tribe (tr), *Economy and Society: A New Translation* (Cambridge: Harvard University Press 2019).
22 Yash Ghai, 'The Rule of Law and Capitalism: Reflections on the Basic Law' in Raymond Wacks (ed.), *Hong Kong, China and 1997: Essays in Legal Theory* (Hong Kong: Hong Kong University Press 1993) 343–365, 355–356.
23 Yash Ghai, 'The Rule of Law and Capitalism: Reflections on the Basic Law' in Raymond Wacks (ed.), *Hong Kong, China and 1997: Essays in Legal Theory* (Hong Kong: Hong Kong University Press 1993) 343–365, 343.

order.[24] Through rational norms, independent judges[25] and competent lawyers,[26] the Basic Law gives security and predictability for businesses, both local and international, to do business with confidence.[27]

Under the Basic Law, the rule of law and a dominant executive, together, sustain Hong Kong's free market economy.[28] To repeat, this exercise in constitutional conservation relies[29] on the three foundational principles that frame the Basic Law: the principle of 'one country, two systems' in Article 1, that '[t]he Hong Kong Special Administrative Region is an inalienable part of the People's Republic of China'; the principle of 'high degree of autonomy' in Article 2, that '[t]he National People's Congress authorizes the Hong Kong Special Administrative Region to exercise a high degree of autonomy'; and the principle of 'Hong Kong people administering Hong Kong'[30] in Article 3, that '[t]he executive authorities and legislature of the Hong Kong Special Administrative Region shall be composed of permanent residents of Hong Kong',[31] 'with patriots as the main body'.[32]

24 Yash Ghai, 'The Rule of Law and Capitalism: Reflections on the Basic Law' in Raymond Wacks (ed.), *Hong Kong, China and 1997: Essays in Legal Theory* (Hong Kong: Hong Kong University Press 1993) 343–365, 346.

25 *The Stock Exchange of Hong Kong Ltd v New World Development Co Ltd* [2006] HKCFA 44 [45] (Ribeiro PJ): 'The purpose of the Basic Law … is to establish the constitutional architecture of that system revolving around the courts of law, catering for the system's separation from that of the Mainland, its continuity with what went before and safeguarding the independence of the judiciary.' See also Michael Ramsden and Stuart Hargreaves, *Hong Kong Basic Law Handbook* (3rd edn) (Hong Kong: Sweet & Maxwell 2022) [2.2].

26 Yash Ghai, 'The Rule of Law and Capitalism: Reflections on the Basic Law' in Raymond Wacks (ed.), *Hong Kong, China and 1997: Essays in Legal Theory* (Hong Kong: Hong Kong University Press 1993) 343–365, 348.

27 Yash Ghai, *Hong Kong's New Constitutional Order: The Resumption of Chinese Sovereignty and the Basic Law* (2nd edn) (Hong Kong: Hong Kong University Press 1999) 241. See Gonzalo Villalta Puig, 'The Misalignment of Commercial Law and Commercial Practice' [2012] 2 *Lloyd's Maritime and Commercial Law Quarterly* 317–336.

28 Albert HY Chen, 'A Comment on the Basic Law as the Constitutional Foundation of Hong Kong's Economic Future' in Say Goo, Douglas Arner and Zhongfei Zhou (eds), *International Financial Sector Reform: Standard Setting and Infrastructure Development* (London: Kluwer Law International 2002) 251–256, 255–256.

29 Priscilla Leung Mei-fun, *The Hong Kong Basic Law: Hybrid of Common Law and Chinese Law* (Hong Kong: LexisNexis 2006) 43.

30 State Council Information Office of the People's Republic of China, *Hong Kong Democratic Progress Under the Framework of One Country, Two Systems* (Beijing: Foreign Language Press 2021) 46: '[W]e must continue to abide by a set of key principles: Hong Kong governed by the people of Hong Kong, a high degree of autonomy for the region, upholding and improving the policy of One Country, Two Systems, Hong Kong governed in accordance with the law, and overall jurisdiction over Hong Kong by the central authorities.'

31 Michael Ramsden and Stuart Hargreaves, *Hong Kong Basic Law Handbook* (3rd edn) (Hong Kong: Sweet & Maxwell 2022) [1], [2], [3].

32 See Decision of the National People's Congress on Improving the Electoral System of the Hong Kong Special Administrative Region (Adopted at the Fourth Session of the Thirteenth National People's Congress on 11 March 2021), Article 1.

The Basic Law prescribes, through Article 11,[33] 'the systems and policies practised in the Hong Kong Special Administrative Region, including the social and economic systems, the system for safeguarding the fundamental rights and freedoms of its residents, the executive, legislative and judicial systems'. Accordingly, as this book explained at the outset, the economic system of Hong Kong is, under Article 5 of the Basic Law, the 'capitalist system and way of life', which 'shall remain unchanged for 50 years', whereas, pursuant to Article 1 of the Constitution, '[t]he socialist system is the basic system of the People's Republic of China'.[34] Within these provisions[35] lies the fundamental systematic difference between Hong Kong and mainland China, the constitutional preservation of which aims to maintain, as the Preamble of the Basic Law proclaims, 'the prosperity and stability of Hong Kong'. Prosperity presupposes stability, which is the basis of development. With the aim of stability, the Basic Law preserves the capitalist system, non-interventionist and fiscally conservative,[36] without change for 50 years from its date of entry into effect on 1 July 1997. It is a prescription[37] to free Hong Kong's market economy from almost all state intervention,[38] be it from the Central People's Government or from the Government of the Region.[39]

The Basic Law revolves around the free market. The structures – economic, political, legal – and the rights and freedoms that the Basic Law establishes for Hong Kong are all to promote the prosperity and stability of the free market: profit-led private ownership and freedom of contract to facilitate market transactions with the assurance of non-intervention; the rule of law to facilitate market transactions with the assurance of certainty; executive dominance to facilitate market transactions with the assurance of effectiveness.[40] The principle of 'one

33 Michael Ramsden and Stuart Hargreaves, *Hong Kong Basic Law Handbook* (3rd edn) (Hong Kong: Sweet & Maxwell 2022) [11.1].
34 State Council Information Office of the People's Republic of China, *Hong Kong Democratic Progress Under the Framework of One Country, Two Systems* (Beijing: Foreign Language Press 2021) 46: 'The socialist system practiced on the mainland, the main body of the country, and the capitalist system in Hong Kong, run in parallel.'
35 David Campbell, 'Economic Ideology and Hong Kong's Governance Structure after 1997' in Raymond Wacks (ed.), *Hong Kong, China and 1997: Essays in Legal Theory* (Hong Kong: Hong Kong University Press 1993) 87–106, 92.
36 Yash Ghai, *Hong Kong's New Constitutional Order: The Resumption of Chinese Sovereignty and the Basic Law* (2nd edn) (Hong Kong: Hong Kong University Press 1999) 242.
37 Yash Ghai, *Hong Kong's New Constitutional Order: The Resumption of Chinese Sovereignty and the Basic Law* (2nd edn) (Hong Kong: Hong Kong University Press 1999) 242.
38 Yash Ghai, 'The Rule of Law and Capitalism: Reflections on the Basic Law' in Raymond Wacks (ed.), *Hong Kong, China and 1997: Essays in Legal Theory* (Hong Kong: Hong Kong University Press 1993) 343–365, 365; David Campbell, 'Economic Ideology and Hong Kong's Governance Structure after 1997' in Raymond Wacks (ed.), *Hong Kong, China and 1997: Essays in Legal Theory* (Hong Kong: Hong Kong University Press 1993) 87–106, 92.
39 Yash Ghai, 'The Rule of Law and Capitalism: Reflections on the Basic Law' in Raymond Wacks (ed.), *Hong Kong, China and 1997: Essays in Legal Theory* (Hong Kong: Hong Kong University Press 1993) 343–365, 365.
40 Yash Ghai, *Hong Kong's New Constitutional Order: The Resumption of Chinese Sovereignty and the Basic Law* (2nd edn) (Hong Kong: Hong Kong University Press 1999) 234.

country, two systems' in the Preamble of the Basic Law[41] translates, most visibly, as 'one country, two *economic* systems'. Hong Kong is an economic entity, a marketplace, a free market. And the Basic Law's spirit of free market constitutionalism is manifest in its various economic functions. Of these functions, Professor Yash Ghai observed:

> The economic provisions of the Basic Law serve four principal (connected and overlapping) purposes to: (a) separate the economic system of the [Hong Kong Special Administrative Region] from the economic system of the [rest of the People's Republic of China]; (b) provide a framework for the operation of a capitalist market; (c) establish key elements of fiscal conservatism; and (d) maintain Hong Kong's status and role as an international trade and finance centre.[42]

The interpretation and application of the provisions of the Basic Law that inform these functions are precisely the subject of this chapter. The chapter demonstrates that most of the economic provisions in the Basic Law have not had much commentary from the courts. Irrespective of the vibrancy of their constitutional jurisprudence, the interpretation of these provisions has been, primarily, legislative rather than judicial in expression. One reason for this phenomenon is their relative novelty. Hong Kong's old Victorian – common law – constitution had no need for its judges to construe such conventions as fiscal prudence, which were already well established in the political branches of the colonial government. Another reason, perhaps a stronger one, is that the non-rights-bearing economic provisions of the Basic Law are, ultimately, too policy oriented to be justiciable[43] with ease. Whatever the reason, much of the analysis that follows necessarily concerns statute law, not case law. The implications of this peculiar phenomenon, which resembles more the methodology of the civil law tradition, are far and wide. To surmise, in the absence of the common law's spontaneity, these provisions necessarily invite legislative direction over the promotion of 'appropriate'[44] environments and policies.

Right to Property

'[N]o advanced civilisation has yet developed', wrote Friedrich Hayek, 'without a government which saw its chief aim in the protection of private

41 See State Council Information Office of the People's Republic of China, *The Practice of the 'One Country, Two Systems' Policy in the Hong Kong Special Administrative Region* (Beijing: Foreign Languages Press 2014).

42 Yash Ghai, 'The Rule of Law and Capitalism: Reflections on the Basic Law' in Raymond Wacks (ed.), *Hong Kong, China and 1997: Essays in Legal Theory* (Hong Kong: Hong Kong University Press 1993) 343–365, 345.

43 Albert HY Chen, 'A Comment on the Basic Law as the Constitutional Foundation of Hong Kong's Economic Future' in Say Goo, Douglas Arner and Zhongfei Zhou (eds), *International Financial Sector Reform: Standard Setting and Infrastructure Development* (London: Kluwer Law International 2002) 251–256, 254.

44 Basic Law of the Hong Kong Special Administrative Region of the People's Republic of China, Articles 109 and 119.

property'.[45] The Basic Law establishes the right to property, both a precondition and a corollary of a free market. It does so through two provisions. First, Article 6 of the Basic Law requires the Region to 'protect the right of private ownership of property'. Second, further to the generality of the earlier declaration, Article 105 of the Basic Law, more specifically, obligates the Region to protect the right to the 'acquisition, use, disposal and inheritance of property'. The right to property is at the core[46] of the capitalist system. With the establishment of that right, the Basic Law accords[47] with the principle of 'one country, two systems' in its Preamble. It moreover accords with the Sino-British Joint Declaration, which, in Article 3(5), provides that '[t]he current social and economic systems in Hong Kong will remain unchanged' and that '[p]rivate property, ownership of enterprises, legitimate right of inheritance and foreign investment will be protected by law'.[48] And, as is evident from the ample judicial commentary on Articles 6 and 105, the most extensive of all economic provisions of the Basic Law, it continues the common law tradition of Hong Kong under British colonial rule, an unassailable bastion of private property protection.

Interpretation and Application

The courts encourage a generous[49] construction of Articles 6 and 105 on the argument that a wider protection of private property rights better meets the inherently capitalist purpose of the provisions.[50] To that effect, in *Harvest Good Development Ltd v Secretary for Justice*[51] (*Harvest Good Development*), the Court of First Instance, through High Court Judge Michael Hartmann, said that 'in the Basic Law, private property rights are rights of real importance' and, further, that 'bearing in mind that the Basic Law entrenches Hong Kong's capitalist system, they are rights … which warrant a generous interpretation'.[52] On Article 105 – the more substantial and specific provision of the two provisions in the Basic Law that establish the right to property – Vice-President Johnson Lam of the Court of Appeal said, in *Hysan Development Co Ltd v Town Planning*

45 FA Hayek, *The Fatal Conceit* (London: Routledge 1988) 32.
46 Michael Ramsden and Stuart Hargreaves, *Hong Kong Basic Law Handbook* (3rd edn) (Hong Kong: Sweet & Maxwell 2022) [6.1].
47 Michael Ramsden and Stuart Hargreaves, *Hong Kong Basic Law Handbook* (3rd edn) (Hong Kong: Sweet & Maxwell 2022) [105.7].
48 The courts endorse reference to the Sino-British Joint Declaration for Basic Law interpretation purposes: *Director of Immigration v Chong Fung Yuen* [2001] HKCFA 48 [6.3] (Li CJ). See too Michael Ramsden and Stuart Hargreaves, *Hong Kong Basic Law Handbook* (3rd edn) (Hong Kong: Sweet & Maxwell 2022) [105.7].
49 Michael Ramsden and Stuart Hargreaves, *Hong Kong Basic Law Handbook* (3rd edn) (Hong Kong: Sweet & Maxwell 2022) [105.1].
50 Malcolm Merry, 'Land' in Johannes Chan and CL Lim (eds), *Law of the Hong Kong Constitution* (3rd edn) (Hong Kong: Sweet & Maxwell 2021) 431–480; Oliver Jones, 'Right to Property' in Johannes Chan and CL Lim (eds), *Law of the Hong Kong Constitution* (3rd edn) (Hong Kong: Sweet & Maxwell 2021) 1129–1149.
51 *Harvest Good Development Ltd v Secretary for Justice* [2007] HKCFI 708.
52 *Harvest Good Development Ltd v Secretary for Justice* [2007] HKCFI 708 [80] (Hartmann J).

Board,[53] that 'we should give a liberal and generous construction to Article 105'.[54] Thus, unsurprisingly, in *Ying Ho Co Ltd v Secretary for Justice*,[55] Justice Kemal Bokhary of the Court of Final Appeal said that 'art.105 is … more protective of property rights than the common law'.[56] There is, nevertheless, a logical limit to the protection; it applies to private property, rather than 'Government properties'.[57]

Real Property and Personal Property Rights

The concept of property has received a broad judicial construction, consistent with the generous approach that the courts of Hong Kong take to the interpretation of Articles 6 and 105.[58] It covers real property and personal property,[59] encompassing choses in possession and choses in action[60] such as inchoate rights,[61] profit and business goodwill[62] and all other forms of property under the common law and, in turn, equity.[63] In line with this approach[64] is Section 3 of the Interpretation and General Clauses Ordinance (Cap 1), which defines property to cover 'money, goods, choses in action and land' as well as 'obligations, easements and every description of estate, interest and profit, present or future, vested or contingent, arising out of or incident to property'.[65]

53 *Hysan Development Co Ltd v Town Planning Board* [2014] HKCA 549.
54 *Hysan Development Co Ltd v Town Planning Board* [2014] HKCA 549 [83] (Lam VP).
55 *Ying Ho Co Ltd v Secretary for Justice* [2004] HKCFA 51.
56 *Ying Ho Co Ltd v Secretary for Justice* [2004] HKCFA 51 [11] (Bokhary PJ); Michael Ramsden and Stuart Hargreaves, *Hong Kong Basic Law Handbook* (3rd edn) (Hong Kong: Sweet & Maxwell 2022) [105.5.1].
57 *Cheung Tak Wing v Director of Administration* [2020] HKCA 124 [84]; Michael Ramsden and Stuart Hargreaves, *Hong Kong Basic Law Handbook* (3rd edn) (Hong Kong: Sweet & Maxwell 2022) [6.4].
58 *Hysan Development Co Ltd v Town Planning Board* [2016] HKCFA 66 [33].
59 *Man Yee Transport Bus Co Ltd v Transport Tribunal* [2008] HKCFI 917 [14] (Cheung J); Michael Ramsden and Stuart Hargreaves, *Hong Kong Basic Law Handbook* (3rd edn) (Hong Kong: Sweet & Maxwell 2022) [105.2].
60 Michael Ramsden and Stuart Hargreaves, *Hong Kong Basic Law Handbook* (3rd edn) (Hong Kong: Sweet & Maxwell 2022) [105.2].
61 *Kong Sau Ching v Kong Pak Yan* [2003] HKCFI 423 [99] (Reyes J).
62 *Kowloon Poultry Laan Merchants Association v Department of Justice* [2002] HKCA 281 [15] (Suffiad J).
63 Article 8, Basic Law; *Director of Immigration v Chong Fung Yuen* [2001] HKCFA 48 [6.1] (Li CJ). See also Oliver Jones, 'Right to Property' in Johannes Chan and CL Lim (eds), *Law of the Hong Kong Constitution* (3rd edn) (Hong Kong: Sweet & Maxwell 2021) 1129–1149; Michael Ramsden and Stuart Hargreaves, *Hong Kong Basic Law Handbook* (3rd edn) (Hong Kong: Sweet & Maxwell 2022) [105.2].
64 Michael Ramsden and Stuart Hargreaves, *Hong Kong Basic Law Handbook* (3rd edn) (Hong Kong: Sweet & Maxwell 2022) [105.2].
65 Interestingly, the concept of property under Articles 6 and 105 could potentially (see Michael Ramsden and Stuart Hargreaves, *Hong Kong Basic Law Handbook* (3rd edn) (Hong Kong: Sweet & Maxwell 2022) [105.2]) cover intellectual property rights, contributory social security credits, statutory licences and legitimate expectations of proprietary interests (maybe, even, rights under government employment contracts): Oliver Jones, 'Right to Property' in Johannes Chan and CL Lim (eds), *Law of the Hong Kong Constitution* (3rd edn)

More specifically, leasehold titles enjoy the express protection of the Basic Law in Article 120: '[A]ll rights in relation to such leases, shall continue to be recognized and protected under the law of the Region.'

Intellectual Property Rights

Intellectual property rights obtain explicit protection from the Basic Law in Article 139 ('[t]he Government … shall … protect by law achievements in scientific and technological research, patents, discoveries and inventions') and in Article 140 ('[t]he Government … shall … protect by law the achievements and the lawful rights and interests of authors in their literary and artistic creation'). Primary legislation such as the Copyright Ordinance (Cap 528), Patents Ordinance (Cap 514), Trade Marks Ordinance (Caps 43 and 559), and Registered Designs Ordinance (Cap 522)[66] elaborate on these protections, with the express sanction of Article 118 of the Basic Law.[67]

Right to Compensation for Lawful Deprivation of Property

The rights that Articles 6 and 105 establish are certainly significant to the conservation of the capitalist system but they are not, in and of themselves, absolute.[68] Ultimately, both provisions demand the protection of the right to property to be 'in accordance with law'. Indeed, Article 105 allows the 'lawful deprivation' of property, albeit subject to the 'right to compensation'. Although the right to property is not absolute,[69] its abrogation or restriction can only be 'in accordance with law', that is, it must be lawful. That form of words – with its call to certainty, precision, and accessibility under the rule of law[70] –

(Hong Kong: Sweet & Maxwell 2021) 1129–1149; Oliver Jones, 'Out with the Owners: The Eurasian Sequels to *JA Pye (Oxford) Ltd v United Kingdom*' (2008) 27 *Civil Justice Quarterly* 260–276, 265–266. See also Michael Ramsden and Stuart Hargreaves, *Hong Kong Basic Law Handbook* (3rd edn) (Hong Kong: Sweet & Maxwell 2022) [105.2–105.3]. The Hong Kong courts could, again potentially, endorse the jurisprudence of the European Court of Human Rights – *Chow Shun Yung v Wei Pih Stella* [2003] HKCFA 27 [36] (Ribeiro J); *Shum Kwok Sher v Hong Kong Special Administrative Region* [2002] HKCFA 27 [59] (Sir Anthony Mason NPJ) – on Article 1 of Protocol No 1 to the Convention for the Protection of Human Rights and Fundamental Freedoms (European Convention on Human Rights, as amended): 'Every natural or legal person is entitled to the peaceful enjoyment of his possessions.'

66 Michael Ramsden and Stuart Hargreaves, *Hong Kong Basic Law Handbook* (3rd edn) (Hong Kong: Sweet & Maxwell 2022) [139.1].

67 Michael Ramsden and Stuart Hargreaves, *Hong Kong Basic Law Handbook* (3rd edn) (Hong Kong: Sweet & Maxwell 2022) [118.1].

68 Oliver Jones, 'Right to Property' in Johannes Chan and CL Lim (eds), *Law of the Hong Kong Constitution* (3rd edn) (Hong Kong: Sweet & Maxwell 2021) 1129–1149.

69 *Securities and Futures Commission v 'C'* [2008] HKCFI 959 [104] (Kwan J).

70 *Shum Kwok Sher v Hong Kong Special Administrative Region* [2002] HKCFA 27 [60], [62–65] (Mason J). See also Oliver Jones, 'Right to Property' in Johannes Chan and CL

enhances[71] the protection that, given this constitutional mandate, the Region must give to the right to property.

In that respect, Chief Justice Andrew Li, Justices Patrick Chan and Roberto Ribeiro, together with former Chief Justice of Australia, Sir Anthony Mason, sitting as a Non–Permanent Judge, said in the Court of Final Appeal's decision in *Leung Kwok Hung v Hong Kong Special Administrative Region*[72] that: 'A law which confers discretionary powers on public officials, the exercise of which may interfere with fundamental rights, must give an adequate indication of the scope of the discretion.'[73] Several years later, Justice Ribeiro, speaking for the same Court in *Hysan Development Co Ltd v Town Planning Board*[74] (*Hysan*), used an identical form of words to make a stance against 'uncharted administrative discretion': 'That phrase and similar phrases … mandate the principle of legal certainty, requiring the subject-matter of the Article to be regulated by laws which are accessible and precisely defined.'[75] His Lordship thus reasoned that the formula secures the protection of property rights, which 'are to be guaranteed by clear and accessible laws'.[76]

Test of Proportionality

To pass constitutional muster, any restriction by law on the constitutional right to property must survive the test of proportionality.[77] For Justice Ribeiro, in *Hysan*, the proportionality analysis comes in four steps, namely:

> (i) [W]hether [the] restrictions pursue a legitimate aim; (ii) whether they are rationally connected with achieving that aim; and (iii) whether they represent a proportionate means of achieving that end, [while] (iv) weighing the detrimental impact of the restrictions against the social benefit gained.[78]

His Lordship intended the fourth step to safeguard[79] especially significant – if not necessarily fundamental – constitutional rights, for it 'requires the Court to

Lim (eds), *Law of the Hong Kong Constitution* (3rd edn) (Hong Kong: Sweet & Maxwell 2021) 1129–1149.

71 Michael Ramsden and Stuart Hargreaves, *Hong Kong Basic Law Handbook* (3rd edn) (Hong Kong: Sweet & Maxwell 2022) [105.1.1].

72 *Leung Kwok Hung v Hong Kong Special Administrative Region* [2005] HKCFA 40.

73 *Leung Kwok Hung v Hong Kong Special Administrative Region* [2005] HKCFA 40 [28–29] (Li CJ, Chan J, Ribeiro J, Mason J).

74 *Hysan Development Co Ltd v Town Planning Board* [2016] HKCFA 66.

75 *Hysan Development Co Ltd v Town Planning Board* [2016] HKCFA 66 [32].

76 *Hysan Development Co Ltd v Town Planning Board* [2016] HKCFA 66 [32]. See further *Interush Limited v Commissioner of Police* [2019] HKCA 70 [6.26].

77 Michael Ramsden and Stuart Hargreaves, *Hong Kong Basic Law Handbook* (3rd edn) (Hong Kong: Sweet & Maxwell 2022) [105.1.1].

78 *Hysan Development Co Ltd v Town Planning Board* [2016] HKCFA 66 [54] (Ribeiro J). See also [135].

79 Michael Ramsden and Stuart Hargreaves, *Hong Kong Basic Law Handbook* (3rd edn) (Hong Kong: Sweet & Maxwell 2022) [105.1.1].

make a value judgment as to whether the impugned law or governmental decision, despite having satisfied the first three requirements, operates on particular individuals with such oppressive unfairness that it cannot be regarded as a proportionate means of achieving the legitimate aim in question'.[80]

Compensable Deprivation

Even if lawful and proportionate, an abrogation of or a restriction on the right to property – real or personal – must still amount to a deprivation if it is to prompt a right to compensation under Article 105. Deprivation is irreversible and occurs through either formal expropriation of the property or such interference with the property as to cause it to lose all economically viable use.[81] In this last respect, Justice Frank Stock in the Court of Appeal's decision in *Fine Tower Associates Ltd v Town Planning Board*[82] held that 'action adversely affecting use of property, despite falling short of formal expropriation, may … nonetheless properly be described as deprivation'[83] and that '*de facto* deprivation for the purpose of establishing a right to compensation, contemplates the removal of any meaningful use, of all economically viable use'.[84] The burden of proof of deprivation is on the claimant;[85] it is a 'case specific'[86] question,[87] of 'fact and degree'[88] and of substance not of form.[89]

Expropriation

Deprivation through expropriation must be direct.[90] That is, the Government of the Region must itself acquire the property rather than compel its transfer to

80 *Hysan Development Co Ltd v Town Planning Board* [2016] HKCFA 66 [54] (Ribeiro J). See Johannes Chan, 'Proportionality after *Hysan*: Fair Balance, Manifestly without Reasonable Foundation and *Wednesbury* Unreasonableness' (2019) 49(2) *Hong Kong Law Journal* 265–294.

81 Michael Ramsden and Stuart Hargreaves, *Hong Kong Basic Law Handbook* (3rd edn) (Hong Kong: Sweet & Maxwell 2022) [105.5]; Oliver Jones, 'Right to Property' in Johannes Chan and CL Lim (eds), *Law of the Hong Kong Constitution* (3rd edn) (Hong Kong: Sweet & Maxwell 2021) 1129–1149.

82 *Fine Tower Associates Ltd v Town Planning Board* [2007] HKCA 332.

83 *Fine Tower Associates Ltd v Town Planning Board* [2007] HKCA 332 [17] (Stock J).

84 *Fine Tower Associates Ltd v Town Planning Board* [2007] HKCA 332 [24] (Stock J).

85 *Man Yee Transport Bus Co Ltd v Transport Tribunal* [2008] HKCFI 917 [13] (Cheung J); Michael Ramsden and Stuart Hargreaves, *Hong Kong Basic Law Handbook* (3rd edn) (Hong Kong: Sweet & Maxwell 2022) [105.5].

86 *Fine Tower Associates Ltd v Town Planning Board* [2007] HKCA 332 [18] (Stock J); *Fine Tower Associates Ltd v Town Planning Board* [2008] HKCFA 65 [1] (Ribeiro J).

87 Michael Ramsden and Stuart Hargreaves, *Hong Kong Basic Law Handbook* (3rd edn) (Hong Kong: Sweet & Maxwell 2022) [105.5].

88 *Fine Tower Associates Ltd v Town Planning Board* [2007] HKCA 332 [17] (Stock J).

89 Michael Ramsden and Stuart Hargreaves, *Hong Kong Basic Law Handbook* (3rd edn) (Hong Kong: Sweet & Maxwell 2022) [105.5].

90 Michael Ramsden and Stuart Hargreaves, *Hong Kong Basic Law Handbook* (3rd edn) (Hong Kong: Sweet & Maxwell 2022) [105.5.1]; Oliver Jones, 'Right to Property' in

a third, private party. In spite of this requirement for direct government acquisition, in *Ying Ho Co Ltd v Secretary for Justice*,[91] Justice Bokhary suggested[92] that expropriation does not always need to be for a public purpose.[93] This interpretation is, nonetheless, not reconcilable with the Chinese text of the provision, which includes the characters 徵用 (*zhengyong*). In English, these characters commonly translate as 'expropriation'. Since the official version of the Basic Law in the Chinese language takes precedence over that in the English language[94] – whereas the two language versions of the Sino-British Joint Declaration are equally authentic[95] – the more accurate interpretation has to be that deprivation exclusively means expropriation. This interpretation has indeed obtained judicial endorsement, albeit from a lower court, the Court of First Instance.[96] In *Harvest Good Development*,[97] High Court Judge Hartmann opined that Article 105 'mean[s] that the Hong Kong Special Administrative Region shall in accordance with law, protect the right of individuals to compensation for the expropriation of their property by the Government or a Government agency'.[98]

Loss of All Economically Viable Use

The loss of all economically viable use of property may constitute deprivation. However, it is not compensable if the legislation in question is one of general application and in pursuit of the public interest.[99] Again, High Court Judge Hartmann said words to that effect in *Harvest Good Development*: 'If therefore the legislation is of a general regulatory nature, authorising deprivation in the public

Johannes Chan and CL Lim (eds), *Law of the Hong Kong Constitution* (3rd edn) (Hong Kong: Sweet & Maxwell 2021) 1129–1149.

91 *Ying Ho Co Ltd v Secretary for Justice* [2004] HKCFA 51.

92 See Michael Ramsden and Stuart Hargreaves, *Hong Kong Basic Law Handbook* (3rd edn) (Hong Kong: Sweet & Maxwell 2022) [105.5.1].

93 *Ying Ho Co Ltd v Secretary for Justice* [2004] HKCFA 51 [11] (Bokhary PJ).

94 Decision of the Standing Committee of the National People's Congress on the English Text of the Basic Law of the Hong Kong Special Administrative Region of the People's Republic of China (Adopted on 28 June 1990).

95 Malcolm Merry, 'Land' in Johannes Chan and CL Lim (eds), *Law of the Hong Kong Constitution* (3rd edn) (Hong Kong: Sweet & Maxwell 2021) 431–480.

96 Michael Ramsden and Stuart Hargreaves, *Hong Kong Basic Law Handbook* (3rd edn) (Hong Kong: Sweet & Maxwell 2022) [105.5.1].

97 *Harvest Good Development Ltd v Secretary for Justice* [2007] HKCFI 708 [138] (Hartmann J); *Weson Investment Ltd v Commissioner of Inland Revenue* [2007] HKCA 23 [79] (Tang VP).

98 *Harvest Good Development Ltd v Secretary for Justice* [2007] HKCFI 708 [138] (Hartmann J); *Weson Investment Ltd v Commissioner of Inland Revenue* [2007] HKCA 23 [79] (Tang VP). See also Albert Chen, 'The Basic Law and the Protection of Property Rights' (1993) 23 *Hong Kong Law Journal* 31–78, 60; Albert HY Chen, 'Constitutional Protection of Property Rights in Hong Kong' (SSRN, 1 May 2007), http://papers.ssrn.com/sol3/papers.cfm?abstract_id=1367587, accessed 1 July 2021.

99 Michael Ramsden and Stuart Hargreaves, *Hong Kong Basic Law Handbook* (3rd edn) (Hong Kong: Sweet & Maxwell 2022) [105.5.2].

interest so as to regulate the rights and duties of society then a deprivation of property under that legislation *may* not constitute a deprivation for which compensation must be made.'[100] In that instance, compensation for deprivation would depend on a proportionality assessment of the fourth stage: 'The real issue … is whether a fair balance has been struck between the aims of the statutory scheme and the hardship visited upon those whose possessory title is extinguished.'[101]

Not Compensable Deprivation

Not all deprivation of property is compensable under the Basic Law. The inevitable deprivation of property that comes with taxation, adverse possession, Government re-entry of land or planning controls, for instance, are not compensable since all are legislative exercises of general regulation for the public interest.[102]

Taxation

Taxation does not constitute compensable deprivation under Article 105. Although, in principle, taxation is a form of expropriation – 'By nature, any tax statute is inequitable in the wide sense of the word. It takes away what a person has earned by his sweat and labour and puts it in general revenue for purposes, many of which have no interest or concern to the taxpayer …'[103] – it is, ultimately, an exercise of government through legislation of general application and in pursuit of the public interest.[104] The Court of First Instance settled this matter[105] in *Weson Investment Ltd v Commissioner of Inland Revenue*, thus:[106]

> [T]ax due and payable under the IRO [Inland Revenue Ordinance (Cap 112)] shall be recoverable as a civil debt due to the Government. … Thus the 'property' being the tax assessed becomes the Government's, and until payment is a debt due to it. So, Article 105 has no application.[107]

100 *Harvest Good Development Ltd v Secretary for Justice* [2007] HKCFI 708 [144] (Hartmann J). See also Michael Ramsden and Stuart Hargreaves, *Hong Kong Basic Law Handbook* (3rd edn) (Hong Kong: Sweet & Maxwell 2022) [105.5.2].
101 *Harvest Good Development Ltd v Secretary for Justice* [2007] HKCFI 708 [185] (Hartmann J).
102 Michael Ramsden and Stuart Hargreaves, *Hong Kong Basic Law Handbook* (3rd edn) (Hong Kong: Sweet & Maxwell 2022) [105.5.4].
103 *Wong Tai Wai David v Commissioner of Inland Revenue* [2003] HKCFI 172 [8] (To J).
104 Michael Ramsden and Stuart Hargreaves, *Hong Kong Basic Law Handbook* (3rd edn) (Hong Kong: Sweet & Maxwell 2022) [105.5.4].
105 Michael Ramsden and Stuart Hargreaves, *Hong Kong Basic Law Handbook* (3rd edn) (Hong Kong: Sweet & Maxwell 2022) [105.5.2].
106 *Weson Investment Ltd v Commissioner of Inland Revenue* [2005] HKCFI 613.
107 *Weson Investment Ltd v Commissioner of Inland Revenue* [2005] HKCFI 613 [42–43] (Gill J).

The Court of Appeal endorsed the construction in these words: 'Article 105 of the Basic Law has no application to legitimate taxation. … When the Government imposes tax on the individual, of necessity it deprives the individual of his property without any right to compensation.'[108] What is more, the Basic Law expressly authorises the practice of taxation under Article 108 and also under Articles 64 and 73. In the same vein, third-party levies, service fees and other public imposts do not constitute compensable deprivation.[109]

Adverse Possession

The acquisition of a possessory title does not constitute compensable deprivation.[110] However unfair it may be to the paper title owner,[111] the Region maintains a title deeds registration system and not a title registration one,[112] such that adverse possession cannot be tantamount to expropriation. It follows that the limitation of actions to recover land and the subsequent extinction of title through adverse possession pursuant to Section 7(2) and Section 17 of the Limitation Ordinance (Cap 347) are compatible with Articles 6 and 105.[113]

Government Re-entry and Resumption

The right to property is not an absolute right and, consequently, Article 105 allows the 'lawful deprivation' of property, which can occur on either re-entry or resumption by the Government of the Region. Under Section 7 of the Government Rights (Re-entry and Vesting Remedies) Ordinance (Cap 126), a right of re-entry to the

108 *Weson Investment Ltd v Commissioner of Inland Revenue* [2007] HKCA 23 [18] (Rogers J). See also *Commissioner of Inland Revenue v Ngai Lik Electronics Co Ltd* [2008] HKDC 331 [8] (Chow J: 'Article 105 … is a provision dealing with the protection of individuals. I cannot see how it can be related to tax matters.').

109 *Julita F Raza v Chief Executive in Council* [2005] HKCFI 2 [90] (Hartmann J); Oliver Jones, 'Right to Property' in Johannes Chan and CL Lim (eds), *Law of the Hong Kong Constitution* (3rd edn) (Hong Kong: Sweet & Maxwell 2021) 1129–1149; Michael Ramsden and Stuart Hargreaves, *Hong Kong Basic Law Handbook* (3rd edn) (Hong Kong: Sweet & Maxwell 2022) [105.5.4].

110 Michael Ramsden and Stuart Hargreaves, *Hong Kong Basic Law Handbook* (3rd edn) (Hong Kong: Sweet & Maxwell 2022) [105.5.3].

111 *Chan Suk Yin v Harvest Good Development* [2006] HKCFA 7 [36] (Lord Hoffmann NPJ). Since adverse possessory title does not bind the head lessor, the leasehold title owner can always surrender the lease to the Region and, therefore, cancel liability for further rent: Malcolm Merry, 'Land' in Johannes Chan and CL Lim (eds), *Law of the Hong Kong Constitution* (3rd edn) (Hong Kong: Sweet & Maxwell 2021) 431–480; Michael Ramsden and Stuart Hargreaves, *Hong Kong Basic Law Handbook* (3rd edn) (Hong Kong: Sweet & Maxwell 2022) [105.5.3].

112 See Malcolm Merry, 'Land' in Johannes Chan and CL Lim (eds), *Law of the Hong Kong Constitution* (3rd edn) (Hong Kong: Sweet & Maxwell 2021) 431–480.

113 *Harvest Good Development Ltd v Secretary for Justice* [2007] HKCFI 708 [191] (Hartmann J); *Hong Kong Kam Lan Koon Ltd v Realray Investments Ltd* [2007] HKCFI 1037 [31] (Lam J).

land accrues to the Government either on breach of a covenant, condition or stipulation in the Government lease or on default in the payment of Government rent or premium for that land.[114] The model 'Conditions of Sale' expressly remove the entitlement to compensation: 'In the event of re-entry by the Government ..., the Purchaser shall not be entitled to ... any payment or compensation whatsoever.' The power of re-entry without compensation is coherent with Article 105 because this provision applies solely to public expropriations rather than private transactions. The right of re-entry is not the only right of the Government of the Region when it comes to land, however. The Government of the Region has the right of resumption as well. The Lands Resumption Ordinance (Cap 124) permits the resumption of Government lands for public purposes. Unlike in respect of the exercise of the right of re-entry to land, the exercise of the right of resumption of land can indeed coexist with compensation, at least in respect of land use that accords with the terms of the Government lease.[115]

Planning Controls

Laws and measures to implement planning[116] or (down)zoning[117] as well as building control laws and measures that affect the use of property[118] or public facilities[119] do not constitute compensable deprivation within the meaning of Article 105. The reason is that they do not deprive the leasehold title owner of a meaningful alternative use of the land, as Justice of Appeal Stock explained in *Fine Tower Associates Ltd v Town Planning Board*.[120] This judicial position is coherent with Article 7 of the Basic Law, which states that '[t]he land and natural resources within the Hong Kong Special Administrative Region shall be

114 See also Government Rent (Assessment and Collection) Ordinance (Cap 515).

115 *R v Board of Arbitrators, ex p Attorney-General* (1955) 39 HKLR 47; *Cheermark Investment Ltd v Director of Lands* [2017] HKCA 606.

116 Malcolm Merry, 'Land' in Johannes Chan and CL Lim (eds), *Law of the Hong Kong Constitution* (3rd edn) (Hong Kong: Sweet & Maxwell 2021) 431–480; Michael Ramsden and Stuart Hargreaves, *Hong Kong Basic Law Handbook* (3rd edn) (Hong Kong: Sweet & Maxwell 2022) [105.5.4].

117 *United Grand Ltd v Town Planning Board* [2007] HKCA 356.

118 *Fine Tower Associates Ltd v Town Planning Board* [2007] HKCA 332 [33] (Stock J): 'There can be no expectation upon the purchase of land that the use permitted by the lease will forever after match the use permitted by town planning regulation.'; *Kaisilk Development Ltd v Urban Renewal Authority* [2002] HKCFI 1224 [19] (Woolley J): 'there never has been a right to compensation in Hong Kong to owners affected by planning or building control and the Basic Law does not change that'; *Kowloon Poultry Laan Merchants Association v Department of Justice* [2002] HKCA 281; *Secretary for Justice v To Kan Chi* [2000] HKCFA 87.

119 *Yook Tong Electric Co Ltd v Commissioner for Transport* [2003] HKCFI 626 [57] (Hartmann J): 'It seems to me that art.105, while it affords protection to the applicant to use its property, does not extend to the use by the applicant of public facilities.'; Michael Ramsden and Stuart Hargreaves, *Hong Kong Basic Law Handbook* (3rd edn) (Hong Kong: Sweet & Maxwell 2022) [105.5.4].

120 *Fine Tower Associates Ltd v Town Planning Board* [2007] HKCA 332 [23] (Stock JA).

State property' and that '[t]he Government of the Hong Kong Special Administrative Region shall be responsible for their management, use and development'. If, however, the laws and measures in question are so 'exceptionally unreasonable'[121] and disruptive to the use of the property as to deprive the property of economic value, then such an interference would very much amount to compensable deprivation.[122] In this regard, to determine actual or de facto deprivation of (real) property for the purposes of Article 105, High Court Judge Anselmo Reyes, on behalf of the Court of First Instance, put forward a three-question test inspired by the jurisprudence of the European Court of Human Rights:[123] that is, (1) whether 'the land could be used in its existing state'; (2) whether 'the land was not valueless and could still be sold in the market'; and (3) whether 'it was possible to seek permission to carry out construction or improvement works on the land'.[124] It goes without saying that no compensation is payable for the expectation of a grant or any other land interest.[125]

Compensation to Correspond to the Real Value

Once established, deprivation is subject to compensation under Article 105. The provision states that '[s]uch compensation shall correspond to the real value of the property concerned at the time [of deprivation] and shall be freely convertible and paid without undue delay'.[126] This mandate functions as a guarantee for 'property rights'.[127] However broad in scope, the guarantee is not without limits: the assessment of compensation for deprivation has to be full and fair, not arbitrary and unrealistic.[128] In that respect, Lord Millett, sitting on the Court of Final Appeal as a Non-Permanent Judge, observed that, while '[in] general, property is worth what it will fetch, and its open market value reflects its real value', Article 105 does not require compensation for 'a speculative price which exceeds the true value of the property'[129] and, furthermore,

121 *Hysan Development Co Ltd v Town Planning Board* [2016] HKCFA 66 [142] (Ribeiro PJ).

122 *Fine Tower Associates Ltd v Town Planning Board* [2005] HKCFI 289 [54] (Hartmann J). See also *Penny's Bay Investment Co Ltd v Director of Lands* [2010] HKCFA 42.

123 *Sporrong and Lönnroth v Sweden* (1982) 5 EHRR 35.

124 *Fine Tower Associates Ltd v Town Planning Board* [2006] HKCFI 1043 [48–50] (Reyes J). See also Malcolm Merry, 'Land' in Johannes Chan and CL Lim (eds), *Law of the Hong Kong Constitution* (3rd edn) (Hong Kong: Sweet & Maxwell 2021) 431–480.

125 Lands Resumption Ordinance (Cap 124), s 12(c).

126 Michael Ramsden and Stuart Hargreaves, *Hong Kong Basic Law Handbook* (3rd edn) (Hong Kong: Sweet & Maxwell 2022) [105.5.5].

127 *Secretary for Transport v Delight World Ltd* [2006] HKCFA 107 [29] (Bokhary PJ); Michael Ramsden and Stuart Hargreaves, *Hong Kong Basic Law Handbook* (3rd edn) (Hong Kong: Sweet & Maxwell 2022) [105.5.5].

128 Malcolm Merry, 'Land' in Johannes Chan and CL Lim (eds), *Law of the Hong Kong Constitution* (3rd edn) (Hong Kong: Sweet & Maxwell 2021) 431–480.

129 *Director of Lands v Yin Shuen Enterprises Ltd* [2003] HKCGA 43 [56] (Lord Millett NPJ). See also *R (SRM Global Master Fund LP) v Commissioners of Her Majesty's Treasury* [2009] EWCA Civ 788.

that compensation is only payable for 'the interest acquired'.[130] Incidentally, the Basic Law establishes no review mechanism for the assessment of compensation. The normal processes for judicial review of administrative action would, therefore, apply.

Real Property

Specifically, for the deprivation of real property, the Lands Resumption Ordinance (Cap 124) in Section 10 confers jurisdiction on the Lands Tribunal to determine the compensation payable. Section 12(d) states that 'the value of the land resumed shall be taken to be the amount which the land if sold by a willing seller in the open market might be expected to realize'. This provision codifies the principle of equivalence that, in the decision of the House of Lords in *Director of Buildings and Lands v Shun Fung Ironworks Ltd*,[131] Lord Nicholls translated into a ready formula, which later served as the template for Hong Kong's legislation.

Personal Property

Although the deprivation of personal property does not have a similar statutory regime to administer it, the academic consensus is that the same approach to the determination of compensation remains applicable.[132] The only caveat relates to personal property of a type that is subject to intense market price fluctuation, which would require a precise and careful study of the time of purchase in order to avoid any miscalculation in payment.[133]

Right to the Acquisition, Use, Disposal and Inheritance of Property

The scope of Article 105 is wider than that of Article 6. The former provision establishes 'the right of individuals and legal persons to the acquisition, use, disposal and inheritance of property'.[134] The restriction of these additional

130 *Director of Lands v Yin Shuen Enterprises Ltd* [2003] HKCGA 43 [57] (Lord Millett NPJ).

131 *Director of Buildings and Lands v Shun Fung Ironworks Ltd* [1995] 2 AC 111 [124–125] (Lord Nicholls of Birkenhead); with approval in *Director of Lands v Yin Shuen Enterprises Ltd* [2003] HKCGA 43 [12] (Lord Millett NPJ).

132 Oliver Jones, 'Right to Property' in Johannes Chan and CL Lim (eds), *Law of the Hong Kong Constitution* (3rd edn) (Hong Kong: Sweet & Maxwell 2021) 1129–1149.

133 Oliver Jones, 'Right to Property' in Johannes Chan and CL Lim (eds), *Law of the Hong Kong Constitution* (3rd edn) (Hong Kong: Sweet & Maxwell 2021) 1129–1149.

134 *Hysan Development Co Ltd v Town Planning Board* [2014] HKCA 549 [60] (Lam VP). Two observations are notable here. First, the right to the acquisition of property is a right to gain ownership on commercial terms. Second, the right to the inheritance of property is subject to the Inheritance (Provision for Family and Dependants) Ordinance (Cap 481): Oliver Jones, 'Right to Property' in Johannes Chan and CL Lim (eds), *Law of the Hong Kong Constitution* (3rd edn) (Hong Kong: Sweet & Maxwell 2021) 1129–1149.

rights does not constitute compensable deprivation[135] and so, in that respect, the right is not actionable.[136] Their restriction, however, can still invalidate[137] the laws and measures in question under Article 105, although not under Article 6,[138] if they fail the 'well-known proportionality test'.[139] In the Court of Appeal, Vice-President Stock formulated the proportionality test in these terms: 'That the restriction pursues a legitimate aim; that the restriction is rationally connected to the legitimate aim; and that the restriction is no more than is necessary to accomplish the aim.'[140] Interestingly, for High Court Judge Andrew Cheung in the Court of First Instance decision in *Hong Kong Special Administrative Region v Au Kwok Kuen*,[141] the right to the use of property does 'require the government (including the police) to take reasonable and appropriate measures to protect Hong Kong residents' homes and other premises against intrusion and their privacy at home against interference'.[142] To put it another way, Articles 105 and 6 jointly provide for a kind of subsidiary right against interference with property – real and personal – by third parties.[143]

Protection of the Ownership of Enterprises and the Investments from Outside the Region

Additional to the call of Article 109 of the Basic Law to maintain 'the status of Hong Kong as an international financial centre', the third paragraph of Article 105 states that: 'The ownership of enterprises and the investments from outside the

135 *HKSAR v Asaduzzaman* [2010] HKCA 606 [24] (Stock VP); *Fine Tower Associates Ltd v Town Planning Board* [2007] HKCA 332 [17] (Stock JA): 'It can safely be postulated as a general proposition that regulatory restriction on use, imposed in the public interest, that does not amount to a taking or deprivation of the property, gives no right to compensation'; *Kaisilk Development Ltd v Urban Renewal Authority* [2003] HKCA 269 [32–33] (Rogers VP); Michael Ramsden and Stuart Hargreaves, *Hong Kong Basic Law Handbook* (3rd edn) (Hong Kong: Sweet & Maxwell 2022) [105.4].

136 Oliver Jones, 'Right to Property' in Johannes Chan and CL Lim (eds), *Law of the Hong Kong Constitution* (3rd edn) (Hong Kong: Sweet & Maxwell 2021) 1129–1149.

137 Michael Ramsden and Stuart Hargreaves, *Hong Kong Basic Law Handbook* (3rd edn) (Hong Kong: Sweet & Maxwell 2022) [105.4].

138 Oliver Jones, 'Out with the Owners: The Eurasian Sequels to *JA Pye (Oxford) Ltd v United Kingdom*' (2008) 27 *Civil Justice Quarterly* 260–276, 275: 'It is .... entirely fitting for art.6 to require any limits on the scope to acquire property to satisfy the "fair balance test".'; Michael Ramsden and Stuart Hargreaves, *Hong Kong Basic Law Handbook* (3rd edn) (Hong Kong: Sweet & Maxwell 2022) [105.4].

139 *Hong Kong Special Administrative Region v Asaduzzaman* [2010] HKCA 606 [25] (Stock VP).

140 *Hong Kong Special Administrative Region v Asaduzzaman* [2010] HKCA 606 [25] (Stock VP).

141 *Hong Kong Special Administrative Region v Au Kwok Kuen* [2010] HKCFI 487.

142 *Hong Kong Special Administrative Region v Au Kwok Kuen* [2010] HKCFI 487 [74] (Cheung J); Michael Ramsden and Stuart Hargreaves, *Hong Kong Basic Law Handbook* (3rd edn) (Hong Kong: Sweet & Maxwell 2022) [105.4].

143 Oliver Jones, 'Right to Property' in Johannes Chan and CL Lim (eds), *Law of the Hong Kong Constitution* (3rd edn) (Hong Kong: Sweet & Maxwell 2021) 1129–1149; Michael Ramsden and Stuart Hargreaves, *Hong Kong Basic Law Handbook* (3rd edn) (Hong Kong: Sweet & Maxwell 2022) [105.4].

Region shall be protected by law.' In *Securities and Futures Commission v 'C'*,[144] the Court of First Instance, in the words of High Court Judge Susan Kwan, restated the argument by counsel that the provision 'extends protection to non-residents … and that the protection is guaranteed to individuals and corporations'.[145] The implication is that Article 105 should be read coherently with Articles 109, 112 and 118 of the Basic Law to protect foreign investments in Hong Kong[146] through the requisite standards of treatment under international investment law, namely, most-favoured-nation treatment, national treatment, fair and equitable treatment and full security and protection treatment. On this interpretation, the Basic Law would, in principle, offer a rule against expropriation, although, in the absence of legislation, it would not automatically create an enforceable, compensable right.[147] Notably, Article 112 requires the Government of the Region to 'safeguard the free flow of capital within, into and out of the Region'.

Right of Private Ownership of Property

Article 6, which should be read in conjunction with Article 105, states that: 'The Hong Kong Special Administrative Region shall protect the right of private ownership of property in accordance with law.' This provision, itself an extension of the proclamation in Article 5 of a 'capitalist system and way of life' to remain unchanged for no less than half a century, recognises private property,[148] which, indisputably, lies protected[149] at the core[150] of

144 *Securities and Futures Commission v 'C'* [2008] HKCFI 959.

145 *Securities and Futures Commission v 'C'* [2008] HKCFI 959 [101] (Kwan J); cf. *Securities and Futures Commission v 'C'* [2009] HKCA 580; Michael Ramsden and Stuart Hargreaves, *Hong Kong Basic Law Handbook* (3rd edn) (Hong Kong: Sweet & Maxwell 2022) [105.6].

146 Michael Ramsden and Stuart Hargreaves, *Hong Kong Basic Law Handbook* (3rd edn) (Hong Kong: Sweet & Maxwell 2022) [105.6].

147 Oliver Jones, 'Right to Property' in Johannes Chan and CL Lim (eds), *Law of the Hong Kong Constitution* (3rd edn) (Hong Kong: Sweet & Maxwell 2021) 1129–1149.

148 Michael Ramsden and Stuart Hargreaves, *Hong Kong Basic Law Handbook* (3rd edn) (Hong Kong: Sweet & Maxwell 2022) [6.4].

149 Yash Ghai, *Hong Kong's New Constitutional Order: The Resumption of Chinese Sovereignty and the Basic Law* (2nd edn) (Hong Kong: Hong Kong University Press 1999) 155; Xiao Weiyun, *One Country, Two Systems: An Account of the Drafting of the Hong Kong Basic Law* (Beijing: Peking University Press 2001) 392–393. Since 2004, the Constitution protects private property further to Article 13, which states (*Amendment to the Constitution of the People's Republic of China* adopted at the Second Session of the Tenth National People's Congress on 14 March 2004): 'Citizens' lawful private property is inviolable.'; 'The state shall protect the right of citizens to own and inherit private property in accordance with the provisions of law.'; 'The state may, in order to meet the demands of the public interest and in accordance with the provisions of law, expropriate or requisition citizens' private property and furnish compensation.': see Michael Ramsden and Stuart Hargreaves, *Hong Kong Basic Law Handbook* (3rd edn) (Hong Kong: Sweet & Maxwell 2022) [6.2].

150 Michael Ramsden and Stuart Hargreaves, *Hong Kong Basic Law Handbook* (3rd edn) (Hong Kong: Sweet & Maxwell 2022) [6.1].

capitalism.[151] In substantive terms, Article 6 'adds nothing'[152] to Article 105.[153] Surplusage, though, it is not;[154] that, at least, has been the presumption.[155] It is a separate provision[156] with a general, albeit complementary purpose, namely, to complete and settle the more specific[157] protections of Article 105.[158] For Vice-President Lam of the Court of Appeal: 'The right of private ownership protected under Article 6 of the Basic Law … should not be overridden without justification.'[159]

Freedom of Choice of Occupation

Like the right to property codified into Articles 6 and 105, the right to freedom of choice of occupation codified into Article 33 of the Basic Law is indispensable to the capitalist system. Historically, Hong Kong has been and, for many commentators, still is the freest market economy in the world. In a free market, economic actors are, in an exercise of self-ownership, free to choose their role in the economy.[160] Article 33 establishes that right for 'Hong Kong residents', which Article 41 of the Basic Law extends[161] to 'persons in the Hong Kong Special Administrative Region other than Hong Kong residents'. It further extends to juridical persons.[162] Commenting on the scope of this provision in the Court of Appeal, Chief Judge Cheung of the High Court in *Leung Sze Ho Albert v The Bar Council of*

151 See Michael Ramsden and Stuart Hargreaves, *Hong Kong Basic Law Handbook* (3rd edn) (Hong Kong: Sweet & Maxwell 2022) [6.2].
152 *Fine Tower Associates Ltd v Town Planning Board* [2007] HKCA 332 [13] (Stock JA); Michael Ramsden and Stuart Hargreaves, *Hong Kong Basic Law Handbook* (3rd edn) (Hong Kong: Sweet & Maxwell 2022) [6.3].
153 *Man Yee Transport Bus Co Ltd v Transport Tribunal* [2008] HKCFI 917 [15] (Cheung J).
154 Michael Ramsden and Stuart Hargreaves, *Hong Kong Basic Law Handbook* (3rd edn) (Hong Kong: Sweet & Maxwell 2022) [6.3].
155 Oliver Jones, 'Out with the Owners: The Eurasian Sequels to *JA Pye (Oxford) Ltd v United Kingdom*' (2008) 27 *Civil Justice Quarterly* 260–276, 275; Oliver Jones, 'Right to Property' in Johannes Chan and CL Lim (eds), *Law of the Hong Kong Constitution* (3rd edn) (Hong Kong: Sweet & Maxwell 2021) 1129–1149; with Michael Ramsden and Stuart Hargreaves, *Hong Kong Basic Law Handbook* (3rd edn) (Hong Kong: Sweet & Maxwell 2022).
156 *Wong Hon Sun v Hong Kong Special Administrative Region* [2009] HKCFA 67 [22] (Bokhary PJ).
157 Michael Ramsden and Stuart Hargreaves, *Hong Kong Basic Law Handbook* (3rd edn) (Hong Kong: Sweet & Maxwell 2022) [6.3].
158 Michael Ramsden and Stuart Hargreaves, *Hong Kong Basic Law Handbook* (3rd edn) (Hong Kong: Sweet & Maxwell 2022) [6.3]; Oliver Jones, 'Right to Property' in Johannes Chan and CL Lim (eds), *Law of the Hong Kong Constitution* (3rd edn) (Hong Kong: Sweet & Maxwell 2021) 1129–1149.
159 *Good Faith Properties Ltd v Cibean Development Company Ltd* [2014] HKCA 475 [11] (Lam VP).
160 *MA v Director of Immigration* [2012] HKCA 514 [139] (Fok JA); *GA v Director of Immigration* [2014] HKCFA 14 [71–73] (Ma CJ).
161 Michael Ramsden and Stuart Hargreaves, *Hong Kong Basic Law Handbook* (3rd edn) (Hong Kong: Sweet & Maxwell 2022) [33.1].
162 *Ngo Kee Construction Co Ltd v The Hong Kong Housing Authority* [2001] HKCFI 867 [57] (Cheung J).

the Hong Kong Bar Association[163] declared that 'Article 33, like other provisions in chapter III, should therefore be given "a generous interpretation"' with reference to its purpose.[164] That generous and purposive[165] interpretation[166] recognises two[167] limbs in the provision: '[F]irst, a resident shall not be forced to work in any or any particular field of occupation against his wish. Secondly, a resident shall have the freedom to work in any or any particular field of occupation of his choice.'[168] In other words, for High Court Judge Lam at first instance, the freedom finds impingement 'both where a person is compelled to take up an occupation against his wishes, and where he is prevented from pursuing an occupation of his choice'.[169]

Article 33 thus operates, in its first limb, as a 'constitutional guarantee'[170] against non-consensual – direct or indirect – government conscription[171] to particular fields of occupation,[172] what, to all intents and purposes, would be 'a form of

163 *Leung Sze Ho Albert v The Bar Council of the Hong Kong Bar Association* [2016] HKCA 510.

164 *Leung Sze Ho Albert v The Bar Council of the Hong Kong Bar Association* [2016] HKCA 510 [2] (Cheung CJHC) (by reference also to the context as evident from the drafting history in the Sino-British Joint Declaration, Article 3(5)); *MA v Director of Immigration* [2012] HKCA 514 [13] (Fok JA). See Michael Ramsden and Stuart Hargreaves, *Hong Kong Basic Law Handbook* (3rd edn) (Hong Kong: Sweet & Maxwell 2022): [33.1], [33.2].

165 Michael Ramsden and Stuart Hargreaves, *Hong Kong Basic Law Handbook* (3rd edn) (Hong Kong: Sweet & Maxwell 2022) [33.1]. In *Lai Chee Ying v Secretary for Security* [2021] 4 HKLRD 695, 710, the Court of First Instance (Anthony Chan J) summed up the essential elements of the purposive approach on which to interpret the Basic Law: '(1) Subject to any binding interpretation by the [NPCSC], in interpreting a particular provision of the [Basic Law], the court construes the language of the text to ascertain the legislative intent as expressed in the language objectively. (2) The court does not construe the language in isolation. It considers the language used in the text in the light of its context and purpose. Put another way, the court ascertains the meaning borne by the language when considered in light of its context and purpose. (3) Whilst in interpreting the provisions in question, the court must avoid a literal, technical, narrow or rigid approach, it cannot give the language a meaning which the language cannot bear. (4) There are two kinds of aids to interpretation: internal and external aids. As its name suggest, the internal aids are derived from what it is found within the [Basic Law], including provisions in the [Basic Law] other than the one in question and the Preamble. External aids are external materials which throw light on the context or purpose of the [Basic Law] or its particular provisions.'

166 *MA v Director of Immigration* [2012] HKCA 514 [13] (Fok JA).

167 Michael Ramsden and Stuart Hargreaves, *Hong Kong Basic Law Handbook* (3rd edn) (Hong Kong: Sweet & Maxwell 2022) [33.2].

168 *Leung Sze Ho Albert v The Bar Council of the Hong Kong Bar Association* [2016] HKCA 510 [7] (Cheung CJHC). The freedom of choice of occupation extends to academia, with its own freedoms under Articles 34 and 137 of the Basic Law.

169 *Leung Sze Ho Albert v The Bar Council of the Hong Kong Bar Association* [2015] HKCFI 1742 [68] (Lam J).

170 *Leung Sze Ho Albert v The Bar Council of the Hong Kong Bar Association* [2016] HKCA 510 [6] (Cheung CJHC).

171 Michael Ramsden and Stuart Hargreaves, *Hong Kong Basic Law Handbook* (3rd edn) (Hong Kong: Sweet & Maxwell 2022) [33.2].

172 In that respect, it follows that the exclusion, by injunction, of an employee from participation in a work activity would need to satisfy the freedom under Article 33 of the Basic Law: *PCCW – HKT Telephone Ltd v David Matthew McDonald Aitken* [2009] HKCFA 11

enslavement'.[173] The second limb, however, does not stand for 'a general right to work';[174] that is, it does not guarantee employment, either generally or in a particular field of occupation.[175] In *GA v Director of Immigration*,[176] Chief Justice Geoffrey Ma explained that Article 33 deals only with the freedom of choice of occupation[177] as a 'narrow',[178] passive, negative right; a right of non-interference. Earlier in the same case, Justice Joseph Fok said in the Court of Appeal that: '[This right] does not imply a right to take up available employment in the first place. Nor does it confer an unqualified right to obtain employment, which is necessarily subject to market forces and to legal constraints.'[179] High Court Judge Hartmann within the Court of First Instance acknowledged the free market imperative when, in *Cheng Chun-Ngai Daniel v Hospital Authority*,[180] his Lordship opined: 'Whether employment can in fact be obtained will depend on the laws of supply and demand as they apply in the market place.'[181] Decisions of personnel – the commercial dynamics of hire and fire, the management, in other words, of human resources – are resolutely beyond the scope of Article 33 and, therefore, unreviewable by the courts:[182] 'Article 33 … does not have the function of turning a commercial decision into a public one.'[183]

Like most constitutional rights and freedoms, the freedom of choice of occupation is hardly absolute. The exercise of the freedom must be in accordance with law and, as such, the choice to enter, practise and exit an occupation ought to be subject to legal constraints, including 'laws and policies relating to labour' per Article 147 of the Basic Law, 'immigration controls' pursuant to Article 154 of the Basic Law as well as professional standards,[184] public morals and even employment

[1] (Bokhary PJ). Note that national service is an exception to the freedom: *Cheng Chun-Ngai Daniel v Hospital Authority* [2004] HKCFI 1023 [55] (Hartmann J); *Financial Services and Systems Ltd v Secretary for Justice* [2007] HKCFI 684 [52] (Fung J). See too Michael Ramsden and Stuart Hargreaves, *Hong Kong Basic Law Handbook* (3rd edn) (Hong Kong: Sweet & Maxwell 2022) [33.2].

173 *Cantor Fitzgerald Europe v Jason Jon Boyer* [2012] HKCFI 256 [31] (Reyes J).

174 *Leung Sze Ho Albert v The Bar Council of the Hong Kong Bar Association* [2016] HKCA 510 [7] (Cheung CJHC).

175 *MA v Director of Immigration* [2012] HKCA 514 [13] (Fok JA); *GA v Director of Immigration* [2014] HKCFA 14 [62] (Ma CJ).

176 *GA v Director of Immigration* [2014] HKCFA 14.

177 *GA v Director of Immigration* [2014] HKCFA 14 [71] (Ma CJ).

178 Michael Ramsden and Stuart Hargreaves, *Hong Kong Basic Law Handbook* (3rd edn) (Hong Kong: Sweet & Maxwell 2022) [33.2].

179 *GA v Director of Immigration* [2012] HKCA 515 [143] (Fok JA).

180 *Cheng Chun-Ngai Daniel v Hospital Authority* [2004] HKCFI 1023.

181 *Cheng Chun-Ngai Daniel v Hospital Authority* [2004] HKCFI 1023 [55–56] (Hartmann J); *Ng King Tat Philip v Post-Release Supervision Board* [2010] HKCFI 2044 [116] (Cheung J).

182 Michael Ramsden and Stuart Hargreaves, *Hong Kong Basic Law Handbook* (3rd edn) (Hong Kong: Sweet & Maxwell 2022) [33.3].

183 *Ngo Kee Construction Co Ltd v The Hong Kong Housing Authority* [2001] HKCFI 867 [57] (Cheung J).

184 *Leung Sze Ho Albert v The Bar Council of the Hong Kong Bar Association* [2016] HKCA 510.

restrictions on prison leavers,[185] all of which are lawful insofar as they can survive the requisite fair balance test.[186] Indeed, Article 142 of the Basic Law functions as a kind of constraint on occupational choice for it empowers professional organisations to 'assess and confer professional qualifications'.[187]

Public Finance

The Basic Law's commitment to relatively unbridled capitalism is most evident in Section 1 (Public Finance, Monetary Affairs, Trade, Industry and Commerce) of Chapter V. This section, as its title implies, deals with the main elements of economic activity, such as private property; public finance, including taxation and public expenditure; private finance, specifically, Hong Kong's status as an international financial centre; monetary affairs; trade; shipping and aviation; and industry and commerce. On taxation and expenditure, the Basic Law constitutionalises the fiscal autonomy of the Region in order to maintain its 'prosperity and stability' as the Preamble declares. It does so in various ways, all adherent to the public finance management principle behind the slogan 'Market Leads, Government Facilitates',[188] a derivation of the laissez-faire, positive non-interventionism under British colonial rule.

Independent Finances

First, Article 106 of the Basic Law erects a firewall to separate the public finances of the Region from those of mainland China: 'The Hong Kong Special Administrative Region shall have independent finances.' The effect of this 'fiscal firewall'[189] is twofold: one, '[t]he Hong Kong Special Administrative Region shall use its financial revenues exclusively for its own purposes'; and, two, '[t]he Central People's Government shall not levy taxes in the Hong Kong Special Administrative Region'. Article 116 of the Basic Law secures the

185 *Ng King Tat Philip v Post-Release Supervision Board* [2010] HKCFI 2044 [117] (Cheung J): '[T]he legitimate aims of the restrictions are not in doubt, namely, rehabilitation, re-integration and the prevention of re-offending.' See too Michael Ramsden and Stuart Hargreaves, *Hong Kong Basic Law Handbook* (3rd edn) (Hong Kong: Sweet & Maxwell 2022) [33.4].

186 Firew Kebede Tiba, 'Freedom of Choice of Occupation and Academic Freedom' in Johannes Chan and CL Lim (eds), *Law of the Hong Kong Constitution* (3rd edn) (Hong Kong: Sweet & Maxwell 2021) 923–954.

187 Firew Kebede Tiba, 'Freedom of Choice of Occupation and Academic Freedom' in Johannes Chan and CL Lim (eds), *Law of the Hong Kong Constitution* (3rd edn) (Hong Kong: Sweet & Maxwell 2021) 923–954; Yash Ghai, *Hong Kong's New Constitutional Order: The Resumption of Chinese Sovereignty and the Basic Law* (2nd edn) (Hong Kong: Hong Kong University Press 1999) 436; Michael Ramsden and Stuart Hargreaves, *Hong Kong Basic Law Handbook* (3rd edn) (Hong Kong: Sweet & Maxwell 2022) [142.1].

188 Legislative Council – Hong Kong, Speech by the Financial Secretary, the Hon John C Tsang moving the Second Reading of the Appropriation Bill 2009 (25 February 2009) [21].

189 Anton Cooray, *Constitutional Law in Hong Kong* (4th edn) (London: Kluwer Law International 2021) 406.

autonomy[190] of the Region's public finances. It is with an assurance that: 'Export quotas, tariff preferences and other similar arrangements, which are obtained or made by the Hong Kong Special Administrative Region or which were obtained or made and remain valid, shall be enjoyed exclusively by the Region.'

That fiscal autonomy[191] finds further expression in the Double Taxation Arrangement between mainland China and the Region of 21 August 2006.[192] Indeed, Hong Kong's fiscal autonomy is so extensive that it escapes the cost of defence since, under Article 14 of the Basic Law, '[e]xpenditure for the garrison shall be borne by the Central People's Government'.[193] In fact,[194] the Court of First Instance, in the words of Deputy High Court Judge Anthony To, was able to say in *Secretary for Justice v Penta-Ocean Construction Co Ltd*[195] that, '[i]n respect of financial matters, the Hong Kong SAR is its own sovereign'.[196]

The Principle of Keeping Expenditure within the Limits of Revenues

Second, to preserve its fiscal autonomy, Article 107 of the Basic Law requires the Region to 'follow the principle of keeping expenditure within the limits of revenues in drawing up its budget, and strive to achieve a fiscal balance, avoid deficits and keep the budget commensurate with the growth rate of its gross domestic product'. This provision prescribes a policy of fiscal caution through a balanced-budget rule and an expenditure rule,[197] both inspired by the work of Nobel Memorial Prize laureate in Economic Sciences, James M Buchanan,[198] a

190 Michael Ramsden and Stuart Hargreaves, *Hong Kong Basic Law Handbook* (3rd edn) (Hong Kong: Sweet & Maxwell 2022) [106.1].
191 Anton Cooray, *Constitutional Law in Hong Kong* (4th edn) (London: Kluwer Law International 2021) 408.
192 Arrangement between the Mainland of China and the Hong Kong Special Administrative Region for the Avoidance of Double Taxation and the Prevention of Fiscal Evasion with respect to Taxes on Income (21 August 2006) and related protocols.
193 Law of the People's Republic of China on the Garrisoning of the Hong Kong Special Administrative Region (Adopted at the Twenty-third Meeting of the Standing Committee of the Eighth National People's Congress on 30 December 1996 and promulgated by Order No 80 of the President of the People's Republic of China on 30 December 1996). See Michael Ramsden and Stuart Hargreaves, *Hong Kong Basic Law Handbook* (3rd edn) (Hong Kong: Sweet & Maxwell 2022) [14].
194 Anton Cooray, *Constitutional Law in Hong Kong* (4th edn) (London: Kluwer Law International 2021) 406.
195 *Secretary for Justice v Penta-Ocean Construction Co Ltd* [2003] HKCFI 361.
196 *Secretary for Justice v Penta-Ocean Construction Co Ltd* [2003] HKCFI 361 [12] (To J).
197 Gonzalo Villalta Puig, 'Fiscal Constitutionalism and Fiscal Culture: A Comparative Study of the Balanced-Budget Rule in the Spanish Constitution and the Hong Kong Basic Law' (2013) 43(1) *Hong Kong Law Journal* 5–53.
198 See James M Buchanan, 'The Balanced Budget Amendment: Clarifying the Arguments' (1997) 90(1–4) *Public Choice* 117–138, 131; James M Buchanan, 'Concerning Future Generations' in JM Ferguson (ed.), *Public Debt and Future Generations* (Chapel Hill: University of North Carolina Press 1964) 55; James M Buchanan, 'The Moral Dimension of Debt Financing' (1985) 23(1) *Economic Inquiry* 1–6; James M Buchanan,

founder of the constitutional political economy research programme to which we subscribe. The balanced-budget rule aims[199] to achieve budgetary balance and avoid budgetary deficit on the premise that the two can lead to unsustainable government debt and, in turn, degrade the economic environment requisite for the status of the Region as an 'international financial centre' under Article 109. The expenditure rule seeks to align the rate of government spending with that of economic production, again on the assumption that increases in public expenditure would result in unsustainable government debt.[200]

Article 107, therefore, is a constitutional mandate for financial stability.[201] It is, in the words of former Chief Executive and Financial Secretary Sir Donald Tsang, a 'guarantee of financial prudence'.[202] That guarantee, necessarily, delimits the scope of the Medium Range Forecast budgetary criteria.[203] Nevertheless, in response to the Asian financial crisis of years past and the recent challenges that the COVID–19 pandemic have posed to the local economy, the Government of the Region, in order to finance a multitude of relief measures, has had to resort to the textual flexibility of Article 107 to shift away from a budgetary surplus paradigm to a budgetary balance paradigm, 'over time'.[204] It is no surprise, then, that with such open, untimed formulations as 'follow the principle' and 'strive to',[205] this policy provision can only be directory rather than mandatory in

'Clarifying Confusion about the Balanced Budget Amendment' (1995) 48(3) *National Tax Journal* 347–355, 355.

199 Michael Ramsden and Stuart Hargreaves, *Hong Kong Basic Law Handbook* (3rd edn) (Hong Kong: Sweet & Maxwell 2022) [107.1].

200 Michael Ramsden and Stuart Hargreaves, *Hong Kong Basic Law Handbook* (3rd edn) (Hong Kong: Sweet & Maxwell 2022) [107.1].

201 Shu-hung Tang, 'Budgetary Guidelines and Fiscal Performance in Hong Kong' (1997) 10 (7) *International Journal of Public Sector Management* 547–571; Shu-hung Tang, 'Art 107 of the Hong Kong Basic Law and the Budgetary Criteria of the Medium Range Forecast: Review and Outlook' (Joint Committee for the Promotion of the Basic Law of Hong Kong, 7 April 2001), http://www.jcpbasiclaw.org.hk/syposium/11/03e.htm, accessed 1 July 2021. Consider the work on Hong Kong of the international Financial Stability Board.

202 Legislative Council – Hong Kong, Speech by the Financial Secretary, the Hon Donald Tsang OBE JP moving the Second Reading of the Appropriation Bill 1997 (12 March 1997) [19], [20].

203 Jermain T Lam, 'Globalization and Fiscal Management in Hong Kong' (2001) 13(2) *Asian Review of Public Administration* 45–62, 49.

204 For the 2022–2023 budget, the budgetary criteria were: '– *Budget surplus/deficit* The Government aims to achieve, over time, a balance in the consolidated account. — *Expenditure policy* The general principle is that, over time, the growth rate of expenditure should be commensurate with the growth rate of the economy. — *Revenue policy* The Government aims to maintain, over time, the real yield from revenue. — *Fiscal reserves* The Government aims to maintain adequate reserves in the long run.': Legislative Council — Hong Kong, Speech by the Financial Secretary, the Hon Paul MP Chan moving the Second Reading of the Appropriation Bill 2022, Appendix A: Medium Range Forecast: Section I: Forecasting Assumptions and Budgetary Criteria [10] (23 February 2022); see Anton Cooray, *Constitutional Law in Hong Kong* (4th edn) (London: Kluwer Law International 2021) 409.

205 Anton Cooray, *Constitutional Law in Hong Kong* (4th edn) (London: Kluwer Law International 2021) 409.

effect[206] and, therefore, unlikely to be justiciable.[207] Indeed, as of the 2020–2021 budget, 'an annual deficit in the Operating Account in each of the coming five financial years' has been the policy practice[208] although with the reassurance that brings the availability of discretionary access to fiscal reserves 'equivalent to 16 months of government expenditure'.[209] In the 2022–2023 Budget Speech, Financial Secretary Paul Chan forecasted that the Region's deficit will turn back into surplus: '[O]ur solid foundation built on the principle of "One Country, Two Systems", [has] turned the consolidated deficit projected in the Original Estimates into a consolidated surplus projected in the Revised Estimates for this financial year.' Apart from a policy of fiscal caution, Article 107 anticipates a narrow tax base as it places a cap on unbalanced budgets and expenditure.[210]

Low Tax Policy and Independent Taxation System

Third, and as a Buchanian[211] companion to Article 107, Article 108 of the Basic Law mandates a 'low tax policy … as reference' while it strengthens the

206 Yash Ghai, *Hong Kong's New Constitutional Order: The Resumption of Chinese Sovereignty and the Basic Law* (2nd edn) (Hong Kong: Hong Kong University Press 1999) 243.

207 Anton Cooray, *Constitutional Law in Hong Kong* (4th edn) (London: Kluwer Law International 2021) 410.

208 Legislative Council – Hong Kong, Speech by the Financial Secretary, the Hon Paul MP Chan moving the Second Reading of the Appropriation Bill 2020 (26 February 2020) [166]; 'The HKSAR Government runs a fiscal deficit in 2019–20, the first time for Hong Kong over the past 15 years. I forecast a deficit for the next five years as well.': Legislative Council – Hong Kong, Speech by the Financial Secretary, the Hon Paul MP Chan moving the Second Reading of the Appropriation Bill 2020 (26 February 2020) [168]. The Government explains: 'The forecast deficit in the Operating Account in the following four years [as of February 2021] is attributed to the fact that recurrent expenditure will be higher than revenue receipts.': Legislative Council – Hong Kong, Speech by the Financial Secretary, the Hon Paul MP Chan moving the Second Reading of the Appropriation Bill 2021 (24 February 2021) [195]. Importantly, the 2022–2023 budget points to a surplus: 'I forecast a deficit in the Operating Account in 2022–23, which will turn into a surplus in 2023–24. There will be a surplus in the Capital Account in each of the five years during the MRF period. Except for the estimated deficit in the Operating Account in 2022–23 which is mainly attributed to the one-off relief measures and anti-epidemic expenditure announced in this Budget, there will be a surplus in the subsequent four years.': Legislative Council – Hong Kong, Speech by the Financial Secretary, the Hon Paul MP Chan moving the Second Reading of the Appropriation Bill 2022 (23 February 2022) [202].

209 Fiscal reserves have been steadily on the decrease from, for instance, 22 months of government expenditure in 2015–2016 (Legislative Council – Hong Kong, Speech by the Financial Secretary, the Hon John C Tsang moving the Second Reading of the Appropriation Bill 2015 (25 February 2015) [171]) but they 'will gradually rebound': Legislative Council – Hong Kong, Speech by the Financial Secretary, the Hon Paul MP Chan moving the Second Reading of the Appropriation Bill 2022 (23 February 2022) [176].

210 Firew Kebede Tiba, 'Freedom of Choice of Occupation and Academic Freedom' in Johannes Chan and CL Lim (eds), *Law of the Hong Kong Constitution* (3rd edn) (Hong Kong: Sweet & Maxwell 2021) 923–954; Anton Cooray, *Constitutional Law in Hong Kong* (4th edn) (London: Kluwer Law International 2021) 410.

211 See, generally, James M Buchanan, *Public Principles of Public Debt: A Defense and Restatement* (Homewood: Richard D Irwin 1958); James M Buchanan and Gordon Tullock, *The Calculus of Consent: Logical Foundations of Constitutional Democracy* (Ann Arbor:

fiscal autonomy of Hong Kong with the establishment of an 'independent taxation system' and the provision for 'laws on its own concerning types of taxes, tax rates, tax reductions, allowances and exemptions, and other matters of taxation'. While the provision pretends[212] to issue a mandate for constitutional economics,[213] the reference to a low tax policy is unlikely, in practice, to be justiciable because of the vagueness of the phrase and the optionality of the command.[214]

Nevertheless, through Article 108, the Region does retain its own tax regime, separate from that of mainland China, and, with it, the two policy features that have historically characterised the territory, namely, a low tax system and a simple tax system. Since its foundation as a port free of customs duties, Hong Kong has been reluctant to obtain revenue through taxation sources. As a matter of policy, the preference instead has been for revenue through non-taxation sources, especially through land premium transactions as all land is subject to leasehold title. This policy has the support of Article 7 of the Basic Law, which declares that: 'The land and natural resources within the Hong Kong Special Administrative Region shall be State property.'[215] The Region, therefore, has long had a narrow taxation base, with correspondingly low taxation rates. It too has long had a simple and stable – *friendly*[216] – tax structure. Under the Inland Revenue Ordinance (Cap 112), the Region has three types of direct, income tax: a profits tax, which applies to profits with a source in Hong Kong irrespective of residence status; a salaries tax, which applies to net chargeable income either at progressive rates (from 2 per cent to 17 per cent) or at a standard rate of 15 per cent, whichever of the two rates is lower; and a property tax, which applies a standard of 15 per cent on the net

University of Michigan Press 1962); James M Buchanan and Richard E Wagner, *Fiscal Responsibility in Constitutional Democracy* (Leiden: Martinus Nijhoff 1978); James M Buchanan and Richard A Musgrave, *Public Finance and Public Choice: Two Contrasting Visions of the State* (Cambridge: MIT Press 1999).

212 Michael Ramsden and Stuart Hargreaves, *Hong Kong Basic Law Handbook* (3rd edn) (Hong Kong: Sweet & Maxwell 2022) [108.1].

213 Anton Cooray, *Constitutional Law in Hong Kong* (4th edn) (London: Kluwer Law International 2021) 410.

214 Anton Cooray, *Constitutional Law in Hong Kong* (4th edn) (London: Kluwer Law International 2021) 411.

215 Article 7 states further: 'The Government of the Hong Kong Special Administrative Region shall be responsible for their management, use and development and for their lease or grant to individuals, legal persons or organizations for use or development. The revenues derived therefrom shall be exclusively at the disposal of the government of the Region.' See also Firew Kebede Tiba, 'Freedom of Choice of Occupation and Academic Freedom' in Johannes Chan and CL Lim (eds), *Law of the Hong Kong Constitution* (3rd edn) (Hong Kong: Sweet & Maxwell 2021) 923–954; Michael Ramsden and Stuart Hargreaves, *Hong Kong Basic Law Handbook* (3rd edn) (Hong Kong: Sweet & Maxwell 2022) [7].

216 InvestHK, The Government of the Hong Kong Special Administrative Region (Setting up in Hong Kong: Tax Basics, 14 May 2020), https://www.investhk.gov.hk/en/setting-hong-kong/tax-basics.html, accessed 1 July 2021.

assessable value of the taxable property. In addition to these income taxes, the Stamp Duty Ordinance (Cap 117) applies a tax on the transfer of Hong Kong stock or property and the Betting Duty Ordinance (Cap 108) applies a tax on the stakes and proceeds of horse races, cash sweeps, lotteries and football matches. The Region has no sales tax or value-added tax, withholding tax, capital gains tax, dividends tax or estate tax. In spite of its narrow base and low and simple profile, the tax system remains efficient, so much so as to allow fiscal reserves worth many months of public expenditure.

The Legislative Council Exercises the Power and Function to Examine and Approve Budgets and to Approve Taxation and Public Expenditure

The 'levying of contributions', noticed Hayek, is 'necessarily an act of coercion and must therefore be done in accordance with general rules laid down by the Legislative Assembly'.[217] This principle is entrenched in the Basic Law, which recognises the plenary authority of the Legislative Council over public finance. That is, the Legislative Council – in accordance with Article 73(2) and (3) of the Basic Law – exercises the power and function[218] '[t]o examine and approve budgets' as well as '[t]o approve taxation and public expenditure' albeit upon the proposal of the Government of the Region, which, under Article 62(4) of the Basic Law,[219] wields the power '[t]o draw up and introduce budgets', subject to the balanced-budget rule. A throwback to the constitutional system under British colonial rule, the Basic Law states in Article 64 that the Government of the Region 'shall obtain approval from the Council for taxation and public expenditure' in spite of Article 48(3) of the Basic Law, which provides that the Chief Executive has '[t]o sign budgets passed by the Legislative Council', with no delegation of the power whatsoever possible.[220]

In these two respects, Hong Kong abides by an autochthonous version of the Westminster system's[221] checks and balances in public finance,[222] which recognises a legislative power of veto,[223] as evidenced by the declaration in the Bill of Rights 1689:

217 FA Hayek, 'A Model Constitution' in Chiaki Nishiyama and Kurt R Leube (eds) *The Essence of Hayek* (Stanford: Hoover Institution Press 1984) 382–406, 403.
218 Michael Ramsden and Stuart Hargreaves, *Hong Kong Basic Law Handbook* (3rd edn) (Hong Kong: Sweet & Maxwell 2022) [73.3.1].
219 Michael Ramsden and Stuart Hargreaves, *Hong Kong Basic Law Handbook* (3rd edn) (Hong Kong: Sweet & Maxwell 2022) [62.2].
220 *Wong Kei Kwong v Principal Assistant Secretary for the Civil Service* [2008] HKCFI 104 [51] (Saunders J). See too Michael Ramsden and Stuart Hargreaves, *Hong Kong Basic Law Handbook* (3rd edn) (Hong Kong: Sweet & Maxwell 2022) [48.3].
221 *Leung Kwok Hung v President of the Legislative Council* [2007] 1 HKLRD 387, 403 (Hartmann J).
222 The Legislative Council under British colonial rule had 'plenary' and 'ample' authority: *Leung Kwok Hung v Secretary for Justice* [2020] HKCA 192 [81]–[82]. See too Michael Ramsden and Stuart Hargreaves, *Hong Kong Basic Law Handbook* (3rd edn) (Hong Kong: Sweet & Maxwell 2022) [73.1.1].
223 Anton Cooray, *Constitutional Law in Hong Kong* (4th edn) (London: Kluwer Law International 2021) 405.

'[t]hat levying Money for or to the Use of the Crowne … without Grant of Parlyament … is Illegall'. This power is a significant concession[224] that the Basic Law makes to an otherwise 'executive-led system'.[225] In principle, the Chief Executive must resign, further to Article 52(3) of the Basic Law, when, 'after the Legislative Council is dissolved [under Article 50 of the Basic Law] because it refuses to pass a budget or any other important bill, the new Legislative Council still refuses to pass the original bill in dispute'.[226] This provision is, in all probability, meant to facilitate consensus between the Chief Executive and the Legislative Council.[227] Notably, in acknowledgement of the 'one country, two systems' principle, Article 48(3) requires the Chief Executive to 'report the budgets and final accounts to the Central People's Government' but – ever respectful of the separation of public finances between Hong Kong and mainland China – it is only 'for the record'.

The Public Finance Ordinance (Cap 2) complements the provisions of the Basic Law on the control and management of public finances.[228] In particular, it outlines the process for the Financial Secretary to prepare, the Finance Committee of the Legislative Council[229] to examine, and the Legislative Council to approve the annual Appropriation Bill, that is, the budget.[230] Of course, the peculiar consequence is that, because the Basic Law mandates financial prudence, the Government of the Region needs to accumulate fiscal reserves, which, unlike the general revenue, it can and does indeed spend[231] without the need for

224 Anton Cooray, *Constitutional Law in Hong Kong* (4th edn) (London: Kluwer Law International 2021) 405–406.

225 While the Legislative Council can dispose of legislation – with the exception of '[b]ills which do not relate to public expenditure or political structure or the operation of the government' under Article 74 of the Basic Law – only the Government of the Region can propose legislation under Article 62(5) also of the Basic Law. See Michael Ramsden and Stuart Hargreaves, *Hong Kong Basic Law Handbook* (3rd edn) (Hong Kong: Sweet & Maxwell 2022) [62.3], [74.1].

226 Article 51 of the Basic Law provides for 'provisional short-term appropriations'.

227 Anton Cooray, *Constitutional Law in Hong Kong* (4th edn) (London: Kluwer Law International 2021) 405–406.

228 *Secretary for Justice v Penta-Ocean Construction Co Ltd* [2003] HKCFI 361 [12] (To J).

229 Rules of Procedure of the Legislative Council of the Hong Kong Special Administrative Region (Made by the Legislative Council of the Hong Kong Special Administrative Region on 2 July 1998 in pursuance of Article 75 of the Basic Law of the Hong Kong Special Administrative Region of the People's Republic of China, Amended to 16 July 2021). See too Michael Ramsden and Stuart Hargreaves, *Hong Kong Basic Law Handbook* (3rd edn) (Hong Kong: Sweet & Maxwell 2022) [73.2].

230 Legislative Council – Hong Kong, 'Report of the Panel on Constitutional Affairs on Arrangements arising from Articles 50 and 51 of the Basic Law' (LC Paper No CB(2) 17/99–00, 8 October 1999); Legislative Council – Hong Kong, 'Report of the Panel on Constitutional Affairs on Articles 50 and 51 of the Basic Law' (LC Paper No CB(2) 1022/99–00, 11 February 2000).

231 'I consider that, with ample fiscal reserves, the Government has to increase public expenditure amid an economic downturn to stimulate the economy and ride out the difficult times with members of the public.': Legislative Council – Hong Kong, Speech by the Financial Secretary, the Hon Paul MP Chan moving the Second Reading of the Appropriation Bill 2020 (26 February 2020) [37].

Legislative Council approval. Further to the Exchange Fund Ordinance (Cap 66),[232] fiscal reserves come under the management of the Monetary Authority within the Exchange Fund,[233] which, further to Article 113 of the Basic Law, is, in turn, 'managed and controlled by the government'.

Ultimately, in spite of the Basic Law's Buchanian call for individual economic liberty through low taxes and balanced budgets, the reality is that this charter has enough textual elasticity to permit significant deviation from the ideal norm. The reality, again, is that Hong Kong has, for now, adopted 'a deficit budget'[234] (although it 'will turn into a surplus in 2023–24');[235] that the Region's public accounts recorded consolidated deficits from 2019–2020 to 2020–2021;[236] and, perhaps most notably, that '[r]ecurrent expenditure of the Government increased from about $150 billion in 1997–98 to about $470 billion in 2020–21, representing a more than three-fold increase'.[237] If government spending and public expenditure are the most reliable indicators not only of the true size of government but also, significantly, of the genuine scope of its intervention in the economy,[238] then the Financial Secretary's data speaks for itself: public expenditure in terms of a percentage of gross domestic product has gone from about 17 per cent in 1997–1998 – the first financial year after China's resumption of the exercise of sovereignty over Hong Kong – to about 32 per cent in the period between 2019–2020 and 2021–2022.[239] These figures suggest that

232 Michael Ramsden and Stuart Hargreaves, *Hong Kong Basic Law Handbook* (3rd edn) (Hong Kong: Sweet & Maxwell 2022) [113.1].

233 'The total assets of the Exchange Fund amounted to HK$4,656.6 billion as at 31 August 2021': Hong Kong Monetary Authority, Press Release: Exchange Fund Abridged Balance Sheet and Currency Board Account (30 September 2021).

234 Legislative Council – Hong Kong, Speech by the Financial Secretary, the Hon Paul MP Chan moving the Second Reading of the Appropriation Bill 2021 (24 February 2021) [165]; Legislative Council – Hong Kong, Speech by the Financial Secretary, the Hon Paul MP Chan moving the Second Reading of the Appropriation Bill 2022 (23 February 2022) [202].

235 Legislative Council – Hong Kong, Speech by the Financial Secretary, the Hon Paul MP Chan moving the Second Reading of the Appropriation Bill 2022 (23 February 2022) [202].

236 Legislative Council – Hong Kong, Speech by the Financial Secretary, the Hon Paul MP Chan moving the Second Reading of the Appropriation Bill 2022 (23 February 2022) [176]. See earlier Legislative Council – Hong Kong, Speech by the Financial Secretary, the Hon Paul MP Chan moving the Second Reading of the Appropriation Bill 2021 (24 February 2021) [166].

237 Legislative Council – Hong Kong, Speech by the Financial Secretary, the Hon Paul MP Chan moving the Second Reading of the Appropriation Bill 2021 (24 February 2021) [167]. The 2022–2023 Budget Speech notes 'the very substantial increase in the recurrent expenditure from $361.8 billion in 2017–18 to over $510 billion in the Original Estimates for this year': Legislative Council – Hong Kong, Speech by the Financial Secretary, the Hon Paul MP Chan moving the Second Reading of the Appropriation Bill 2022 (23 February 2022) [178].

238 Milton Friedman is said to have said: 'Keep your eye on one thing and one thing only: how much government is spending.' See *The Economist*, 'The Triumph of Big Government' (20–26 November 2021).

239 Legislative Council – Hong Kong, Speech by the Financial Secretary, the Hon Paul MP Chan moving the Second Reading of the Appropriation Bill 2021 (24 February

the government's role in the Region's economy has been in expansion. Arguably, Hong Kong's specific conditions have required the Government of the Region to increase in size and role. In only one financial year, for example, the Region's 'civil service establishment increased by 6,082 posts'.[240] To be fair, '[t]he civil service establishment recorded zero growth in this [2021–2022] financial year'[241] and the Government of the Region will 'continue to examine carefully any new initiatives that will incur recurrent expenditure and strictly control the growth of the civil service, so as to ensure that our long-term financial commitments are commensurate with the increase in our revenue'.[242] Budgetary questions aside, redistribution and spending in the three policy areas that most affect people's livelihood – 'education, social welfare and healthcare'[243] – are certainly legitimate actions of governance in aid of a fairer prosperity.[244] The problem is the market distortion that might come – however, improbably – with greater government involvement in the market process.[245]

Private Finance

Status as an International Financial Centre

The Basic Law provides a constitutional framework not only for public finance but also for private finance, including the monetary and financial systems, over which the Region enjoys competence. Article 109 declares that the Government of the Region ought to 'provide an appropriate economic and legal environment for the maintenance of the status of Hong Kong as an international financial centre'. Aware that much of the wealth of the Region depends on its role as an entrepôt for cross-border financial transactions, the drafters of the Basic Law attempted, through this provision, to honour China's sovereign pledge to maintain the 'prosperity and stability' of Hong Kong as its Preamble proclaims. The phrase

2021) Appendix B 19. Notably, the 2022–2023 budget reduces public expenditure in terms of percentage of gross domestic product to 28.4 per cent: Legislative Council – Hong Kong, Speech by the Financial Secretary, the Hon Paul MP Chan moving the Second Reading of the Appropriation Bill 2022 (23 February 2022) Appendix B 18.

240 Legislative Council – Hong Kong, Speech by the Financial Secretary, the Hon Paul MP Chan moving the Second Reading of the Appropriation Bill 2021 (24 February 2021) [185].

241 Legislative Council – Hong Kong, Speech by the Financial Secretary, the Hon Paul MP Chan moving the Second Reading of the Appropriation Bill 2022 (23 February 2022) [192].

242 Legislative Council – Hong Kong, Speech by the Financial Secretary, the Hon Paul MP Chan moving the Second Reading of the Appropriation Bill 2022 (23 February 2022) [178].

243 Legislative Council – Hong Kong, Speech by the Financial Secretary, the Hon Paul MP Chan moving the Second Reading of the Appropriation Bill 2021 (24 February 2021) [172].

244 See *The Economist*, 'The Triumph of Big Government' (20–26 November 2021).

245 See *The Economist*, 'The Triumph of Big Government' (20–26 November 2021).

'appropriate … legal environment' is, at one level, an implicit constitutional acknowledgement of the consequentialness of the rule of law[246] to Hong Kong's relevance in the global economy.[247] In relation to an 'appropriate … economic environment', the Competition Ordinance (Cap 619) – and the Competition Commission that it establishes – promotes competitiveness in the Region's markets through prohibitions on conduct that prevents, restricts or distorts competition and on mergers that substantially weaken competition. The Financial Services Development Council advises the Government of the Region on the further promotion of Hong Kong as an international financial centre.

As a constitutional provision without equal elsewhere, Article 109 provides continuity of and consistency with the tradition of positive non-interventionism under British colonial rule. Government non-intervention in the market process does not entail the complete absence of all government-driven coordination whatsoever in the economy. Coordination is not tantamount to intervention. The rise of Hong Kong as a hub for finance was, admittedly, spontaneous, serendipitous for the most part. Its free port, open market, rule of law, limited government and strategic location combined to turn Hong Kong into a meeting point for bankers, investors, and creditors all over. However, as Chapter 2 demonstrates, the forces of spontaneity and serendipity were not wild horses; British colonial rule carefully corralled them in the spirit of positive non-interventionism. The freedom of the market has never been and cannot ever be absolute, not even in Hong Kong. Article 109 constitutionalises the proper discretion of the executive authorities to appropriately coordinate various aspects of the market, while still letting the market be itself.

Certainly, to the most libertarian of free market thinkers, Article 109 might open up the potential for distortion of the market process by the state, however improbably. Indeed, Article 109 is the first in a triad of provisions, together with Articles 118 and 119 of the Basic Law, that direct the Government of the Region to coordinate, to support the market process, either through the provision of a certain 'economic and legal' environment or the formulation of 'appropriate policies'. Several were the opinions in the Basic Law consultation process that faulted this type of policy provision as the expression of a rather wistful, 'unrealistic'[248] conception of the free market, as if the spontaneous outcome and order of free competition – free trade and free commerce –

246 Michael Ramsden and Stuart Hargreaves, *Hong Kong Basic Law Handbook* (3rd edn) (Hong Kong: Sweet & Maxwell 2022) [109.1]. See Berry Fong-Chung Hsu, 'Legal Facets of Hong Kong SAR Economic Development: Colonial Legacy and Constitutional Constraint' in Ming K Chan and Alvin Y So (eds), *Crisis and Transformation in China's Hong Kong* (Armonk: ME Sharpe 2002) 220–241.

247 Syed Kemal Bokhary, 'The Economic and Legal Environment Provided by the Rule of Law in Hong Kong' (2007) 5(1) *Trust Quarterly Review* 9. See too Syed Kemal Bokhary, 'The Rule of Law in an Evolving Democracy' (2010) 16(2) *Canterbury Law Review* 225–242.

248 The Secretariat of the Consultative Committee for the Basic Law of the Hong Kong Special Administrative Region of the People's Republic of China, *The Draft Basic Law of the Hong Kong Special Administrative Region of the People's Republic of China (for Solicitation of Opinions): Consultation Report* (Volume 5, 1 October 1988) p 730 para [2].

could somehow be controllable,[249] reducible to policy. Whether a government – *any* government – can and should provide an appropriate environment for the maintenance of the status as an international financial centre or some other commercial operation is, at a philosophical level, debatable. The reality is that, while Article 109 allows the prospect of economic intervention, in principle at least, the provision equally mandates it to be 'appropriate', that is, to be *positively* supportive of the free market. And the provision equally does not mandate the Government of the Region to act. Conduct by omission – by non-intervention – is within the scope of Article 109.

The purpose of Article 109 and its two companion provisions is doubtlessly commendable. They reveal a laudable concern by the framers to maintain 'the prosperity and stability of Hong Kong', as the Preamble of the Basic Law resolutely affirms. Because of their policy character, these are provisions with negligible judicial commentary – they are seemingly non-justiciable – and their development can only ever be largely legislative in drive.

Free Operation of Financial Business and Financial Markets

Reinforcing Article 109 is Article 110 of the Basic Law, a further free market provision in Hong Kong's economic constitution. It assigns competence to the Government of the Region over monetary and financial policies, away from the jurisdiction of mainland China, in order to safeguard the free operation of financial business and markets,[250] virtually as 'its own sovereign'.[251] Article 110 thus states that: 'The Government of the Hong Kong Special Administrative Region shall, on its own, formulate monetary and financial policies, safeguard the free operation of financial business and financial markets, and regulate and supervise them in accordance with law.'

The provision, said Chief Justice Ma in the Court of Final Appeal decision in *Securities and Futures Commission v Yiu Hoi Ying Charles*,[252] presents 'a requirement to safeguard, regulate and supervise Hong Kong's business and financial markets'.[253] These functions are the remit of the Public Finance Ordinance (Cap 2).[254] This instrument of primary legislation provides 'the statutory framework'[255] for the control and management of the Region's public finances and, more specifically, the Securities and Futures Ordinance (Cap 571),[256] under which the Securities and Futures Commission

249 See Michael Ramsden and Stuart Hargreaves, *Hong Kong Basic Law Handbook* (3rd edn) (Hong Kong: Sweet & Maxwell 2022) [109.2].

250 See Douglas W Arner and Berry FC Hsu, 'Hong Kong Markets and Exchanges' in Michael Blair, George Walker and Stuart Willey (eds), *Financial Markets and Exchanges Law* (3rd ed) (Oxford: Oxford University Press 2021).

251 *Secretary for Justice v Penta-Ocean Construction Co Ltd* [2003] HKCFI 361 [12] (To J).

252 *Securities and Futures Commission v Yiu Hoi Ying Charles* [2018] HKCFA 44.

253 *Securities and Futures Commission v Yiu Hoi Ying Charles* [2018] HKCFA 44 [3] (Ma CJ).

254 Michael Ramsden and Stuart Hargreaves, *Hong Kong Basic Law Handbook* (3rd edn) (Hong Kong: Sweet & Maxwell 2022) [110.1].

255 *Secretary for Justice v Penta-Ocean Construction Co Ltd* [2003] HKCFI 361 [12] (To J).

256 Michael Ramsden and Stuart Hargreaves, *Hong Kong Basic Law Handbook* (3rd edn) (Hong Kong: Sweet & Maxwell 2022) [110.1].

operates.[257] Banks and other financial institutions come under the purview of the Monetary Authority, which, pursuant to the Exchange Fund Ordinance (Cap 66), plays a double role as a kind of central bank and premier financial regulator to promote the general stability and effective working of the Region's financial system.[258] The Insurance Authority is an equally important regulator in that respect.

Free Flow of Capital

Further reinforcing Article 109 is Article 112, which establishes the free movement of capital in its promotion of open capital and other financial markets.[259] The provision is that '[m]arkets for foreign exchange, gold, securities, futures and the like shall continue' and that '[t]he Government of the Hong Kong Special Administrative Region shall safeguard the free flow of capital within, into and out of the Region'. Much like Article 110, Article 112 has received virtually no judicial commentary.

Monetary Affairs

The next three provisions of the Basic Law – Articles 111, 112 and 113 – comprise a set of constitutional norms for the regulation of monetary affairs. First, Article 111 prescribes '[t]he Hong Kong dollar, as the legal tender in the Hong Kong Special Administrative Region'. This provision vests in the Government of the Region '[t]he authority to issue Hong Kong currency', which, in an exercise of fiscal prudence, 'must be backed by a 100 percent reserve fund', 'will be soundly based' and be 'consistent with the object of maintaining the stability of the currency'. The Legal Tender Notes Issue Ordinance (Cap 65), which regulates the issue of bank and currency notes as legal tender, and the Coinage Ordinance (Cap 454), which regulates the issue of coins as legal tender, administer the Hong Kong dollar note and coin.[260] Second,

257 *Securities and Futures Commission v Yiu Hoi Ying Charles* [2018] HKCFA 44 [3] (Ma CJ). See also the Companies Ordinance (Cap 622).

258 Deposit taking and cheque-related banking business comes under the regulation of the Banking Ordinance (Cap 155) (see also the Deposit Protection Scheme Ordinance (Cap 581)); money-lending business under the Money Lenders Ordinance (Cap 163); insurance business under the Insurance Ordinance (Cap 41); and, provident fund business under the Mandatory Provident Fund Schemes Ordinance (Cap 485). For a conflict resolution mechanism, see the Financial Institutions (Resolution) Ordinance (Cap 628). The exemption of banks from the Money Lenders Ordinance (Cap 163), which 'has the legitimate aim of preserving the currency peg', does not contravene the Basic Law: *Hang Seng Bank Ltd v Tsang Chiu Wa* [2010] HKDC 174 [16] (Chan J). See Michael Ramsden and Stuart Hargreaves, *Hong Kong Basic Law Handbook* (3rd edn) (Hong Kong: Sweet & Maxwell 2022) [110.2]. For coordination and cooperation among regulators and operators are the Financial Stability Committee and the Council of Financial Regulators in conjunction with various memoranda of understanding.

259 Michael Ramsden and Stuart Hargreaves, *Hong Kong Basic Law Handbook* (3rd edn) (Hong Kong: Sweet & Maxwell 2022) [112.1].

260 Michael Ramsden and Stuart Hargreaves, *Hong Kong Basic Law Handbook* (3rd edn) (Hong Kong: Sweet & Maxwell 2022) [111.1].

Article 112, which – with its additional provision for financial markets and capital movement – is a kind of catch-all provision that makes the Hong Kong dollar 'freely convertible', an indispensable quality in a free market with international financial centre status. Third, Article 113 establishes the Exchange Fund 'primarily for regulating the exchange value of the Hong Kong dollar' and, therefore, it serves to promote confidence in the local legal tender.[261] Pursuant to the Exchange Fund Ordinance (Cap 66), the Monetary Authority maintains the stability of the external exchange value of the Hong Kong dollar within a band of 7.75–7.85 Hong Kong dollars to one United States dollar. It does so through the Linked Exchange Rate System, a currency board that backs the stock and flow of the monetary base by foreign reserves. This triad of monetary provisions has not been the subject of much judicial commentary. Their development has been legislatively driven.

Trade

The sense of economic freedom that runs through Chapter V very obviously informs the regulation of trade, which the Basic Law frees for Hong Kong through a set of four interdependent provisions: Articles 114, 115, 116, and 117.

Status of a Free Port

First, under Article 114, '[t]he Hong Kong Special Administrative Region shall maintain the status of a free port and shall not impose any tariff unless otherwise prescribed by law'.[262] Hong Kong has indeed been a port free of customs duties since the period under British colonial rule and that history of freedom to trade has shaped its modern status as an international financial centre.

Policy of Free Trade and the Free Movement of Goods

Article 115 develops Article 114 with a remarkable expression of economic freedom.[263] The provision, thus, mandates the Region to 'pursue the policy of free trade and safeguard the free movement of goods' and – in express acknowledgement of the freedom of (direct and indirect) foreign investment that sustains the status of the Region as an international financial centre – 'intangible assets and capital'. In this last respect, the overlap between Article 112, which directs the Government of the Region to 'safeguard the free flow of capital', and Article 115, which directs the Region to 'safeguard the free movement of … capital', is notable and shows a concern by the framers to constitutionally bind Hong Kong's status at the centre of international finance.

261 Michael Ramsden and Stuart Hargreaves, *Hong Kong Basic Law Handbook* (3rd edn) (Hong Kong: Sweet & Maxwell 2022) [111.2].
262 Michael Ramsden and Stuart Hargreaves, *Hong Kong Basic Law Handbook* (3rd edn) (Hong Kong: Sweet & Maxwell 2022) [114.1].
263 Michael Ramsden and Stuart Hargreaves, *Hong Kong Basic Law Handbook* (3rd edn) (Hong Kong: Sweet & Maxwell 2022) [115.1].

Separate Customs Territory

Article 116 protects the freedom of trade with a declaration of Hong Kong as 'a separate customs territory' tantamount to a grant of jurisdiction, with competence in external trade relations, a competence which the Import and Export Ordinance (Cap 60) develops. Therefore, under this clause, the Region may, 'using the name "Hong Kong, China", participate in relevant international organizations and international trade agreements (including preferential trade arrangements), such as the General Agreement on Tariffs and Trade and arrangements regarding international trade in textiles'. It suffices to recall that Hong Kong joined the World Trade Organization at its formation on 1 January 1995 and has remained a dutiful member ever since.[264] The Region is now a signatory to an ever larger number of preferential trade agreements and arrangements. Article 115 has the reinforcement of Articles 151 and 156, which, respectively, authorise the Region to conduct 'economic, trade' external relations through the conclusion of treaties and such other arrangements[265] and establish 'economic and trade missions in foreign countries', as and when necessary.

Own Certificates of Origin

Article 117 completes this constitutional tetralogy of free trade with the affirmation that: 'The Hong Kong Special Administrative Region may issue its own certificates of origin for products in accordance with prevailing rules of origin.'[266] Partly due to their policy-oriented, non-legalistic nature, these four provisions have not had the benefit of much meaningful commentary by the courts. Their true scope, therefore, is the measure of the Region's participation in the multilateral trading system, a subject that Chapter 6 addresses.

Travel

Free trade, at its most basic, is free movement, a freedom to travel within and across territorial borders.[267] The Basic Law makes that association in a range of provisions that promote the freedoms of movement.

264 Michael Ramsden and Stuart Hargreaves, *Hong Kong Basic Law Handbook* (3rd edn) (Hong Kong: Sweet & Maxwell 2022) [116.1].
265 Michael Ramsden and Stuart Hargreaves, *Hong Kong Basic Law Handbook* (3rd edn) (Hong Kong: Sweet & Maxwell 2022) [151.3], [151.3.3].
266 Michael Ramsden and Stuart Hargreaves, *Hong Kong Basic Law Handbook* (3rd edn) (Hong Kong: Sweet & Maxwell 2022) [117.1].
267 Yash Ghai, 'The Rule of Law and Capitalism: Reflections on the Basic Law' in Raymond Wacks (ed.), *Hong Kong, China and 1997: Essays in Legal Theory* (Hong Kong: Hong Kong University Press 1993) 343–365, 344.

Shipping and Aviation

Article 126 of the Basic Law declares that 'ships shall enjoy access to the ports of the Hong Kong Special Administrative Region' – with the obvious exception of 'foreign warships' – while Article 127 permits the free operation of '[p]rivate shipping business and shipping-related businesses and private container terminals'. The Shipping and Port Control Ordinance (Cap 313) regulates ports and vessels in Hong Kong and its waters,[268] a policy area of strategic importance since Hong Kong is one of the world's busiest container ports.

Article 128 calls on the Government of the Region to maintain 'the status of Hong Kong as a centre of international and regional aviation', with provision elsewhere in Section 4 of Chapter V to manage civil aviation as well as to negotiate and conclude air service agreements. Aviation comes under the regulation of a host of legislation, including the Civil Aviation Ordinance (Cap 448).[269] Yet, perhaps surprisingly, in spite of its status as the most open of open markets, the Region, historically, has not followed an open skies approach to the regulation of aviation.[270] Neither provision has attracted significant judicial commentary.

Freedom of Movement: Freedom of Emigration and Freedom to Travel

More generally, under Article 31 of the Basic Law, 'Hong Kong residents[271] shall have freedom of movement within the Hong Kong Special Administrative Region and freedom of emigration to other countries and regions'. That is, '[t]hey shall have freedom to travel and to enter or leave the Region'. This provision informs Article 8 of the Hong Kong Bill of Rights[272] under the Hong Kong Bill of Rights Ordinance (Cap 383), which, in paragraph 1, states that '[e]veryone lawfully within Hong Kong shall, within Hong Kong, have the right to liberty of movement and freedom to choose his residence' and, in paragraph 2, that '[e]veryone shall be free to leave Hong Kong'. For persons from foreign states and regions, the Government of the Region may and does, under Article 154, 'apply immigration controls on entry into, stay in and departure from the Region'. As this provision hints, the

268 Michael Ramsden and Stuart Hargreaves, *Hong Kong Basic Law Handbook* (3rd edn) (Hong Kong: Sweet & Maxwell 2022) [126.1].

269 *Hong Kong Aircrew Officers Association v The Director-General of Civil Aviation* [2009] HKCFI 527 [11]–[12] (Cheung J). See Michael Ramsden and Stuart Hargreaves, *Hong Kong Basic Law Handbook* (3rd edn) (Hong Kong: Sweet & Maxwell 2022) [128.1].

270 Miron Mushkat and Roda Mushkat, 'The Political Economy of Hong Kong's "Open Skies" Legal Regime: An Empirical and Theoretical Exploration' 10 (2009) *San Diego International Law Journal* 381–438, 384.

271 See Basic Law of the Hong Kong Special Administrative Region of the People's Republic of China, Article 24. See too Michael Ramsden and Stuart Hargreaves, *Hong Kong Basic Law Handbook* (3rd edn) (Hong Kong: Sweet & Maxwell 2022) [24].

272 Michael Ramsden and Stuart Hargreaves, *Hong Kong Basic Law Handbook* (3rd edn) (Hong Kong: Sweet & Maxwell 2022) [31.1]. See the International Covenant on Civil and Political Rights on which the Hong Kong Bill of Rights relies.

right to liberty of movement is not absolute.[273] Article 8(3) of the Hong Kong Bill of Rights allows the right to come under such restriction[274] – 'by restraint or provision of law'[275] – as is 'necessary to protect national security, public order (*ordre public*), public health or morals or the rights and freedoms of others'. Hong Kong's COVID-19 protective measures, notably the quarantine requirement for inbound travellers,[276] illustrate this qualification.

Industries and Trades

Articles 118 and 119 complete Hong Kong's economic constitution with policy declarations in aid of the 'development' of industries and trades. Article 118[277] is the more general of the two provisions, with a requirement for the Government of the Region to 'provide an economic and legal environment for encouraging investments, technological progress and the development of new industries'. Article 119,[278] more specifically, obligates the Government of the Region to support trading activity, that is, to 'formulate appropriate policies to promote and co-ordinate the development of various trades such as manufacturing, commerce, tourism, real estate, transport, public utilities, services, agriculture and fisheries'. These two provisions welcomingly recognise the interrelationship between the certainty of the rule of law and the profitability of economic activity, including the development of an appropriate regime for the protection[279] of intellectual property[280] ('technological progress' reads Article 118) and even the environment. Nevertheless, they also confer on the Government of the Region the power to intervene in the market process, an issue we will return to in Chapter 5.

In conjunction with Article 109 and its call on the Government of the Region to 'provide an appropriate economic and legal environment', Articles 118 and 119, on face value, stand opposite to laissez-faire capitalism. In the Basic Law consultation process, the general concern was that they could potentially inverse the *individual-self-interest-for-collective-total-utility* dynamics of the neoclassical economic model – the supply and demand equilibrium of the invisible hand – for they reserve to the Government of the Region the power of

273 Michael Ramsden and Stuart Hargreaves, *Hong Kong Basic Law Handbook* (3rd edn) (Hong Kong: Sweet & Maxwell 2022) [31.2].
274 Simon NM Young, 'Restricting Basic Law Rights in Hong Kong' (2004) 34(1) *Hong Kong Law Journal* 109–132.
275 *Lau Kwok Fai Bernard v Commissioner of Police* [2006] HKCA 408 [9] (Stock JA).
276 Compulsory Quarantine of Certain Persons Arriving at Hong Kong Regulation (Cap 599C).
277 Michael Ramsden and Stuart Hargreaves, *Hong Kong Basic Law Handbook* (3rd edn) (Hong Kong: Sweet & Maxwell 2022) [118.2].
278 Michael Ramsden and Stuart Hargreaves, *Hong Kong Basic Law Handbook* (3rd edn) (Hong Kong: Sweet & Maxwell 2022) [119.1].
279 Michael Ramsden and Stuart Hargreaves, *Hong Kong Basic Law Handbook* (3rd edn) (Hong Kong: Sweet & Maxwell 2022) [118.1].
280 Paul Tackaberry, 'Intellectual–Property Laws in the Hong Kong SAR: Localization and Internationalization' (1997) 42(3) *McGill Law Journal* 579–602, 582.

economic intervention.[281] More particularly, the concern was that the provisions could have a distortive effect be it in 'investments' or 'new industries' pursuant to Article 118 or in any of the 'privileged treatment'[282] sectors as in Article 119, from 'real estate' to 'commerce' from 'public utilities' to 'services'. Economic intervention can be construed as an 'act of favouritism',[283] something that, the Basic Law Consultative Committee noted at the time, 'will pose a serious threat to the principle of "positive non-intervention"'.[284] In principle, then, these provisions could risk the adoption of policy that could, unwittingly, allow non-market forces to determine which industries and trades to favour for development, to the likely loss of efficiency-through-competition. To quote a concern at the time: '[I]t is unfair and improper to ask the government to subsidize a particular industry.'[285]

The more historically accurate interpretation, however, is that Articles 109, 118 and 119 are strictly in accordance with the Region's constitutional tradition of positive non-interventionism. Positive non-interventionism does encourage and indeed require the government to actively coordinate the market process, precisely in order to support it. The Basic Law faithfully articulates that tradition. With qualifying adjectives in their wording such as 'appropriate' and positive verbs such as 'encouraging' or 'promote and coordinate', these three provisions have the maintenance of the prosperity and stability of Hong Kong as their unquestionable raison d'être. Needless to say, the power of intervention is merely a discretion, one that the government is free not to exercise. But when the government does exercise it, the power of intervention is, in fact, a power of coordination that can and does have a legitimate corrective application and outcome,

281 The Consultative Committee for the Basic Law of the Hong Kong Special Administrative Region of the People's Republic of China (BLCC) noted concerns about the interventionist potential of Article 118: Michael Ramsden and Stuart Hargreaves, *Hong Kong Basic Law Handbook* (3rd edn) (Hong Kong: Sweet & Maxwell 2022) [118.2]. As for Article 119, the BLCC did not adopt a proposal to delete the phrase that directs the Government of the Region to 'promote and coordinate': Michael Ramsden and Stuart Hargreaves, *Hong Kong Basic Law Handbook* (3rd edn) (Hong Kong: Sweet & Maxwell 2022) [119.1].

282 The Secretariat of the Consultative Committee for the Basic Law of the Hong Kong Special Administrative Region of the People's Republic of China, *The Draft Basic Law of the Hong Kong Special Administrative Region of the People's Republic of China (for Solicitation of Opinions): Consultation Report* (Volume 5, 1 October 1988) p 772 para [3.1].

283 The Secretariat of the Consultative Committee for the Basic Law of the Hong Kong Special Administrative Region of the People's Republic of China, *The Draft Basic Law of the Hong Kong Special Administrative Region of the People's Republic of China (for Solicitation of Opinions): Consultation Report* (Volume 5, 1 October 1988) p 772 para [3.1].

284 The Secretariat of the Consultative Committee for the Basic Law of the Hong Kong Special Administrative Region of the People's Republic of China, *The Draft Basic Law of the Hong Kong Special Administrative Region of the People's Republic of China (for Solicitation of Opinions): Consultation Report* (Volume 5, 1 October 1988) p 773 para [3.1].

285 The Secretariat of the Consultative Committee for the Basic Law of the Hong Kong Special Administrative Region of the People's Republic of China, *The Draft Basic Law of the Hong Kong Special Administrative Region of the People's Republic of China (for Solicitation of Opinions): Consultation Report* (Volume 5, 1 October 1988) p 771 para [2.2]. See Michael Ramsden and Stuart Hargreaves, *Hong Kong Basic Law Handbook* (3rd edn) (Hong Kong: Sweet & Maxwell 2022) [118.2].

either in resolution of a market failure or otherwise in pursuance of the public interest. They express the *positive* in Hong Kong's established tradition of positive non-interventionism. It is the *non-interventionism* that makes coordination possible to facilitate, promote, support, guide, but never disrupt. These provisions reveal a prudent sense of market reality in the inevitable realisation that absolute economic freedom is not and cannot be feasible. Every now and then, the public interest may demand public policy to channel market forces towards appropriate and adapted market purposes, precisely with the intention to intensify the dynamics of the free market. These policy provisions are part of the policy toolkit; a restatement of positive non-interventionism; and, at the end of the day, a powerful restatement of classical liberal economic thought.

On the Justiciability of the Basic Law as an Economic Constitution

The generality of Articles 118 and 119, like other policy-oriented provisions in Chapter V of the Basic Law, raises the practical question of justiciability.[286] The design and implementation of the Region's taxation and expenditure policies are 'a fundamentally political process'; to ask the courts to review such policies is to ask them to resolve fundamentally political questions.[287] Moreover, Chapter V provisions are, arguably, too aspirational – both in form and in substance – to be meaningfully enforceable by the courts.[288] '[T]he role of the court is to defer to the legislature in matters of policy', said Chief Judge Ma of the High Court in *Leung TC William Roy v Secretary for Justice*.[289] In that same vein, High Court Judge Hartmann, in *Clean Air Foundation Ltd v The Government of Hong Kong Special Administrative Region*, said that 'policy ... is for Government'[290] and, in *Chan To Foon v The Director of Immigration*, commented that 'an aspirational covenant' – such as the International Covenant on Civil and Political Rights – cannot create absolute obligations.[291] Just as Justice Brandeis of the Supreme

286 The (non-)justiciability of the economic policy provisions of the Basic Law has long been the subject of study in Douglas Arner, Richard Cullen and Evan Gibson, 'Fiscal Policy and Financial System' in Johannes Chan and CL Lim (eds) *Law of the Hong Kong Constitution* (3rd edn) (Hong Kong: Sweet & Maxwell 2021) 387–430. See too Michael Littlewood, *Taxation without Representation: The History of Hong Kong's Troublingly Successful Tax System* (Hong Kong: Hong Kong University Press 2010) 248.

287 Douglas Arner, Richard Cullen and Evan Gibson, 'Fiscal Policy and Financial System' in Johannes Chan and CL Lim (eds) *Law of the Hong Kong Constitution* (3rd edn) (Hong Kong: Sweet & Maxwell 2021) 387–430, 428.

288 Albert HY Chen, 'A Comment on the Basic Law as the Constitutional Foundation of Hong Kong's Economic Future' in Say Goo, Douglas Arner and Zhongfei Zhou (eds), *International Financial Sector Reform: Standard Setting and Infrastructure Development* (London: Kluwer Law International 2002) 251–256, 254.

289 *Leung TC William Roy v Secretary for Justice* [2006] HKCA 360 [52] (Ma CJ).

290 *Clean Air Foundation Ltd v The Government of Hong Kong Special Administrative Region* [2007] HKCFI 757 [36] (Hartmann J).

291 *Chan To Foon v The Director of Immigration* [2001] HKCFI 295 [72] (Hartmann J); the reference was to the International Covenant on Civil and Political Rights (adopted 16 December 1966, entered into force 23 March 1976) 999 UNTS 171.

Court of the United States stated in *Ashwander v Tennessee Valley Authority*[292] that courts are not disposed to the resolution of political questions, Sir Anthony Mason, sitting as a Non-Permanent Judge on the Court of Final Appeal, remarked, in *'C' v Director of Immigration*,[293] that judicial review is not suitable for cases that exhibit 'a lack of judicially manageable standards, such as matters of economic or social policy', or 'a political character and a high political content where a political rather than a legal solution may be called for'.[294]

The Basic Law's economic provisions are, certainly, a Buchanian charter of constitutional economics, in spite of the fact that, within that charter, several provisions are not likely to be judicially enforceable due to their open terms. Apart from those guarantees with traceable origins in the English common law tradition – such as the right to property – the other provisions are, more or less, subject to construction by political actors within the political process. They have, thus far, remained beyond the purview of judicial review.[295] Arguably, they guide more than they prescribe. In this respect, it suffices to note that the Government of the Region has not considered itself under obligation to literally abide by the balanced-budget rule in Article 107 on a year-to-year basis. Whether Article 107 like the other economic provisions of the Basic Law are judicially enforceable, ultimately, the text is amenable to final interpretation by the Standing Committee of the National People's Congress pursuant to Article 158 of the Basic Law.[296] This power of interpretation, Chief Justice Ma recounted in the Court of Final Appeal decision in *Vallejos Evangeline Banao v Commissioner of Registration*,[297] is 'plenary in that it covers all articles in the Basic Law and may be exercised even in the absence of any legal proceedings'.[298]

That being said, we are in no position to conclusively foreclose the justiciability of the economic provisions of the Basic Law.[299] As High Court Judge Russell Coleman recently remarked, although certain legal questions may 'arise in a political or socio-economic context', this is no excuse for the courts to shirk their constitutional obligations, for '[t]hat would be to abrogate the very duty imposed on the members of the independent judiciary which Hong Kong enjoys, and which independence is guaranteed under the Basic Law in the clearest of terms'.[300]

292 *Ashwander v Tennessee Valley Authority* 297 US 288 (1936) (Brandeis J).
293 *'C' v Director of Immigration* [2013] HKCFA 22.
294 *'C' v Director of Immigration* [2013] HKCFA 22 [81] (Mason NPJ).
295 Firew Kebede Tiba, 'Freedom of Choice of Occupation and Acadmic Freedom' in Johannes Chan and CL Lim (eds), *Law of the Hong Kong Constitution* (3rd edn) (Hong Kong: Sweet & Maxwell 2021) 923–954.
296 *Lau Kong Yung v The Director of Immigration* [1999] HKCFA 4 [159–163] (Li CJ).
297 *Vallejos Evangeline Banao v Commissioner of Registration* [2013] HKCFA 17.
298 *Vallejos Evangeline Banao v Commissioner of Registration* [2013] HKCFA 17 [102] (Ma CJ).
299 See Shue Sing Churk, 'Forced to Go Capitalist: Revisiting the Economic Provisions of Hong Kong's Basic Law' (2015) 3(1) *The Chinese Journal of Comparative Law* 144–160.
300 *Secretary for Justice v Persons Unlawfully and Wilfully Conducting Etc. (1957/2019)* [2019] 5 HKLRD 500, 508 (Coleman J).

Conclusion

Hong Kong's economic constitution articulates an ideal, that of economic liberty. This ideal it received from the Victorian common law tradition of free market constitutionalism, which, over many decades, evolved into the convention of positive non-interventionism, an autochthonous adaptation of the laissez-faire neoclassical economic model of competitive capitalism. In this respect and in many more, the Basic Law delivers for the Region an efficacious economic constitution as is evident from the codification of the right to property, including, as its corollaries, the right to compensation for the lawful deprivation of property and the right of private ownership of property; the freedom of choice of occupation; independent finances; fiscal prudence under a balanced budget; an independent, low tax system; maintenance of the status as an international financial centre; the free operation of financial business and markets; the free flow of capital; maintenance of the status of a free port; the policy of free trade and the free movement of goods; a separate customs territory with its own certificates of origin; access for ships to the ports; maintenance of the status as a centre of international and regional aviation; and freedom of movement. This constitutional catalogue covers almost all conceivable facets of the ideal of economic liberty, what we label as free market constitutionalism. Through the realisation of that ideal with full constitutional force, the Basic Law has ushered in a renewed legal culture of market openness facilitative of efficient trade and commerce. The Basic Law's economic provisions perform an invaluable function unparalleled in the world as an authoritative testament of the enduring idea and ideal of economic liberty. The charter's vision of Hong Kong as a market free from unnecessary obstacles has provided rigorous, trustworthy[301] reassurances to investors, producers, traders and consumers, both at home and abroad, that the Region is a land – a world, in fact – of opportunity and profit. This ideal is worthy of praise and admiration.

301 Francis Fukuyama, *Trust: The Social Virtues and The Creation of Prosperity* (New York: Free Press 1996).

5

FREE MARKET CONSTITUTIONALISM AND HONG KONG'S INTERNAL ECONOMIC POLICY

Introduction

In October 2006, just a month before his death, Milton Friedman, who had, throughout his career, so admiringly praised Hong Kong's commitment to economic liberty, penned these words:

> It had to happen. Hong Kong's policy of 'positive noninterventionism' was too good to last. It went against all the instincts of government officials, paid to spend other people's money and meddle in other people's affairs. That's why it was sadly unsurprising to see Hong Kong's current leader, Donald Tsang, last month declare the death of the policy on which the territory's prosperity was built.[1]

Yet, from 1995, Hong Kong ranked as the 'freest economy in the world' for 25 consecutive years on the Index of Economic Freedom published annually by The Heritage Foundation. The Region lost the title to Singapore in 2020 and then only for non-economic considerations; indeed, a year later, it was removed from the Index altogether.[2] As at September 2022, however, Canada's Fraser Institute continued to rank Hong Kong as the world's freest economy.[3] What, then, explains the divergent pictures offered by Friedman and the rankings? And can they be reconciled?

1 Milton Friedman, 'Hong Kong Wrong' *The Wall Street Journal* (6 October 2006), https://www.wsj.com/articles/SB116009800068684505, accessed 2 May 2022.
2 See Jamie Peck, Rachel Bok and Jun Zhang, 'Hong Kong — A Model on the Rocks?' (2020) *Territory, Politics, Governance*, https://doi.org/10.1080/21622671.2020.1837221, accessed 2 May 2022.
3 James Gwartney et al., *Economic Freedom of the World 2022: Annual Report* (Vancouver: Fraser Institute 2022) vi.

DOI: 10.4324/9780429341229-5

In this chapter, we study the internal implementation of the Basic Law's *free market constitutionalism*. The first section examines the economic philosophy of the Region's five Chief Executives to date, as evidenced in their Policy Addresses – the British colonial rule equivalent of the Governor's Speech – with a particular focus on industrial policy as in the policy that 'singles out [an] industrial sector of the economy for specific public support'.[4] It demonstrates that, in spite of some deviation from the economic policies of their colonial forebears, each has stayed within the broad contours of free market constitutionalism. The second section reviews the economic jurisprudence of the Region's courts in respect of social welfare and public housing. The third section closes the chapter, concluding that, although the Region's successive governments and even the judiciary have leaned toward interventionism at times, this is not foregone; ultimately, the text of the Basic Law is flexible enough to simultaneously accommodate both a modicum of interventionism and interpretations in closer alignment with Hong Kong's traditions of free market constitutionalism.

Economic Philosophy of the Chief Executives

Chapter 2 concludes that the Victorian economic constitution of Hong Kong under British colonial rule performed reasonably well as it facilitated steady improvements in the standard of living.[5] Nevertheless, the drafters of the Basic Law foresaw that a prosperous and stable future for Hong Kong under Chinese sovereignty would depend on express constitutional provisions to solidify otherwise uncodified principles such as 'private property, the rule of law, freedom of occupation and movement, low taxes, a limit on the scope and size of the state, free movement of capital, a convertible (fully backed) currency, free entry into any line of business, unregulated prices, free trade, and the retention of a free port'.[6] None of the clauses in Chapter V of the Basic Law, which deals with the economy, specifically addresses the regulation of business, much less inflicts any costs on doing business in terms of environmental controls, fringe benefits of labour and the like. Indeed, the principle in Article 5 of the Basic Law – that Hong Kong's 'previous capitalist system and way of life shall remain unchanged for 50 years' – logically implies that the free market constitutionalism which the territory practised under British colonial rule and which, ultimately, translated into non-intervention in the private sector should equally remain unchanged.[7]

4 Leung-chuen Chau et al., *Industrial Development in Singapore, Taiwan, & South Korea* (Singapore: World Scientific 2001) 235.
5 Brian CH Fong and Tai-Lok Lui, 'Introduction: "One Country, Two Systems" from Theory to Practice: Emerging Social and Institutional Fractures in Hong Kong since 1997' in Brian CH Fong and Tai-Lok Lui (eds), *Hong Kong 20 Years After the Handover: Emerging Social and Institutional Fractures After 1997* (Cham: Palgrave Macmillan 2018) xvii–xxv, xix.
6 Alvin Rabushka, 'A Free-Market Constitution for Hong Kong: A Blueprint for China' (1989) 8(3) *Cato Journal* 641–656, 649–650.
7 Alvin Rabushka, 'A Free-Market Constitution for Hong Kong: A Blueprint for China' (1989) 8(3) *Cato Journal* 641–656, 649.

Unlike other fast-growing Asian economies, Hong Kong never had an industrial policy under British colonial rule, for it was not essential; not to mention the fact that any industrial policy would have been tantamount to '[a] departure from free market principles'.[8] Chapter V of the Basic Law, however, imposes obligations on an executive – otherwise vested with almost complete economic management prerogatives – to 'provide an appropriate economic and legal environment for the maintenance of the status of Hong Kong as an international financial centre'[9] and 'on its own, formulate monetary and financial policies, safeguard the free operation of financial business and financial markets, and regulate and supervise them in accordance with law'.[10] These provisions, by default, allow an interpretation compatible with established constitutional tradition, as drafter Xiao Weiyun maintained, in that the words 'appropriate economic and legal environment' presumably mean 'effective economic policies previously in practice for a long time, [but which, nevertheless, permit the government to] implement and continuously improve previous laws on finance'.[11] Yet, the wording is also capable of interpretation to legitimate state intervention in the economy if, for instance, it serves to maintain 'the status of Hong Kong as an international financial centre'.

Indeed, the Basic Law empowers and mandates the Government of the Region to 'provide an economic and legal environment for encouraging investments, technological progress and the development of new industries';[12] 'formulate appropriate policies to promote and co-ordinate the development of various trades such as manufacturing, commerce, tourism, real estate, transport, public utilities, services, agriculture and fisheries, and pay regard to the protection of the environment';[13] and, even 'formulate policies to develop Western and traditional Chinese medicine and … to improve medical and health services'.[14] These provisions could, arguably, be open to an interpretation that justifies high-profile industrial policies, the kind that favour rent-seeking and favouritism,[15] neither of which is conducive to free market constitutionalism. Of course, the same provisions are equally open to an interpretation that

8 Leung-chuen Chau et al., *Industrial Development in Singapore, Taiwan, & South Korea* (Singapore: World Scientific 2001) 235. See also Henry Wai-chung Yeung, 'Neoliberalism, *Laissez-Faire* Capitalism and Economic Crisis: The Political Economy of Deindustrialisation in Hong Kong' (2000) 4(2) *Competition & Change* 121–169.

9 Basic Law of the Hong Kong Special Administrative Region of the People's Republic of China, Article 109.

10 Basic Law of the Hong Kong Special Administrative Region of the People's Republic of China, Article 110(2).

11 Weiyun Xiao, *One Country, Two Systems: An Account of the Drafting of the Hong Kong Basic Law* (Beijing: Peking University Press 2001) 407.

12 Basic Law of the Hong Kong Special Administrative Region of the People's Republic of China, Article 118.

13 Basic Law of the Hong Kong Special Administrative Region of the People's Republic of China, Article 119.

14 Basic Law of the Hong Kong Special Administrative Region of the People's Republic of China, Article 138.

15 See Dieter Helm, 'Government Failure, Rent-Seeking, and Capture: The Design of Climate Change Policy' (2010) 26(2) *Oxford Review of Economic Policy* 182–196.

coheres with Hong Kong's positive non-interventionist tradition, the kind that mandates the Government of the Region to proactively 'draw up appropriate measures to facilitate continued development of each sector' and 'coordinate the interests and divergences of all sectors, proceeding from Hong Kong's overall, long-term interests so that each sector will have a proper role to play, to develop harmoniously and together safeguard the social stability and economic prosperity of Hong Kong'.[16]

It was commonplace to suggest that the Basic Law was a replication of the constitution under British colonial rule, itself 'a product of a bygone era'[17] of 'non-intrusive'[18] administration. In that respect, scholar of public administration Anthony Cheung remarked that, with the promulgation of the Basic Law, '[o] ld wine was put into new bottles', in that he viewed the instrument as, more or less, a continuation of the 'ancient regime'.[19] Undoubtedly, the Basic Law was inspired by the executive-led system in operation under British colonial rule.[20] It is equally beyond doubt that Deng Xiaoping's China recognised in Hong Kong's colonial governance, devoid as it was of party politics,[21] the qualities of 'high efficiency, stability, and eas[iness] to control'.[22] Beijing intended to resume the prosperity and stability of Hong Kong's governance under British colonial rule and concluded that the Region's central leadership should be with the Chief Executive, *de facto* successor of the Governor, who should have 'close to unlimited power in terms of appointment and patronage, only weakly checked by a restricted legislature'.[23] Like the Governor, the Chief Executive is thus charged with implementing the law;[24] presenting regular

16 Weiyun Xiao, *One Country, Two Systems: An Account of the Drafting of the Hong Kong Basic Law* (Beijing: Peking University Press 2001) 422.

17 Brian CH Fong, 'Executive-Legislative Disconnection in the HKSAR: Uneasy Partnership Between Chief Executives and Pro-Government Parties, 1997–2016' in Brian CH Fong and Tai-Lok Lui (eds), *Hong Kong 20 Years After the Handover: Emerging Social and Institutional Fractures After 1997* (Cham: Palgrave Macmillan 2018) 45–72, 65.

18 Steve Tsang, 'Government and Politics in Hong Kong: A Colonial Paradox' in Judith M Brown and Rosemary Foot (eds), *Hong Kong's Transitions, 1842–1997* (London: Macmillan Press 1997) 62–83, 73.

19 Anthony BL Cheung, *Governance in Hong Kong: In Search of Identity, Legitimate and Trust* (Hong Kong: The Hong Kong Institute of Education 2009) 2.

20 Tsz Ken Yau, 'Housing Question and Social Discontent After 1997: History and Continuity of Home Ownership' in Brian CH Fong and Tai-Lok Lui (eds), *Hong Kong 20 Years After the Handover: Emerging Social and Institutional Fractures After 1997* (Cham: Palgrave Macmillan 2018) 177–202, 184.

21 Ngok Ma, 'From Executive Dominance to Fragmented Authority: An Institutional and Political Analysis' in Brian CH Fong and Tai-Lok Lui (eds), *Hong Kong 20 Years After the Handover: Emerging Social and Institutional Fractures After 1997* (Cham: Palgrave Macmillan 2018) 21–44, 23.

22 Qianhong Qin and Jing Fu, *Evaluating Executive-Legislative Branch Relations of the Hong Kong Special Administrative Region* (Hong Kong: City University Press 2018) 60.

23 Mathew YH Wong, *Comparative Hong Kong Politics: A Guidebook for Students and Researchers* (Singapore: Palgrave Macmillan 2017) 149.

24 Basic Law of the Hong Kong Special Administrative Region of the People's Republic of China, Article 48(2).

policy addresses to the Legislative Council;[25] and assenting to legislation in light of the 'overall interests of the Region'.[26]

The Basic Law institutes, in effect, a corporatist model of government. Accordingly, interest groups enjoy significant representation on the Chief Executive Election Committee and the various functional constituencies. The Election Committee, which, at its establishment, consisted of only 400 members, grew to 800 four years later and stood at 1,200 from 2012 until the reforms to the electoral system in 2021. It was returned by four groups of both corporate and individual electors: the industrial, commercial and financial sectors; the professional sectors; the labour, social services and religious sectors; and what could be broadly described as the political sector. The functional constituencies comprise certain designated professions plus corporate persons; doctors, lawyers, accountants, social workers and teachers all have representation as do banks, sundry mega-companies, corporate members of chambers of commerce and industry bodies, as well as trade unions to represent employees.

Chief Executive Tung Chee-hwa

Tung Chee-hwa, the inaugural Chief Executive and a former OOCL shipping businessman, launched Hong Kong's contemporary era of relatively active industrial policy.[27] In his first Policy Address, Tung pledged fidelity to his own take on what we call free market constitutionalism in these words:

> Our efforts will be directed to increasing our external competitiveness, increasing friendliness to business within Hong Kong and to promoting a healthy competitive environment. We will do everything to remove obstacles and constraints to business development. We will give the private sector freedom to set its own direction, to explore and to seize opportunities.[28]

In the same Policy Address, however, he announced a policy to build 85,000 public flats every year to offset the risk of a housing bubble.[29] This announcement was followed, a year later, by another, similarly significant, announcement: a plan to spend HK$235 billion (US$30.32 billion) on infrastructure contracts over five years,

25 Basic Law of the Hong Kong Special Administrative Region of the People's Republic of China, Article 64.
26 Basic Law of the Hong Kong Special Administrative Region of the People's Republic of China, Article 49.
27 Cheung-kwok Law, *Industrial Economics and Industrial Policy of Hong Kong* (Hong Kong: Education Bureau 2016) 8–9.
28 Chee-hwa Tung, *The Chief Executive's Policy Address 1997* (Hong Kong: Government of the Hong Kong Special Administrative Region 1997) [17].
29 Kim Ming Lee, Benny Ho Pong To and Kar Ming Yu, 'Financialization and Economic Inequality in Hong Kong: The Cost of the Finance-led Growth Regime' in Brian CH Fong and Tai-Lok Lui (eds), *Hong Kong 20 Years after the Handover: Emerging Social and Institutional Fractures After 1997* (Cham: Palgrave Macmillan 2018) 127–151, 135.

in spite of a projected deficit of over HK$20 billion (US$2.58 billion) in the fiscal year 1998–1999.[30] The public housing scheme particularly exposed the inaugural Government of the Region to the concern of both the propertied middle class and property developers,[31] suffice to note that property prices fell by 40 per cent in only nine months. Presumably after lobbying, the Chief Executive decided, just a year later, to abandon the scheme.[32] Moreover, pressure for an increase in government spending to support the economy from the Legislative Council, exerted by the coalition of seven mainstream political parties that won the general election of May 1998, moved the Chief Executive to respond with a HK$32 billion package in June that year.[33]

In his 1998 Policy Address, Tung identified for subsidy, as 'strategic growth domains', the areas of innovation and technology, global satellite communication links, the film industry and traditional Chinese medicine.[34] This plan, however, was soon overtaken by the Asian financial crisis, which, eventually, ushered in the collapse of Hong Kong's share and property prices, leaving many borrowers unable to repay their loans,[35] raising the average unemployment rate to six per cent from 1998 to 2003 and unleashing deflation throughout Asia.[36]

These events all came to a head in August 1998, when a speculative attack on the Hong Kong dollar, which had risked a meltdown of the Region's money and credit markets, prompted Financial Secretary Sir Donald Tsang and Secretary for Financial Services Rafael Hui to draw US$15.2 billion from the Exchange Fund to purchase shares of selected companies over a two-week period. The significance of the episode was such that the Government of the Region became, for a short time, the largest shareholder of HSBC. Concurrently, the Monetary Authority tightened the Hong Kong dollar supply.[37] This one-off intervention succeeded: speculators,

30 Edward KY Chen, 'The Economic Setting' in David G Lethbridge and Sek Hong Ng (eds), *The Business Environment in Hong Kong* (Hong Kong: Oxford University Press 2000) 1–51, 43.
31 Tze Ken Yau, 'Housing Question and Social Discontent After 1997: History and Continuity of Home Ownership' in Brian CH Fong and Tai-Lok Lui (eds), *Hong Kong 20 Years after the Handover: Emerging Social and Institutional Fractures After 1997* (Cham: Palgrave Macmillan 2018) 177–202, 187.
32 By 2003, the Government of the Region had suspended its scheme for selling rental public housing to tenants, with the upshot that even low-income families had to buy on the private market: Eliza WY Lee, 'Social Mobilization, Blame Avoidance, and Welfare Restructuring in Hong Kong' in Ming Sing (ed.), *Politics and Government in Hong Kong: Crisis under Chinese Sovereignty* (New York: Routledge 2009) 162–175, 167.
33 Tim Summers, *China's Hong Kong* (Newcastle upon Tyne: Agenda Publishing 2019) 58.
34 Anthony BL Cheung, *Can Hong Kong Exceptionalism Last? Dilemmas of Governance and Public Administration over Five Decades 1970s–2020* (Hong Kong: City University Press 2021) 149.
35 Chor-yiu Sin, 'The Economic Fundamental and Economic Policy Uncertainty of Mainland China and Their Impacts on Taiwan and Hong Kong' (2015) 40 *International Review of Economics and Finance* 298–311, 301.
36 Yue Chim Richard Wong, *Fixing Inequality in Hong Kong* (Hong Kong: Hong Kong University Press 2017) 257.
37 See Kui-wai Li, *Economic Freedom: Lessons of Hong Kong* (Singapore: World Scientific 2012).

surprised, were worsted and the economy stabilised.[38] Although popular and certainly effective, the intervention appeared, in principle at least, to deviate from Hong Kong's traditional commitment to positive non-interventionism.[39]

Precisely on this interpretative question, Tung's Financial Secretary, Antony Leung – who as former Chairman of Asia of JP Morgan Chase was not a career-tenured[40] bureaucrat, unlike his predecessors – laid out his economic philosophy in his maiden Budget Speech in these words:

> Some may have the impression that, to maintain Hong Kong's economic freedom, the Government should be passive and distance itself from the economy. I disagree. I am of the view that the Government should have a clear vision of the direction of economic development and be a proactive market enabler.[41]

By the time Tung delivered his last Policy Address in 2004,[42] terms such as 'free market' or 'economic liberty' found no mention; instead stating, '[t]he Government will actively facilitate the development and expansion of our core industries';[43] and '[t]he Government will actively provide the necessary support and co-ordination in respect of policy, infrastructure and software [for growth]'.[44]

Chief Executive Donald Tsang

Tung resigned in March 2005, and was succeeded by veteran civil servant Sir Donald Tsang, the former Chief Secretary. In September 2006, Tsang, a putative disciple of Sir Philip Haddon-Cave,[45] remarked, after a summit on China's 11th Five-Year Plan, that Hong Kong 'no longer has a policy of positive non-intervention'.[46] A month later, he stated in his Policy Address:

38 See Berry FC Hsu and Douglas W Arner, 'Reevaluating the Efficient Capital Markets Hypothesis: The Case of Hong Kong' (2009) 43 *The International Lawyer* 1429–1449.
39 See Katherine Lynch, 'The Temptation to Intervene: Problems Created by Government Intervention in the Hong Kong Stock Market' (1999) 29 *Hong Kong Law Journal* 129–149.
40 See John P Burns, 'Administrative Reform in Hong Kong: An Institutional Analysis of Food Safety' (2008) 17 *Research in Public Policy Analysis and Management* 21–38.
41 Antony Leung, *The 2002–03 Budget Speech by the Financial Secretary* (Hong Kong: Government of the Hong Kong Special Administrative Region 2002) [42].
42 Tai-lok Lui, 'The Unfinished Chapter of Hong Kong's Long Political Transition' (2020) 40(2) *Critique of Anthropology* 270–276, 274.
43 Chee-hwa Tung, *The Chief Executive's Policy Address 2004* (Hong Kong: Government of the Hong Kong Special Administrative Region 2004) [19].
44 Chee-hwa Tung, *The Chief Executive's Policy Address 2004* (Hong Kong: Government of the Hong Kong Special Administrative Region 2004) [27].
45 Anthony BL Cheung, *Can Hong Kong Exceptionalism Last? Dilemmas of Governance and Public Administration over Five Decades 1970s–2020* (Hong Kong: City University Press 2021) 150.
46 Joseph Yu-shek Cheng, *Political Development in Hong Kong* (Singapore: World Scientific 2020) 524.

> I welcome the participation of the business community, the Legislative Council and members of the public in discussing when and to what extent the Government should ever intervene in the market, under the rubric of 'Big Market, Small Government' and public expenditure not exceeding 20% of GDP. These discussions would be far more profitable than prolonging philosophical debates over abstract slogans or terminology.[47]

Tsang's notion of 'Big Market, Small Government' meant – for, at least, one commentator – that 'government will only do the things which the market does not do'.[48] This interpretative nuance, however minor, marked somewhat of a departure from Hong Kong's traditional understanding of positive non-interventionism or laissez-faire. In effect, this approach signified that, although the size of the public sector should be kept in check, the government may and should indeed intervene for the sake of specific industries.

The Great Recession between 2007 and 2009, which unfolded during Tsang's second term, inflicted unprecedented pain on economies all over the world.[49] However, Hong Kong's economic constitution operated efficiently and resiliently throughout the global financial crisis.[50] Financial meltdown in the United States, the United Kingdom and continental Europe left the Region relatively unscathed, with no permanent loss of gross domestic product (GDP) or any fundamental revision of its financial and macroeconomic structures.[51] On the contrary, between 2009 and 2013, Hong Kong recorded unemployment rates averaging just 4 per cent while property prices rose by 134 per cent.[52] The obligation under the Basic Law to balance the budget was honoured during the crisis. Fiscal reserves, for example, stood ample enough for the Government of the Region to operate for no less than 21 months without revenue.[53]

With the treasury's chests full, in July 2010, Tsang tabled the Region's first-ever minimum wage bill before the Legislative Council. This development did not, at least initially, shy away Financial Secretary John Tsang, in his Budget Speech of 23

47 Donald Tsang, *The Chief Executive's Policy Address 2006* (Hong Kong: Government of the Hong Kong Special Administrative Region 2006) [68]–[69].

48 JJ Woo, *The Evolution of the Asian Developmental State: Hong Kong and Singapore* (New York: Routledge 2019) 76.

49 See Andrew Farlow, *Crash and Beyond: Causes and Consequences of the Global Financial Crisis* (Oxford: Oxford University Press 2013).

50 See Eric C Ip, 'Constitutional Finance: The Role of the Hong Kong Basic Law During the Global Financial Crisis' (2019) 49(1) *Hong Kong Law Journal* 295–314.

51 Suwina Cheng, Gladie Lui and Connie Shum, 'Did Corporate Governance Safeguard Investor Interest in the Global Financial Crisis? Evidence from Hong Kong SAR' (2015) 21(4) *Asia Pacific Business Review* 534–550, 534.

52 Yue Chim Richard Wong, *Fixing Inequality in Hong Kong* (Hong Kong: Hong Kong University Press 2017) 257.

53 See Wilson Wong and Raymond Yuen, 'Economic Policy' in WM Lam, PLT Lui and W Wong (eds), *Contemporary Hong Kong Government and Politics* (Hong Kong: Hong Kong University Press 2012) 251, 253.

February 2011, from conventions of fiscal prudence. He, in fact, was sensitive to preclude cash handouts and tax rebates on the grounds that they might stoke inflation. But the welfarist policy tide that the prospect of a statutory minimum wage had started proved too strong. Just one week later, the Financial Secretary revised his budget to spend HK$40 billion (US$5.16 billion) on entitlements, of which HK$36 billion (US$4.65 billion) were cash handouts. Overnight a HK$3.9 billion (US$0.13 billion) surplus became a HK$8.5 billion (US$1.1 billion) deficit.[54] The Chief Executive tried to justify 'appropriate government intervention' – in the rhetorical context of what we are referring to as free market constitutionalism – in his last Policy Address:

> Market forces represent collective wisdom. The Government should not step in without good reason. But neither should it adopt a completely hands-off approach. When the market fails, the Government should intervene as appropriate. The introduction of subsidised housing and the statutory minimum wage, for example, highlights the importance of appropriate government intervention.[55]

The local business elite shared hardly any other principle of economic philosophy, let alone a firm commitment to the free market.[56] After all, it took Hong Kong almost 20 years to 'adopt something as uncontroversial as a general competition law'.[57] It was not until June 2012, the last month of Tsang's tenure as Chief Executive, that the Legislative Council finally enacted into law the Competition Ordinance (Cap 619), which only entered into full force in December 2015. The purpose of the law, according to its Long Title, is 'to prohibit conduct that prevents, restricts or distorts competition in Hong Kong; to prohibit mergers that substantially lessen competition in Hong Kong; to establish a Competition Commission and a Competition Tribunal'. Interestingly, this enactment followed the European Union's model of competition law, which commentators generally perceive to be more interventionist than its antitrust counterpart in the United States, long under the influence of the Chicago School of neoclassical, free market economics.[58] Arguably, this policy choice could be interpreted as another step away from the Region's traditional positive non-interventionism, although, admittedly, still within the broad contours of free market constitutionalism.

54 Kin-ping Kwong and Chiew Ping Yew, 'Is Hong Kong dying?' in Yongnian Zheng and Chiew Ping Yew (eds), *Hong Kong under Chinese Rule: Economic Integration and Political Gridlock* (Singapore: World Scientific 2013) 165–183, 170.

55 Donald Tsang, *The Chief Executive's Policy Address 2011–12* (Hong Kong: Government of the Hong Kong Special Administrative Region 2011) [190], [194].

56 Ngok Ma, 'Reinventing the Hong Kong State or Rediscovering It? From Low Interventionism to Eclectic Corporatism' (2009) 38(3) *Economy and Society* 492–519, 509–510.

57 Thomas K Cheng, 'Sherman vs. Goliath?: Tackling the Conglomerate Dominance Problem in Emerging and Small Economies – Hong Kong as a Case Study' (2017) 37 (1) *Northwestern Journal of International Law & Business* 35–105, 98.

58 Thomas K Cheng and Kelvin Hiu Fai Kwok, *Hong Kong Competition Law: Comparative and Theoretical Perspectives* (New York: Cambridge University Press 2021) 123.

Chief Executive Leung Chun-ying

After the 2012 Chief Executive Election, Leung Chun-ying, a real estate services businessman, became the Region's third Chief Executive. In his first Policy Address, the new Chief Executive coined the phrase '"appropriately proactive" governance', while ringing some of the main slogans of free market constitutionalism:

> To address housing shortage, we have introduced and implemented the policy of 'Hong Kong property for Hong Kong people' to give priority to the needs of local home buyers over non-Hong Kong residents. We have also introduced the Buyer's Stamp Duty and, through administrative means, disallowed delivery bookings for expectant Mainland mothers with no ties to Hong Kong. These measures are examples of 'appropriately proactive' governance.[59]

On 17 January 2013, Leung established a Financial Services Development Council to tout Hong Kong's financial services; appointed an Economic Development Commission to formulate strategies and policies enhancing long-term development; and, pushed for an expansion of the financial services industry into offshore renminbi (RMB) business, the legal services of arbitration and mediation, high-value maritime services, innovation and technology and testing and certification.[60] A year later, on 15 January 2014, amid ever widening income inequality, Leung unveiled a social welfare programme of a size previously alien to Hong Kong's public finance traditions at a cost of some HK$20 billion (US$2.58 billion). Toward the end of 2015, Leung created the office of Secretary for Innovation and Technology to spearhead Hong Kong's reindustrialisation.[61] And in his penultimate Policy Address, delivered in 2016, he stated the Government of the Region's commitment to the renewal of Hong Kong as a technology hub for the banking and financial sector, empowering the Innovation and Technology Bureau to coordinate the area, along with the establishment of a Chinese Medicine Development Committee to lead research and development in the discipline, and a Maritime and Port Board to bring along maritime services.[62]

On 9 December 2016, Leung announced that he would not seek re-election.[63] In his last Policy Address, the Chief Executive celebrated that, throughout his term

59 CY Leung, *The Chief Executive's Policy Address 2013* (Hong Kong: Government of the Hong Kong Special Administrative Region 2013) [20].
60 Anthony BL Cheung, *Can Hong Kong Exceptionalism Last? Dilemmas of Governance and Public Administration over Five Decades 1970s–2020* (Hong Kong: City University Press 2021) 153.
61 Anthony BL Cheung, *Can Hong Kong Exceptionalism Last? Dilemmas of Governance and Public Administration over Five Decades 1970s–2020* (Hong Kong: City University Press 2021) 153.
62 See CY Leung, *The Chief Executive's Policy Address 2016* (Hong Kong: Government of the Hong Kong Special Administrative Region 2016) [68], [233], [15].
63 See Joseph Yu-shek Cheng, 'Overall Evaluation of the C. Y. Leung Administration' in Joseph Yu-shek Cheng (ed.), *Evaluation of the C. Y. Leung Administration* (Hong Kong: City University Press 2020) 1–30.

in office, The Heritage Foundation had continued to rank Hong Kong as the world's freest economy[64] while maintaining a policy of economic activism: 'Apart from reinforcing the competitive edges of traditional industries, the Government also strives to promote the development of emerging industries.'[65]

Chief Executive Carrie Lam

Leung's successor was Carrie Lam, a former Chief Secretary, Secretary for Development and Director of Social Welfare.[66] In her first Policy Address, in October 2017, she resorted to rhetoric not dissimilar to that of Leung:

> While upholding the free market principle, the Government has to actively enhance its role in boosting our economic vibrancy through efforts in various areas, including land supply, talent, government-to-government business, policy directions, investment, business-friendly environment and taxation.[67]

A year later, seemingly with the intention to alleviate the concerns of the business sector, Lam denied that the Region was turning into a 'welfare society', although she insisted that:

> [I]t is the Government's responsibility to use the resources derived from the community for the good of the community, invest for the future, relieve people's burdens and enable people from different walks of life to share the fruits of our economic growth.[68]

While successive governments had certainly succeeded in making the Region attractive for global finance, many residents still struggled with income inequality,[69] especially in relation to the affordability of housing costs. For decades, land use in Hong Kong had been left to the management of the private sector on free market principles; that is, until September 2018, when Lam proposed 'Lantau Tomorrow Vision', a project to reclaim 1,700 hectares near Lantau Island and house 1.1

64 CY Leung, *The Chief Executive's Policy Address 2017* (Hong Kong: Government of the Hong Kong Special Administrative Region 2017) [2].
65 CY Leung, *The Chief Executive's Policy Address 2017* (Hong Kong: Government of the Hong Kong Special Administrative Region 2017) [3]–[4].
66 TW Lim, 'The "Nanny", the "Fighter" and the "Puppet": A Brief Political Biographical History of Carrie Lam Cheng Yuet-ngor Including the Earliest Days of Her Chief Executive Appointment' (2018) 35 *East Asia* 379–394, 380.
67 Carrie Lam, *The Chief Executive's Policy Address 2017* (Hong Kong: Government of the Hong Kong Special Administrative Region 2017) [38].
68 Carrie Lam, *The Chief Executive's Policy Address 2018* (Hong Kong: Government of the Hong Kong Special Administrative Region 2017) [11].
69 Heribert Dieter, 'Inequality and Social Problems in Hong Kong: The Reasons for the Broad Support of the Unrest' (2020) 74(4) *Australian Journal of International Affairs* 341–347, 346.

million people at a cost of some HK$500 billion (US$63.8 billion).[70] In 2021, she launched another project – 'Northern Metropolis' – to redevelop 2,270 hectares of rural land near the Hong Kong–Shenzhen border as a new residential and commercial centre.[71] In support, big land developers donated farmland to the Government of the Region for housing development; they felt that they owed a kind of corporate social responsibility to narrow the income gap. The Government of the Region readily assumed the donations, signalling its greater involvement in the economy.[72]

In 2020, the year of the outbreak of the COVID-19 pandemic, Chief Executive Lam continued to advertise her Government's role as a 'facilitator' and 'promoter' that 'will join hands with enterprises to explore more market opportunities and assist professional service providers to go beyond Hong Kong'.[73] She reported the injection of HK$1 billion (US$0.13 billion) each into the CreateSmart Initiative and the Film Development Fund to support the creative industries[74] and announced the establishment of an Agricultural Park to 'facilitate the development of agro-technology and modernisation of farm management'.[75] She also announced that the environmental, construction, information and technology, property management, creative and legal sectors would receive public stimulus.[76]

In her last Policy Address, Lam explained that the Region's economic restructuring processes benefitted from guidance by mainland China's policies:

> Driven by changes to the external environment, guided by the direction of the Mainland policies and led by the market forces, all these restructuring processes have been attributed to the remarkable acumen, brilliant versatility and 'can-do' spirit of Hong Kong entrepreneurs.[77]

Chief Executive John Lee

In this line, former Chief Secretary John Lee, elected Chief Executive in May 2022 to succeed Lam, announced, in his election manifesto, his plan for Hong Kong to

70 Heribert Dieter, 'Inequality and Social Problems in Hong Kong: The Reasons for the Broad Support of the Unrest' (2020) 74(4) *Australian Journal of International Affairs* 341–347, 345.
71 Sonny Shiu-Hing Lo, *Casino Capitalism, Society and Politics in China's Macau* (Newcastle upon Tyne: Cambridge Scholars Publishing 2020) 32.
72 Sonny Shiu-Hing Lo, *Casino Capitalism, Society and Politics in China's Macau* (Newcastle upon Tyne: Cambridge Scholars Publishing 2020) 33.
73 Carrie Lam, *The Chief Executive's Policy Address 2020* (Hong Kong: Government of the Hong Kong Special Administrative Region 2020) [37].
74 Carrie Lam, *The Chief Executive's Policy Address 2020* (Hong Kong: Government of the Hong Kong Special Administrative Region 2020) [74].
75 Carrie Lam, *The Chief Executive's Policy Address 2020* (Hong Kong: Government of the Hong Kong Special Administrative Region 2020) [80].
76 Carrie Lam, *The Chief Executive's Policy Address 2020* (Hong Kong: Government of the Hong Kong Special Administrative Region 2020) [135].
77 Carrie Lam, *The Chief Executive's Policy Address 2021* (Hong Kong: Government of the Hong Kong Special Administrative Region 2021) [39].

foster 'a freer and more transparent business environment based on the rule of law, thereby strengthening its vibrancy and enhancing its overall competitiveness', in accordance with China's 14th Five-Year Plan.[78] '[T]he administration must adopt a proactive and forward-looking attitude to foster economic growth', the manifesto read.[79] In his inauguration speech, given on 1 July 2022, Lee reiterated the Government of the Region's commitment to 'strengthening … established sectors and reinforcing Hong Kong's status as an international financial, transportation and trading centre', with emphasis on developing the Region into 'an international innovation and technology hub'.[80] In his first Policy Address, delivered to the Legislative Council on 19 October 2022, Lee emphasised the Region's identity as 'a free, open and international metropolis connecting with the Mainland and the world'.[81]

Overall, Chief Executives and their Financial Secretaries have deployed Article 107 of the Basic Law – 'the principle of keeping expenditure within the limits of revenues in drawing up [a Government] budget, and strive to achieve a fiscal balance, avoid deficits and keep the budget commensurate with the growth rate of its gross domestic product' – to legitimate reductions of government spending. And, at the same time, they have operated under Articles 109, 118 and 119 of the Basic Law to fund what they consider to be 'appropriate' infrastructure projects and industrial interests.[82]

Economic Jurisprudence of the Courts

The courts of Hong Kong have been consistent in their development of a jurisprudence that coheres with the spirit of free market constitutionalism. In *Wong Shu Wan v Wu Kwok Yau Simon*,[83] decided in the same year as the Sino-British Joint Declaration was signed, Justice of Appeal Derek Cons contrasted the spirit of self-sufficiency in the territory with the welfare state back in the United Kingdom:

> The general situation may not be quite the same here in Hong Kong where the individual does not have the cushion of the welfare state behind him and

78 John Lee, *Starting a New Chapter for Hong Kong Together: Election Manifesto of Chief Executive Election 2022* (Hong Kong: John Lee Ka-chiu Election Campaign Office 2022) 19.

79 John Lee, *Starting a New Chapter for Hong Kong Together: Election Manifesto of Chief Executive Election 2022* (Hong Kong: John Lee Ka-chiu Election Campaign Office 2022) 19.

80 John Lee, 'CE's speech at Inaugural Ceremony of Sixth-term Government' (1 July 2022), https://www.info.gov.hk/gia/general/202207/01/P2022070100398p.htm, accessed 3 July 2022.

81 John Lee, *The Chief Executive's Policy Address 2022* (Hong Kong: Government of the Hong Kong Special Administrative Region 2022) [144].

82 Leo Goodstadt, *A City Mismanaged: Hong Kong's Struggle for Survival* (Hong Kong: Hong Kong University Press 2018) 30.

83 *Wong Shu Wan v Wu Kwok Yau Simon* CACV 97/1984.

> usually starts to realise the importance of personal financial responsibility at an early age. It may therefore be possible that by his middle twenties a single man, although subsequently changing his parental family for one of his own, will have established a sufficiently stable pattern of life for the court to assess quite accurately how he would have adapted himself over that period.[84]

Through its development of positive non-interventionism, old Hong Kong was able to avoid the problem of government debt that often comes with excessive spending on public benefits and services.[85] The unavailability of redistributed income, like systematic social inequality, were seen in the territory as inevitable evils of the free market and necessary motivations for hard work.[86] Residents were, voluntarily, self-sufficient. Indeed, as Friedrich Hayek put it, the use of 'coercive' governmental powers to achieve '"positive" justice' can lead to 'the destruction of individual freedom', since, he explained, that kind of justice is, ultimately, 'a mirage or an illusion which cannot be achieved'.[87] In *Re Lam Kin Chung*,[88] the High Court of Justice – the predecessor of the Court of First Instance – took pride 'in a society like ours, thriving on its *laissez-faire* tradition with little disciplined monitoring'.[89] In *The Queen v Hui Siu-yan, Edward*,[90] the same Court unequivocally decided that 'international commercial activities' should not be subject to 'unwarranted curtailment', for it 'fall[s] foul of Hong Kong's reputation for *laissez-faire*'.[91]

More recently, the Court of Appeal, in *Secretary for Justice v Wong Chi Fung (Criminal Contempt)*,[92] explained the significance of the rule of law to a Region that is an international financial centre:

> The importance of the rule of law to Hong Kong is self-evident. It distinguishes Hong Kong as a modern civilised and open society from anarchy where the rule of might prevails. It renders all the rights and freedoms guaranteed under our laws, including the Basic Law, which we all enjoy and cherish, real and meaningful in actuality. It enables Hong Kong citizens to flourish. It ensures that

84 *Wong Shu Wan v Wu Kwok Yau Simon* CACV 97/1984 (Cons JA).
85 Florence Meng-soi Fong and Chack-kie Wong, 'Setting the Poverty Line: Policy Implications for Squaring the Welfare Circle in Hong Kong' in Maggie KW Lau and David Gordon (eds), *Poverty in a Rich Society: The Case of Hong Kong* (Hong Kong: The Chinese University Press 2017) 57–88, 63.
86 Tsz Ken Yau, 'Housing Question and Social Discontent After 1997: History and Continuity of Home Ownership' in Brian CH Fong and Tai-Lok Lui (eds), *Hong Kong 20 Years After the Handover: Emerging Social and Institutional Fractures After 1997* (Cham: Palgrave Macmillan 2018) 177–202, 178.
87 FA Hayek, 'The Principles of a Liberal Social Order' in Chiaki Nishiyama and Kurt R Leube (eds), *The Essence of Hayek* (Stanford: Hoover Institution Press 1984) 363–381, 375.
88 *Re Lam Kin Chung* HCMP 216/1991.
89 *Re Lam Kin Chung* HCMP 216/1991 [14] (Liu J).
90 *The Queen v Hui Siu-yan, Edward* [1994] 1 HKCLR 200.
91 *The Queen v Hui Siu-yan, Edward* [1994] 1 HKCLR 200, 210 (Jerome Chan J).
92 *Secretary for Justice v Wong Chi Fung (Criminal Contempt)* [2019] 2 HKLRD 1236.

> Hong Kong will continue to thrive as an international financial centre. The rule of law is the very fabric and foundation of our society.[93]

In a similar vein, Geoffrey Ma, Chief Justice of the Hong Kong Court of Final Appeal between 2010 and 2021, extra-judicially remarked: 'A *laissez faire* policy (sometimes called positive non-intervention) is often said to apply to Hong Kong's economic policy … [while] the weakness with having rules and regulations in abundance seeking to govern every aspect of commerce – in particular, the resolution of disputes – is that flexibility is perhaps sacrificed, and flexibility is key to justice.'[94]

On matters of distribution and redistribution of resources, the courts have staunchly maintained the custom of non-intervention. In *Chan To Foon v Director of Immigration*,[95] the Court of First Instance categorised the International Covenant on Economic, Social and Cultural Rights (ICESCR) as more 'aspirational' than strictly obligatory, in marked contrast with its enthusiasm for the implementation of the International Covenant on Civil and Political Rights:

> Hong Kong may therefore recognise the rights protected by the ICESCR. But they are rights which, having regard to this Territory's existing social difficulties, may only be guaranteed progressively; that is, as and when those difficulties are overcome … [the ICESCR] is an aspirational covenant, not one that creates absolute obligations.[96]

The case made apparent the reluctance of the Hong Kong judiciary to enforce such ICESCR entitlements as the right to social security, including social insurance;[97] the right to an adequate standard of living, including food, clothing and housing;[98] the right to the enjoyment of the 'highest attainable standard of physical and mental health';[99] the right to education;[100] and, the right to take part in cultural life,[101] any and all of which may depend on positive state action. The ruling in *Chan To Foon v Director of Immigration* drew sharp criticism from the Committee on Economic, Social and Cultural Rights, the United Nations body that monitors the implementation of the

93 *Secretary for Justice v Wong Chi Fung (Criminal Contempt)* [2019] 2 HKLRD 1236, 1260 (Poon JA).
94 Geoffrey Ma, 'The Bapsybanoo Marchioness of Winchester Lecture 2018: The Dependency of Business and Finance on the Common Law in Hong Kong: A Paradigm Jurisdiction' (7 November 2018) [3].
95 *Chan To Foon v Director of Immigration* [2001] 3 HKLRD 109.
96 *Chan To Foon v Director of Immigration* [2001] 3 HKLRD 109, 132 (Hartmann J).
97 International Covenant on Economic, Social and Cultural Rights, Article 9.
98 International Covenant on Economic, Social and Cultural Rights, Article 11.
99 International Covenant on Economic, Social and Cultural Rights, Article 12.
100 International Covenant on Economic, Social and Cultural Rights, Article 13.
101 International Covenant on Economic, Social and Cultural Rights, Article 15.

ICESCR.[102] Two decades later, the Court of Appeal in *Lubiano Nancy Almorin v Director of Immigration*[103] continued to maintain a non-interventionist stance:

> It would not be a task which the Court finds itself institutionally equipped to adjudicate upon due to the aspirational and generic formulation in the ICESCR which addresses interests within the spheres of socio-economic and cultural rights … which is a function institutionally within the province of the executive and the legislative arm of the Government.[104]

This statement echoed an earlier opinion of the Court of Final Appeal, which had ruled in *Fok Chun Wa v Hospital Authority*[105] that 'it would not usually be within the province of the courts to adjudicate on the merits or demerits of government socio-economic policies'.[106] In *Choi King Fung v Hong Kong Housing Authority*,[107] a case back in 2017 asserting rights to equality and social welfare, the Court of First Instance, elaborating on the proper role of judicial review in public housing policy, said thus:

> The courts are not entrusted by the Basic Law with the function of formulating housing policies. They are not equipped to devise housing or welfare policies and examine the wide range of ramifications that such policies may entail, to make the 'difficult and agonising judgments' that have to be made in distributive decisions allocating [public rental housing] resources to one sector or another.[108]

Indeed, the Basic Law contains several clauses, described by one commentator as 'curious',[109] namely, that 'Hong Kong residents shall have the right to social welfare in accordance with law';[110] that '[t]he welfare benefits and retirement security of the labour force shall be protected by law';[111] and, that '[o]n the basis of the previous social welfare system, the Government of the Hong Kong Special Administrative Region shall, on its own, formulate policies on the development and improvement of this system in the light of the

102 Committee on Economic, Social and Cultural Rights, Concluding Observations: China (Hong Kong), UN Doc E/C.12/1/Add.58 (21 May 2001) [178].
103 *Lubiano Nancy Almorin v Director of Immigration* [2020] 5 HKLRD 107.
104 *Lubiano Nancy Almorin v Director of Immigration* [2020] 5 HKLRD 107, 135 (Lam V–P, Barma and Au JJA).
105 *Fok Chun Wa v Hospital Authority* (2012) 15 HKCFAR 409.
106 *Fok Chun Wa v Hospital Authority* (2012) 15 HKCFAR 409, 437 (Ma CJ).
107 *Choi King Fung v Hong Kong Housing Authority* [2017] HKCFI 459.
108 *Choi King Fung v Hong Kong Housing Authority* [2017] HKCFI 459 (Lam J).
109 Alvin Rabushka, 'A Free-Market Constitution for Hong Kong: A Blueprint for China' (1989) 8(3) *Cato Journal* 641–656, 649.
110 Basic Law of the Hong Kong Special Administrative Region of the People's Republic of China, Article 36.
111 Basic Law of the Hong Kong Special Administrative Region of the People's Republic of China, Article 36.

economic conditions and social needs'.[112] The Basic Law does not define 'social welfare'; it presumably refers to schemes run by the Region's Social Welfare Department, including the Comprehensive Social Security Assistance (CSSA) scheme, Support for Self-reliance Scheme, and the Social Security Allowance Scheme, encompassing Old Age Allowance, Old Age Living Allowance and Disability Allowance.[113] In particular, the CSSA scheme, dating back to the early 1970s, is no more than an administrative measure subject to fiscal affordability; it is certainly not a mandatory social entitlement.[114] Notably, the Basic Law permits no scope to dismantle the social welfare system operative under British colonial rule,[115] although a comprehensive social security scheme would hardly be sustainable in the Region, given its narrow tax base. The cost of the social welfare system is borne nearly entirely by taxpayers who derive little direct benefit from it, as the poorest 65 per cent of residents pay hardly any tax at all.[116]

We think it important, however, to clarify that neither free market constitutionalism nor Hong Kong's customary positive non-interventionism is incompatible with an expectation 'that some minimum of food, shelter, and clothing, sufficient to preserve health and the capacity to work, can be assured to everybody'.[117] In *Chan Noi Heung and Others v The Chief Executive in Council*, the Court of First Instance ruled: 'All societies that consider themselves to be built on principles of social justice – and Hong Kong stands among them – recognise that every worker, no matter how humble his labour, is entitled to a liveable wage.'[118] Although positive non-interventionism 'raises a strong burden of proof against government interference', it does not forbid any intervention whatsoever, no matter how minimal or necessary.[119] Indeed, classical economic liberal thought, to which we subscribe, encourages taxation for the compassionate provision of essential public goods – education, health, housing – to buttress basic human dignity and, more generally, the common good.

112 Basic Law of the Hong Kong Special Administrative Region of the People's Republic of China, Article 145.

113 Karen Kong, 'Right to Social Welfare, in Johannes Chan and CL Lim (eds), *Law of the Hong Kong Constitution* (3rd edn) (Hong Kong: Sweet & Maxwell 2021) 955–989, 958.

114 Anthony BL Cheung, *Can Hong Kong Exceptionalism Last? Dilemmas of Governance and Public Administration over Five Decades 1970s–2020* (Hong Kong: City University Press 2021) 145.

115 Leo Goodstadt, *A City Mismanaged: Hong Kong's Struggle for Survival* (Hong Kong: Hong Kong University Press 2018) 30.

116 Michael Littlewood, *Taxation without Representation: The History of Hong Kong's Troublingly Successful Tax System* (Hong Kong: Hong Kong University Press 2010) 291.

117 FA Hayek, *The Road to Serfdom* (New York: Routledge 2014) 148.

118 *Chan Noi Heung and Others v The Chief Executive in Council* HCAL 126/2006, [1] (Hartmann J).

119 Yue Chim Richard Wong, *Fixing Inequality in Hong Kong* (Hong Kong: Hong Kong University Press 2017) 299.

To rebut the charge that 'positive non-interventionism was adopted by the Government of the Region as an excuse to escape from its social welfare obligations', one need look no further than its role in housing policy, especially in encouraging home ownership.[120] The total share of the Region's budget spent on housing as well as education, health and social welfare increased from 38.3 per cent in 1971–1972 to 52.2 per cent in 2015–2016. Within government spending, the fastest rise was in social welfare, from 1.9 per cent to 14.3 per cent.[121] In fact, in May 2011, the Tsang Government adopted a statutory minimum wage on the premise that it would reduce poverty across households.[122] These and the other anti-poverty measures of successive Chief Executives, even if open to improvement,[123] were popular and justified as income inequality in the Region has, in relative terms, been greater than in other developed economies:[124] over one-third of its income is controlled by the wealthiest 10 per cent, whereas the bottom 10 per cent share just 2 per cent.[125] Hong Kong's Gini coefficient climbed from 0.45 in 1981 to 0.52 in 1996 and then to 0.537 in 2011 and 0.539 in 2016.[126] As at 2022, the Region had not yet adopted a comprehensive retirement scheme.[127]

Against this background, the Court of Final Appeal's decision in *Kong Yunming v Director of Social Welfare*[128] (*Kong Yunming*) seemed to be an outlier in the non-interventionist economic jurisprudence of the Hong Kong judiciary or, perhaps, a signpost of a new era of judicial activism in the protection of ICESCR entitlement rights from the government's socioeconomic policies.[129] On 17 December 2013, the Court unanimously quashed part of an order of the Chief Executive in Council that required all recipients of the CSSA scheme to have been Hong Kong residents

120 Tze Ken Yau, 'Housing Question and Social Discontent After 1997: History and Continuity of Home Ownership' in Brian CH Fong and Tai-Lok Lui (eds), *Hong Kong 20 Years after the Handover: Emerging Social and Institutional Fractures After 1997* (Cham: Palgrave Macmillan 2018) 177–202, 177.
121 Yue Chim Richard Wong, *Fixing Inequality in Hong Kong* (Hong Kong: Hong Kong University Press 2017) 227.
122 Yue Chim Richard Wong, *Fixing Inequality in Hong Kong* (Hong Kong: Hong Kong University Press 2017) 262.
123 Hung Wong, 'Is Poverty Eradication Impossible? A Critique on the Misconceptions of the Hong Kong Government' in Maggie KW Lau and David Gordon (eds), *Poverty in a Rich Society: The Case of Hong Kong* (Hong Kong: The Chinese University Press 2017) 179–201, 183.
124 Maggie KW Lau, 'Introduction' in Maggie KW Lau and David Gordon (eds), *Poverty in a Rich Society: The Case of Hong Kong* (Hong Kong: The Chinese University Press 2017) 1–8, 1.
125 Luke Marsh, 'The Strategic Use of Human Rights Treaties in Hong Kong's Cage-Home Crisis: No Way Out?' (2016) 3 *Asian Journal of Law and Society* 159–188, 183.
126 Joseph Yu-shek Cheng, 'Overall Evaluation of the C. Y. Leung Administration' in Joseph Yu-shek Cheng (eds), *Evaluation of the C. Y. Leung Administration* (Hong Kong: City University Press 2020) 1–30, 3.
127 Leo Goodstadt, *A City Mismanaged: Hong Kong's Struggle for Survival* (Hong Kong: Hong Kong University Press 2018) 38.
128 *Kong Yunming v Director of Social Welfare* (2013) 16 HKCFAR 950.
129 See Pok Yin S Chow, 'After *Kong Yunming v Director of Social Welfare*: The Status of Socioeconomic Rights in Hong Kong' (2018) 29(2) *Public Law Review* 133–146.

for no fewer than seven years. Arguably, the *Kong Yunming* doctrine 'is distinct from [that of] the lower courts … which did not impose a standard as to the justifications provided by the Government but merely endorsed Government decisions by adopting a deferential approach to socio-economic policies [...] It demonstrated the more structured and detailed enquiry required by the proportionality analysis and the heavier burden on the Government to justify its decision'.[130] On this view and all in all, *Kong Yunming* should be regarded as 'the landmark authority of the [Court of Final Appeal] on the right to social welfare in Hong Kong'.[131] Undoubtedly, the decision removed an obstacle to access by new immigrants to welfare benefits and broke new ground with its declaration that 'any restriction subsequently placed on [social welfare rights in Article 36 of the Basic Law] is also subject to constitutional review by the Courts on the basis of a proportionality analysis'.[132] The Court, speaking through Justice Roberto Ribeiro, thus affirmed the standing of the right to social welfare as self-sufficient, enforceable independently of the right of equality.

Despite its singularity, *Kong Yunming* is no outlier. It is noteworthy that the Court stuck to rule under the Basic Law: '[t]he Article 36 right to social welfare is not a fundamental right but a right which intrinsically involves the Government setting rules determining eligibility and benefit levels';[133] that 'Article 145 does not preclude the elimination or reduction of particular welfare benefits if that proves necessary to develop, improve or maintain the sustainability of the welfare system as a whole';[134] such that 'reducing standard payments in 1999 in relation to larger households and reducing standard payments across-the-board in 2003 and 2004' were 'rational measures … genuinely' pursuant to a 'legitimate aim of curbing expenditure on CSSA with a view to ensuring the financial sustainability of the social security system'.[135]

The Court's lead judgment, authored by Justice Ribeiro, struck down the impugned residence requirement, not on the basis of idealistic socioeconomic philosophy but on the much narrower, lawyerly grounds of administrative illogic.[136] The test propounded by the Court was lenient to the Government of the Region:

130 Karen Kong, 'Right to Social Welfare', in Johannes Chan and CL Lim (eds), *Law of the Hong Kong Constitution* (3rd edn) (Hong Kong: Sweet & Maxwell 2021) 955–989, 972–973.

131 Karen Kong, 'Right to Social Welfare, in Johannes Chan and CL Lim (eds), *Law of the Hong Kong Constitution* (3rd edn) (Hong Kong: Sweet & Maxwell 2021) 955–989, 964.

132 Karen Kong, 'Right to Social Welfare, in Johannes Chan and CL Lim (eds), *Law of the Hong Kong Constitution* (3rd edn) (Hong Kong: Sweet & Maxwell 2021) 955–989, 968. Basic Law of the Hong Kong Special Administrative Region of the People's Republic of China, Article 36: 'Hong Kong residents shall have the right to social welfare in accordance with law. The welfare benefits and retirement security of the labour force shall be protected by law.'

133 *Kong Yunming v Director of Social Welfare* (2013) 16 HKCFAR 950, 970 (Ribeiro PJ).

134 *Kong Yunming v Director of Social Welfare* (2013) 16 HKCFAR 950, 968 (Ribeiro PJ).

135 *Kong Yunming v Director of Social Welfare* (2013) 16 HKCFAR 950, 998 (Ribeiro PJ).

136 See Eric C Ip, '*Kong Yunming* Manifest Unreasonableness: The Doctrinal Future of Constitutional Review of Welfare Policy in Hong Kong' (2014) 44(1) *Hong Kong Law Journal* 55–66.

> Where the disputed measure involves the implementation of the Government's socio-economic policy choices regarding the allocation of limited public funds without impinging upon fundamental rights or involving possible discrimination on inherently suspect grounds, the Court has held that it has a duty to intervene only where the impugned measure is 'manifestly without reasonable justification'.[137]

The manifest unreasonableness standard suggests that the impugned act should be invalidated only in extreme circumstances.[138] A reviewing court will only need to scrutinise the act according to a deferential standard that resembles *Wednesbury* unreasonableness as in irrationality.[139] The justification for restraint in welfare rights adjudication is rooted in traditional concerns about comity with the political branches, and also in a deeper commitment to non-interventionist economic thinking.[140] The Government of the Region reacted to the decision with a warning that social welfare expenditure could become a severe fiscal burden.[141]

Conclusion

The Hong Kong Basic Law never purported to transform the Region into a welfare state. A 'charter of capitalism',[142] it, instead, sought to 'freeze' the Victorian constitution under British colonial rule as it stood on 4 April 1990.[143] Its provisions were drafted to ringfence the Hong Kong way of life, as underpinned by the positive non-interventionist tradition, to the furthest extent. Nevertheless, on reversion to China on 1 July 1997, demand within and beyond ruling circles for more active state intervention began to rise.[144] Anthony Cheung, who was Secretary for Transport and Housing between 2012 and 2017 under Chief Executive CY Leung, observed:

137 *Kong Yunming v Director of Social Welfare* (2013) 16 HKCFAR 950, 969–970 (Ribeiro PJ).
138 Paul Daly, *A Theory of Deference in Administrative Law: Basis, Application and Scope* (New York: Cambridge University Press 2012) 181.
139 Alec Stone Sweet, 'The Necessity of Balancing: Hong Kong's Flawed Approach to Proportionality, and Why It Matters' (2020) 50(2) *Hong Kong Law Journal* 541–568, 558.
140 See Eric C Ip, '*Kong Yunming* Manifest Unreasonableness: The Doctrinal Future of Constitutional Review of Welfare Policy in Hong Kong' (2014) 44(1) *Hong Kong Law Journal* 55–66.
141 Leo Goodstadt, *A City Mismanaged: Hong Kong's Struggle for Survival* (Hong Kong: Hong Kong University Press 2018) 33.
142 Yash Ghai, 'The Rule of Law and Capitalism: Reflections on the Basic Law' in Raymond Wacks (ed.), *Hong Kong, China and 1997: Essays in Legal Theory* (Hong Kong: Hong Kong University Press 1993) 343–365, 345.
143 Raymond Wacks, 'One Country, Two Grundnormen? The Basic Law and the Basic Norm' in Raymond Wacks (ed.), *Hong Kong, China and 1997: Essays in Legal Theory* (Hong Kong: Hong Kong University Press) 169–170.
144 Anthony BL Cheung, *Can Hong Kong Exceptionalism Last? Dilemmas of Governance and Public Administration over Five Decades 1970s–2020* (Hong Kong: City University Press 2021) 144.

> Among the post-1997 [Chief Executives], both Tung Chee-hwa and Leung Chun-ying, as outsiders, were known for embracing proactive government. For the two former civil servants brought up in the tradition of fiscal conservatism, Donald Tsang had formally discarded positive non-interventionism after becoming [Chief Executive] while Carrie Lam is also noted for more proactive steering and policy intervention.[145]

As we illustrate in the first section of this chapter, the Region's receptivity to the adoption of industrial policies does suggest a modest shift of economic philosophy away from the laissez-faire paradigm of old but one that is, nevertheless, in close alignment with the contemporary policy trends of developed economies across the world. These policy trends favour industrial diversification and reform, which, normally, feature extensive research funding and significant public procurement.[146] On trend perhaps but state funding of large-scale projects is, arguably, questionable in terms of efficacy.[147] Ultimately, industrial policy in itself departs from the idea that the market ought to be driven by the free decisions of private entrepreneurs, not those of public officials.[148] As Hayek put it:

> The unconscious collaboration of individuals in the market leads to the solution of problems which, although no individual mind has even formulated these problems in a market economy, would have to be consciously solved on the same principle in a planned system. Under the price system the solution of these problems is impersonal and social in the strict sense of the term.[149]

In all fairness, be it admitted that the industrial policy of the Hong Kong Special Administrative Region has, thus far, remained comparatively modest, as it has not been supplemented by further initiatives and resources, leaving the business sector to itself for its financing decisions.[150] Hong Kong's industrial policy has not crept so far as to 'impos[e] heavy costs on industry after industry to meet increasingly detailed and extensive government requirements'.[151] On the contrary, Hong

145 Anthony BL Cheung, *Can Hong Kong Exceptionalism Last? Dilemmas of Governance and Public Administration over Five Decades 1970s–2020* (Hong Kong: City University Press 2021) 279.
146 Justin Yifu Lin, 'Industrial Policy Revisited: A New Structural Economics Perspective' (2013) 21(2) *Revue d'économie du développement* 55–78, 59.
147 Anthony BL Cheung, *Can Hong Kong Exceptionalism Last? Dilemmas of Governance and Public Administration over Five Decades 1970s–2020* (Hong Kong: City University Press 2021) 156.
148 Katsuro Sakoh, 'Japanese Economic Success: Industrial Policy or Free Market?' (1984) 4(2) *Cato Journal* 521–548, 537.
149 FA Hayek, *Freedom and the Economic System* (Chicago: The University of Chicago Press 1939) 15.
150 Jue Wong, 'Innovation and Government Intervention: A Comparison of Singapore and Hong Kong' (2018) 47 *Research Policy* 399–412, 401.
151 See Milton Friedman and Rose Friedman, *Free to Choose: A Personal Statement* (Orlando: Harcourt 1980) 181.

Kong's economic liberty, buttressed by the Basic Law, is as, if not more, vibrant as anywhere else in the world: low taxes, transparent market rules, stable finances are an ongoing success.[152] The divergent pictures offered by Friedman and the rankings, which we mention at the outset of this chapter, can indeed be reconciled. And free market constitutionalism has proved and continues to prove resilient: the Asian financial crisis and the severe acute respiratory syndrome (SARS) outbreak were shocks, but Hong Kong rebounded and soared to unmatched prosperity, thanks to China's rapid growth and mainland support through such initiatives as the Closer Economic Partnership Arrangement.[153]

As for Hong Kong's courts, they have yielded an economic jurisprudence that coheres with the ambit of free market constitutionalism. *Kong Yunming* affirmed that the right to social welfare in the Basic Law has minimal content.[154] Although holding the impugned law unconstitutional,[155] the Court set a deferential manifest unreasonableness standard, which has closed the backdoor on judicial promotion of welfarism under the guise of constitutional interpretation.[156]

152 Andrew Sheng, 'Financial Sector in Hong Kong, China' in Ulrich Volz, Peter J Morgan and Naoyuki Yoshino (eds), *Routledge Handbook of Banking and Finance in Asia* (New York: Routledge 2019) 39–53, 41.

153 Andrew Sheng, 'Financial Sector in Hong Kong, China' in Ulrich Volz, Peter J Morgan and Naoyuki Yoshino (eds), *Routledge Handbook of Banking and Finance in Asia* (New York: Routledge 2019) 39–53, 41.

154 Michael Ramsden, 'Judging Socio-economic Rights in Hong Kong' (2018) 16(2) *International Journal of Constitutional Law* 447–469, 450.

155 See Po Jen Yap and Thomas Wong, 'Public Welfare and the Judicial Over-Enforcement of Socio-Economic Rights in Hong Kong' (2014) 44 *Hong Kong Law Journal* 41.

156 Eric C Ip, '*Kong Yunming* Manifest Unreasonableness: The Doctrinal Future of Constitutional Review of Welfare Policy in Hong Kong' (2014) 44(1) *Hong Kong Law Journal* 55, 66.

6

FREE MARKET CONSTITUTIONALISM AND HONG KONG'S EXTERNAL ECONOMIC POLICY

Introduction

Earlier chapters establish that the Hong Kong Basic Law is recognisable as an economic constitution with the principles of the free market as its motivation, what we call *free market constitutionalism*. The previous chapter studies their internal implementation. This chapter studies their external implementation. The Basic Law confers onto the Hong Kong Special Administrative Region of the People's Republic of China both an external personality[1] to act under the name of 'Hong Kong, China' further to Article 151 and an external capacity to act as a 'separate customs territory'[2] further to Article 116, all in pursuit of the 'policy of free trade'[3] under Article 115. Hong Kong – historically, the world's free port – is a founding member of the World Trade Organization (WTO); mainland China, as in the entire customs territory of China, only joined years later.[4] The Region is a signatory to bilateral, regional and plurilateral trade agreements, as well as arrangements, with numerous customs territories. It is through these instruments and instrumentalities of trade that Hong Kong's economic constitution has a significant external function.

1 See Eric C Ip, 'Comparative Subnational Foreign Relations Law in the Chinese Special Administrative Regions' (2016) 65(4) *International and Comparative Law Quarterly* 953–968.
2 Matthew Kennedy, 'Overseas Territories in the WTO' (2016) 65(3) *International and Comparative Law Quarterly* 741–762.
3 Zeng Huaqun, 'Unprecedented International Status: Theoretical and Practical Aspects of the HKSAR's External Autonomy' (2008) 9(3) *Journal of World Investment & Trade* 275–298; Roda Mushkat, 'Hong Kong's Exercise of External Autonomy: A Multi-Faceted Appraisal' (2006) 55(4) *International and Comparative Law Quarterly* 945–962; Sun Zhichao, 'International Legal Personality of the Hong Kong Special Administrative Region' (2008) 7(2) *Chinese Journal of International Law* 339–352.
4 Joseph CK Yam, 'The WTO: China's Future and Hong Kong's Opportunity' (2001) 21(1) *Cato Journal* 1–12.

DOI: 10.4324/9780429341229-6

The WTO's periodic Trade Policy Review of Hong Kong corroborates the commitment of the Government of the Region to a 'free market philosophy'.[5] For the WTO Secretariat, Hong Kong remains one of the most open market economies in the world, with 'some of the highest rankings in world indicators of economic freedom, competitiveness, and ease of doing business'.[6] Even though the Region has begun, gradually and appropriately, to follow the global trend for greater government support of the market[7] – especially in the aftermath of the COVID-19 pandemic – free trade and low taxes[8] remain at the heart of the doctrine of 'big market, small government',[9] a topic that Chapter 5 explores. Indeed, in true commitment to the free market, Hong Kong is – by constitutional ordination, no less – a free port and a separate customs territory.[10] Notably, it is the largest free zone in the world.[11] It ranks worldwide as the sixth largest exporter and fifth largest importer of goods and the eighth largest exporter and twelfth largest importer of services.[12] As a global centre for trade,[13] exports and imports of goods and non-factor services represent 375 per cent of the Region's gross domestic product.[14] Particularly, for trade in goods, the Region serves as an entrepôt between mainland China – its largest trading partner – and the rest of the world.[15]

Hong Kong's port – the fourth largest in the world[16] – predominantly conduits re-exports from and re-imports to mainland China.[17] For trade in services, the

5 World Trade Organization, *Trade Policy Review Report by the Secretariat: Hong Kong, China (Revision)* (25 January 2011) WT/TPR/S/241/Rev.1 vii [4].
6 World Trade Organization, *Trade Policy Review Report by the Secretariat: Hong Kong, China (Revision)* (28 January 2015) WT/TPR/S/306/Rev.1 [1].
7 World Trade Organization, *Trade Policy Review Report by the Secretariat: Hong Kong, China (Revision)* (25 January 2011) WT/TPR/S/241/Rev.1 viii [11].
8 World Trade Organization, *Trade Policy Review Report by the Secretariat: Hong Kong, China (Revision)* (25 January 2011) WT/TPR/S/241/Rev.1 viii [14]. Hong Kong has a neutral direct tax system mainly reliant on stamp duty revenue from the lease of (state-owned) land: World Trade Organization, *Trade Policy Review Report by the Secretariat: Hong Kong, China (Revision)* (25 January 2011) WT/TPR/S/241/Rev.1 viii–ix [14–15].
9 World Trade Organization, *Trade Policy Review Report by the Secretariat: Hong Kong, China (Revision)* (25 January 2011) WT/TPR/S/241/Rev.1 viii [13].
10 World Trade Organization, *Trade Policy Review Report by the Secretariat: Hong Kong, China (Revision)* (30 January 2019) WT/TPR/S/380/Rev.1 [3.1].
11 World Trade Organization, *Trade Policy Review Report by the Secretariat: Hong Kong, China (Revision)* (28 January 2015) WT/TPR/S/306/Rev.1 [1.21].
12 World Trade Organization, *Trade Policy Review Report by the Secretariat: Hong Kong, China (Revision)* (30 January 2019) WT/TPR/S/380/Rev.1 [1.22].
13 World Trade Organization, *Trade Policy Review Report by the Secretariat: Hong Kong, China (Revision)* (30 January 2019) WT/TPR/S/380/Rev.1 [1].
14 World Trade Organization, *Trade Policy Review Report by the Secretariat: Hong Kong, China (Revision)* (30 January 2019) WT/TPR/S/380/Rev.1 [1.4], [1.22].
15 World Trade Organization, *Trade Policy Review Report by the Secretariat: Hong Kong, China (Revision)* (30 January 2019) WT/TPR/S/380/Rev.1 [1.29]: 'Total two-way trade between HKC and Mainland China amounted to US$561 billion in 2017.'
16 World Trade Organization, *Trade Policy Review Report by the Secretariat: Hong Kong, China (Revision)* (28 January 2015) WT/TPR/S/306/Rev.1 [19].
17 World Trade Organization, *Trade Policy Review Report by the Secretariat: Hong Kong, China (Revision)* (28 January 2015) WT/TPR/S/306/Rev.1 [1.21].

Region is 'a regional or even global centre in sectors such as financial services, and maritime and air transport'.[18] In fact, services trade comprises the largest sector of the Region's economy,[19] with significant exports of financial, transport and travel services.[20] Trade aside, Hong Kong 'is one of the largest destinations and sources of direct investment in the world … the fourth-largest recipient of direct investment inflows worldwide … and the sixth-largest source of direct investment outflows'.[21] Much of this remarkably high transactional volume is attributable to the Region's foreign investment regime, which is 'one of the world's most liberal and transparent'.[22] Under the Basic Law, Hong Kong is free of restrictions on investment, capital flows or foreign exchange. With the exception of regulatory measures in the banking and broadcasting services sectors, foreign investors receive national treatment, and no minimum capital requirements apply to investments.[23]

External Trade Policy and Practice

The external trade policy of Hong Kong revolves around its membership of the WTO.[24] It has a twofold objective, namely, to support the multilateral trading system[25] and to make it more free, more open.[26] Indeed, the words of the 12th WTO Ministerial Conference of June 2022 articulate the Region's external economic policy: 'We resolve to strengthen the rules-based, non-discriminatory, open, fair, inclusive, equitable and transparent multilateral trading system with the WTO at its core.'[27] And to realise that objective – that is, to progressively expand and effectively liberalise

18 World Trade Organization, *Trade Policy Review Report by the Secretariat: Hong Kong, China (Revision)* (28 January 2015) WT/TPR/S/306/Rev.1 [16].

19 World Trade Organization, *Trade Policy Review Report by the Secretariat: Hong Kong, China (Revision)* (25 January 2011) WT/TPR/S/241/Rev.1 ix [17]; World Trade Organization, *Trade Policy Review Report by the Secretariat: Hong Kong, China (Revision)* (28 January 2015) WT/TPR/S/306/Rev.1 [6].

20 World Trade Organization, *Trade Policy Review Report by the Secretariat: Hong Kong, China (Revision)* (28 January 2015) WT/TPR/S/306/Rev.1 [6]: 'Services remain the dominant sector of the economy, accounting for 93% of GDP and 88% of total employment (2012).'

21 World Trade Organization, *Trade Policy Review Report by the Secretariat: Hong Kong, China (Revision)* (30 January 2019) WT/TPR/S/380/Rev.1 [1.35].

22 World Trade Organization, *Trade Policy Review Report by the Secretariat: Hong Kong, China (Revision)* (25 January 2011) WT/TPR/S/241/Rev.1 vii [1].

23 World Trade Organization, *Trade Policy Review Report by the Secretariat: Hong Kong, China (Revision)* (30 January 2019) WT/TPR/S/380/Rev.1 [2.41].

24 World Trade Organization, *Trade Policy Review Report by the Secretariat: Hong Kong, China (Revision)* (30 January 2019) WT/TPR/S/380/Rev.1 [2.10].

25 World Trade Organization, *Trade Policy Review Report by the Secretariat: Hong Kong, China (Revision)* (28 January 2015) WT/TPR/S/306/Rev.1 [7].

26 World Trade Organization, *Trade Policy Review Report by the Secretariat: Hong Kong, China (Revision)* (30 January 2019) WT/TPR/S/380/Rev.1 [2.6].

27 World Trade Organization, *MC12 Outcome Document* (22 June 2022) WT/MIN(22)/24 [1].

global trade – Hong Kong works with the WTO and its other members to reinforce and renovate the rules of the trading system[28] against any form of discriminatory protectionism.

The principal legislation that implements Hong Kong's external trade policy is the Import and Export Ordinance (Cap 60).[29] This legal instrument, together with its subordinate regulations,[30] administers the customs territory and its customs procedures with provision for the regulation and control of the import of goods into the Region and the export of goods from the Region. In support of that statutory framework, the Secretary for Commerce and Economic Development proposes trade and investment policies for the Government of the Region.[31] The Trade and Industry Department – which is responsible for the issue of certificates of origin, import and export licences and Hong Kong Service Supplier certificates – implements those policies with the assistance, if necessary, of a global network of Economic and Trade Offices.[32] New policies are subject to public consultation, with the exception of trade agreements and arrangements, which do not require ratification by the Legislative Council prior to their entry into force.[33] Apart from the negotiation and conclusion of agreements and arrangements with trading partners, which can often require careful impact assessments, the Region's external trade practice presents relatively little complication.

Trade in Goods

Since Hong Kong is a free port, it is, correspondingly, free of customs duties.[34] With respect to other WTO members and on a most-favoured-nation basis, the

28 World Trade Organization, *Trade Policy Review Report by the Secretariat: Hong Kong, China (Revision)* (30 January 2019) WT/TPR/S/380/Rev.1 [2.10].
29 World Trade Organization, *Trade Policy Review Report by the Secretariat: Hong Kong, China (Revision)* (30 January 2019) WT/TPR/S/380/Rev.1 [2.4].
30 See the Import and Export (General) Regulations (Cap 60A), the Import and Export (Strategic Commodities) Regulations (Cap 60G) and the Import and Export (Registration) Regulations (Cap 60E): World Trade Organization, *Trade Policy Review Report by the Secretariat: Hong Kong, China (Revision)* (30 January 2019) WT/TPR/S/380/Rev.1 [3.1].
31 World Trade Organization, *Trade Policy Review Report by the Secretariat: Hong Kong, China (Revision)* (30 January 2019) WT/TPR/S/380/Rev.1 [2.8].
32 World Trade Organization, *Trade Policy Review Report by the Secretariat: Hong Kong, China (Revision)* (30 January 2019) WT/TPR/S/380/Rev.1 [2.9]. To further support the administration of Hong Kong's external economic relations is a global network of Economic and Trade Offices (with offices outside mainland China in Bangkok, Berlin, Brussels, Dubai, Geneva, Jakarta, London, New York, San Francisco, Singapore, Sydney, Tokyo, Toronto and Washington DC) and statutory bodies such as Invest Hong Kong, the Hong Kong Trade Development Council, the Hong Kong Export Credit Insurance Corporation and the Hong Kong Productivity Council.
33 World Trade Organization, *Trade Policy Review Report by the Secretariat: Hong Kong, China (Revision)* (30 January 2019) WT/TPR/S/380/Rev.1 [2.5].
34 World Trade Organization, *Trade Policy Review Report by the Secretariat: Hong Kong, China (Revision)* (28 January 2015) WT/TPR/S/306/Rev.1 [9].

Region applies zero rates to all tariff lines[35] and does not apply any tariff rate quotas.[36] It follows from this uniquely liberal tariff regime that Hong Kong's customs procedures are among the simplest of WTO members.[37] Imports into the Region do not need certification of origin[38] and, with electronic submission,[39] customs declarations are easy and fast to process.[40]

Hong Kong's external trade practice record is liberal almost without equal; its trade, however, is not completely without restraints. In relation to customs duties, while the Region has bound its agricultural goods schedules,[41] the bulk of its other tariffs[42] are not subject to WTO bindings,[43] a moot point, ultimately, because they are 100 per cent duty free since Hong Kong is a free port. Aside from tariffs, other fiscal barriers to imports include a first registration tax (FRT) on new motor vehicles[44] and excise duties on four commodity groups,[45] namely, liquor (subject, that is, to an alcohol volume content in excess of 30 per cent),[46] tobacco, hydrocarbon oil and methyl alcohol.[47] These internal taxes are collectable at the customs border and their calculation requires a preliminary process of customs valuation.[48] In addition are trade

35 World Trade Organization, *Trade Policy Review Report by the Secretariat: Hong Kong, China (Revision)* (28 January 2015) WT/TPR/S/306/Rev.1 [3.15]; World Trade Organization, *Trade Policy Review Report by the Secretariat: Hong Kong, China (Revision)* (25 January 2011) WT/TPR/S/241/Rev.1 viii [8]. Curiously, Hong Kong benefits from Russia's Generalized System of Preferences, although it is of no practical significance: World Trade Organization, *Trade Policy Review Report by the Secretariat: Hong Kong, China (Revision)* (30 January 2019) WT/TPR/S/380/Rev.1 [2.40].

36 World Trade Organization, *Trade Policy Review Report by the Secretariat: Hong Kong, China (Revision)* (30 January 2019) WT/TPR/S/380/Rev.1 [3.20].

37 World Trade Organization, *Trade Policy Review Report by the Secretariat: Hong Kong, China (Revision)* (25 January 2011) WT/TPR/S/241/Rev.1 viii [9].

38 World Trade Organization, *Trade Policy Review Report by the Secretariat: Hong Kong, China (Revision)* (30 January 2019) WT/TPR/S/380/Rev.1 [3.17].

39 World Trade Organization, *Trade Policy Review Report by the Secretariat: Hong Kong, China (Revision)* (25 January 2011) WT/TPR/S/241/Rev.1 viii [9].

40 World Trade Organization, *Trade Policy Review Report by the Secretariat: Hong Kong, China (Revision)* (28 January 2015) WT/TPR/S/306/Rev.1 [9].

41 World Trade Organization, *Trade Policy Review Report by the Secretariat: Hong Kong, China (Revision)* (25 January 2011) WT/TPR/S/241/Rev.1 viii [8].

42 World Trade Organization, *Trade Policy Review Report by the Secretariat: Hong Kong, China (Revision)* (28 January 2015) WT/TPR/S/306/Rev.1 [9].

43 World Trade Organization, *Trade Policy Review Report by the Secretariat: Hong Kong, China (Revision)* (25 January 2011) WT/TPR/S/241/Rev.1 viii [8].

44 World Trade Organization, *Trade Policy Review Report by the Secretariat: Hong Kong, China (Revision)* (30 January 2019) WT/TPR/S/380/Rev.1 [3.25]; World Trade Organization, *Trade Policy Review Report by the Secretariat: Hong Kong, China (Revision)* (28 January 2015) WT/TPR/S/306/Rev.1 [9].

45 World Trade Organization, *Trade Policy Review Report by the Secretariat: Hong Kong, China (Revision)* (30 January 2019) WT/TPR/S/380/Rev.1 [3.23].

46 World Trade Organization, *Trade Policy Review Report by the Secretariat: Hong Kong, China (Revision)* (30 January 2019) WT/TPR/S/380/Rev.1 [3.23].

47 World Trade Organization, *Trade Policy Review Report by the Secretariat: Hong Kong, China (Revision)* (28 January 2015) WT/TPR/S/306/Rev.1 [9].

48 World Trade Organization, *Trade Policy Review Report by the Secretariat: Hong Kong, China (Revision)* (28 January 2015) WT/TPR/S/306/Rev.1 [3.15]; World Trade

declaration fees and, if applicable, licensing administrative charges.[49] Importantly, however, Hong Kong does not charge value-added or goods and services taxes.[50]

Non-fiscal barriers to imports take the form of import controls. In all fairness, prohibitions and restrictions[51] – effective through licensing schemes[52] – are relatively few.[53] And they are uncontroversial because they either serve to comply with unavoidable international legal obligations or confidently come under the usual WTO general exceptions for the protection of health, safety, security and the environment.[54] Interestingly, the Region operates a Rice Control Scheme, which makes provision for an emergency reserve stock of this staple food.[55] Export controls also apply but these are, again, insignificant, with quantitative restrictions on infant formula[56] as the only noteworthy quirk. Apart from these minor peculiarities, Hong Kong has no behind-the-border barriers. Thus, the Region, with no investigating authorities[57] for dumping and subsidisation, has, correspondingly, never taken any countervailance action against unfair trade practices. It has never undertaken emergency safeguard measures either.[58] In the same way, Hong Kong's regimes on technical barriers to trade and sanitary and phytosanitary standards are notable for their simplicity and transparency.[59] Moreover, the Region is free of local content requirements.[60]

Organization, *Trade Policy Review Report by the Secretariat: Hong Kong, China (Revision)* (25 January 2011) WT/TPR/S/241/Rev.1 viii [9].

49 World Trade Organization, *Trade Policy Review Report by the Secretariat: Hong Kong, China (Revision)* (30 January 2019) WT/TPR/S/380/Rev.1 [3.26].

50 World Trade Organization, *Trade Policy Review Report by the Secretariat: Hong Kong, China (Revision)* (30 January 2019) WT/TPR/S/380/Rev.1 [3.24].

51 World Trade Organization, *Trade Policy Review Report by the Secretariat: Hong Kong, China (Revision)* (30 January 2019) WT/TPR/S/380/Rev.1 [3.27].

52 World Trade Organization, *Trade Policy Review Report by the Secretariat: Hong Kong, China (Revision)* (30 January 2019) WT/TPR/S/380/Rev.1 [3.29].

53 World Trade Organization, *Trade Policy Review Report by the Secretariat: Hong Kong, China (Revision)* (25 January 2011) WT/TPR/S/241/Rev.1 viii [10].

54 World Trade Organization, *Trade Policy Review Report by the Secretariat: Hong Kong, China (Revision)* (30 January 2019) WT/TPR/S/380/Rev.1 [6]; World Trade Organization, *Trade Policy Review Report by the Secretariat: Hong Kong, China (Revision)* (28 January 2015) WT/TPR/S/306/Rev.1 [10].

55 World Trade Organization, *Trade Policy Review Report by the Secretariat: Hong Kong, China (Revision)* (25 January 2011) WT/TPR/S/241/Rev.1 x [22]. Not as obviously relevant are the special controls that Hong Kong applies to the origin of textile imports and exports: World Trade Organization, *Trade Policy Review Report by the Secretariat: Hong Kong, China (Revision)* (25 January 2011) WT/TPR/S/241/Rev.1 viii [10].

56 World Trade Organization, *Trade Policy Review Report by the Secretariat: Hong Kong, China (Revision)* (30 January 2019) WT/TPR/S/380/Rev.1 [7].

57 World Trade Organization, *Trade Policy Review Report by the Secretariat: Hong Kong, China (Revision)* (30 January 2019) WT/TPR/S/380/Rev.1 [3.38].

58 World Trade Organization, *Trade Policy Review Report by the Secretariat: Hong Kong, China (Revision)* (30 January 2019) WT/TPR/S/380/Rev.1 [3.38].

59 World Trade Organization, *Trade Policy Review Report by the Secretariat: Hong Kong, China (Revision)* (30 January 2019) WT/TPR/S/380/Rev.1 [6].

60 World Trade Organization, *Trade Policy Review Report by the Secretariat: Hong Kong, China (Revision)* (30 January 2019) WT/TPR/S/380/Rev.1 [3.39].

Trade in Services

Hong Kong's trade in services regime largely follows the liberal[61] approach that it takes to the regulation of trade in goods, even though its commitments under the General Agreement on Trade in Services (GATS) are not consistently extensive.[62] On the whole, the Region's 'applied regime is quite liberal',[63] even in such mainstay sectors as financial services where the customs territory is a regional and global hub.[64] The proof is in Hong Kong's commitment to a standstill negative-list practice, with almost no reservations.[65]

The few protectionist exceptions that the Region does come under relate to its unique position as an entrepôt: Hong Kong, after all, boasts the world's largest air-cargo airport[66] (and has the potential of further growth as an international aviation hub with a third runway in construction). In this particular respect, while the Region has a generally open approach to air transport services – as is manifest from the host of air transport agreements[67] to which it is a party – it is, for strategic reasons no doubt, less open to trade in support services such as cargo ground handling as well as maintenance services. These are dependent on a restrictive licence system.[68] Hong Kong does not subscribe to the Treaty on Open Skies.[69]

Multilateral and Plurilateral Trade Relations

World Trade Organization

Membership

Hong Kong is an active participant in the multilateral trading system and subscribes to several important multilateral and plurilateral trade organisations and initiatives. It is, of course, a member of the WTO – a founder, in fact. Within the WTO, the

61 World Trade Organization, *Trade Policy Review Report by the Secretariat: Hong Kong, China (Revision)* (28 January 2015) WT/TPR/S/306/Rev.1 [16].
62 World Trade Organization, *Trade Policy Review Report by the Secretariat: Hong Kong, China (Revision)* (28 January 2015) WT/TPR/S/306/Rev.1 [16].
63 World Trade Organization, *Trade Policy Review Report by the Secretariat: Hong Kong, China (Revision)* (28 January 2015) WT/TPR/S/306/Rev.1 [16].
64 World Trade Organization, *Trade Policy Review Report by the Secretariat: Hong Kong, China (Revision)* (28 January 2015) WT/TPR/S/306/Rev.1 [16].
65 World Trade Organization, *Trade Policy Review Report by the Secretariat: Hong Kong, China (Revision)* (28 January 2015) WT/TPR/S/306/Rev.1 [16].
66 World Trade Organization, *Trade Policy Review Report by the Secretariat: Hong Kong, China (Revision)* (28 January 2015) WT/TPR/S/306/Rev.1 [20].
67 World Trade Organization, *Trade Policy Review Report by the Secretariat: Hong Kong, China (Revision)* (28 January 2015) WT/TPR/S/306/Rev.1 [20].
68 World Trade Organization, *Trade Policy Review Report by the Secretariat: Hong Kong, China (Revision)* (28 January 2015) WT/TPR/S/306/Rev.1 [20].
69 World Trade Organization, *Trade Policy Review Report by the Secretariat: Hong Kong, China (Revision)* (25 January 2011) WT/TPR/S/241/Rev.1 ix [18].

Region remains supportive of the Doha Development Agenda – a top priority,[70] in spite of the little recent progress in negotiations for agricultural and non-agricultural market access – and is manifestly receptive to reform proposals in aid of efficiency and transparency.[71] The Region was indeed the first WTO member to accept and implement the terms of the Agreement on Trade Facilitation to simplify import and export customs procedures.

With an unquestionable commitment to free and open trade, Hong Kong is a dutiful and enthusiastic member of the WTO. Examples of that firm support abound. To mention a few, the Region hosted the Sixth WTO Ministerial Conference in December 2005 and the WTO Secretariat consistently commends its 'excellent record of providing notifications'.[72] More tellingly, perhaps, the Region has never been a respondent to a WTO dispute. Indeed, Hong Kong has always been a non-confrontational member of the WTO and has shied away from complaints and disputes generally.

Disputes

Hong Kong has only been a complainant twice. It made its first complaint during the final years of British colonial rule, in the 1990s against Turkey (*Turkey – Restrictions on Imports of Textile and Clothing Products* (WT/DS29)). On 12 February 1996, the territory requested consultations with Turkey in relation to 'the unilateral imposition of quantitative restrictions by Turkey on imports of a broad range of textile and clothing products from Hong Kong as from 1 January 1996'.[73] Hong Kong considered that those restrictions were against Articles XI and XIII of the General Agreement on Tariffs and Trade (GATT) 1994 and did not come under Article XXIV of GATT 1994, which makes no provision for discriminatory quantitative restrictions.[74] The European Communities (now the European Union) joined the consultations[75] – as the territory's complaint derived from a customs union agreement between Turkey and the European Communities – and the parties resolved the dispute amicably and informally. However, they never notified a mutually agreed solution.

Decades later, Hong Kong made its second ever complaint … and it was against the United States (US). On 30 October 2020, the Region requested consultations with the US over its origin marking requirements on Hong Kong

70 World Trade Organization, *Statement by Hong Kong, China* (1 December 2009) WT/MIN(09)/ST/6.

71 World Trade Organization, *Strengthening the WTO* (16 October 2009) WT/MIN(09)/W/1.

72 World Trade Organization, *Trade Policy Review Report by the Secretariat: Hong Kong, China (Revision)* (30 January 2019) WT/TPR/S/380/Rev.1 [4].

73 World Trade Organization, *Turkey: Restrictions on Imports of Textile and Clothing Products – Request for Consultations by Hong Kong, China* (15 February 1996) WT/DS29/1, G/L/64 1.

74 World Trade Organization, *Turkey: Restrictions on Imports of Textile and Clothing Products – Request for Consultations by Hong Kong, China* (15 February 1996) WT/DS29/1, G/L/64 1.

75 World Trade Organization, *Turkey: Restrictions on Imports of Textile and Clothing Products – Acceptance by Turkey of the Request to Join Consultations by the European Communities under Article 4.11 of the DSU* (23 April 1996) WT/DS29/9.

goods.[76] In spite of the Region's well-established status as a 'separate customs territory' – with constitutional authorisation by Article 116 of the Basic Law – the US Office of Trade (US Customs and Border Protection) notified, by way of a general notice on the Federal Register of 11 August 2020, that the mark on the designation of origin label on goods from the Region must, after 25 September 2020, 'indicate that the origin is "China"' for the purposes of Section 304 of the Tariff Act of 1930 (Title 19 (Customs Duties) US Code). For the US, this was 'due to the determination that Hong Kong is no longer sufficiently autonomous to justify differential treatment in relation to China'.[77] In its request to the Chairperson of the WTO Dispute Settlement Body for the establishment of a panel, the Region outlined the background to the matter thus:

> Prior to the imposition of the revised origin marking requirement …, the United States has required, and therefore permitted, goods produced in Hong Kong, China to be marked to indicate that their origin is 'Hong Kong'. The United States' prior treatment of goods of Hong Kong, China origin was consistent with the fact that the United States generally permits goods originating within the territory of other WTO Members, including separate customs territory Members, to be marked with the English name of that territory.[78]

Hong Kong claimed that the measures that result from these US origin marking requirements breach the law of the WTO, specifically that they are contrary to Articles I:1, IX:1 and X:3(a) of the GATT 1994; Articles 2(c), 2(d) and 2(e) of the Agreement on Rules of Origin; and Article 2.1 of the Agreement on Technical Barriers to Trade:

> The United States measures … are inconsistent with the United States' obligations under the following provisions of the GATT 1994 …
>
> 1. Article I:1 of the GATT 1994, because in respect of the rules and formalities of importation pertaining to marks of origin, the United States does not extend to products of Hong Kong, China origin immediately and unconditionally the same advantages, favours, privileges, or immunities that the United States extends to like products originating in the territory of other countries;
> 2. Article IX:1 of the GATT 1994, because the United States does not accord to the products of Hong Kong, China treatment with regard to

76 World Trade Organization, *United States: Origin Marking Requirement – Request for Consultations by Hong Kong, China* (3 November 2020) WT/DS597/1, G/L/1365, G/RO/D/8, G/TBT/D/53. For background, see Shawn B Jensen, 'International Agreements between the United States and Hong Kong under the United States – Hong Kong Policy Act' (1993) 7(2) *Temple International and Comparative Law Journal* 167–190.

77 Brenda B Smith, Executive Assistant Commissioner, Office of Trade, US Customs and Border Protection, Department of Homeland Security, [CBP Dec 2015] *General Notice: Country of Origin Marking of Products of Hong Kong* [FR Doc 2020–17599], Federal Register / Vol 85 No 155 / 11 August 2020, 48551–48552.

78 World Trade Organization, *United States: Origin Marking Requirement – Request for the Establishment of a Panel by Hong Kong, China* (15 January 2021) WT/DS597/5 1–2.

marking requirements no less favourable than the treatment that the United States accords to like products of other countries;

3. Article X:3(a) of the GATT 1994, because the United States does not administer its origin marking requirements in a uniform, impartial, and reasonable manner; ...[79]

In November 2020, the US entered into consultations but announced that, in its assessment, the measures relate to 'issues of national security not susceptible to review or capable of resolution by WTO dispute settlement'[80] and, moreover, that 'the President determined that the situation with respect to Hong Kong, China, constitutes a threat to the national security of the United States'.[81] Consultations failed to broker a compromise and, on 14 January 2021, the Region requested the establishment of a panel, which, on 22 February 2021, the Dispute Settlement Body established. The terms of reference of the Panel are:

> To examine, in the light of the relevant provisions of the covered agreements cited by the parties to the dispute, the matter referred to the DSB [Dispute Settlement Body] by Hong Kong, China in document WT/DS597/5 and to make such findings as will assist the DSB in making the recommendations or in giving the rulings provided for in those agreements.[82]

The WTO Director–General composed the Panel on 29 April 2021[83] with Beatriz Leycegui Gardoqui of Mexico as chairperson. The dispute receives the title of *US – Origin Marking (Hong Kong, China)* (WT/DS597). Brazil, Canada, China, the EU, India, Japan, Korea, Norway, Russia – which requested[84] to join the consultations although the US declined[85] – Singapore, Switzerland, Turkey and Ukraine have all reserved their third-party rights. On 26 October 2021, the Panel issued a communication to announce that '[i]n the light of the complexity of the issues presented in this dispute, the Panel expects to issue its final report to the parties in the second quarter of 2022'.[86] On 21 June 2022, the Panel issued a further communication to advise that 'the Panel

79 World Trade Organization, *United States: Origin Marking Requirement – Request for the Establishment of a Panel by Hong Kong, China* (15 January 2021) WT/DS597/5 2.

80 World Trade Organization, *United States: Origin Marking Requirement – Communication from the United States* (13 November 2020) WT/DS597/2.

81 World Trade Organization, *United States: Origin Marking Requirement – Communication from the United States* (13 November 2020) WT/DS597/2.

82 World Trade Organization, *United States: Origin Marking Requirement – Constitution of the Panel Established at the Request of Hong Kong, China (Note by the Secretariat)* (30 April 2021) WT/DS597/6 [2].

83 World Trade Organization, *United States: Origin Marking Requirement – Constitution of the Panel Established at the Request of Hong Kong, China (Note by the Secretariat)* (30 April 2021) WT/DS597/6 [2].

84 World Trade Organization, *United States: Origin Marking Requirement – Request to Join Consultations (Communication from Russia)* (17 November 2020) WT/DS597/3.

85 World Trade Organization, *United States: Origin Marking Requirement – Communication from the United States* (26 November 2020) WT/DS597/4.

86 World Trade Organization, *United States: Origin Marking Requirement – Communication from the Panel* (27 October 2021) WT/DS597/7.

now expects to issue its final report to the parties in the last quarter of 2022'.[87] The findings of the Panel are likely to have significant implications for the future development of the external economic constitution of Hong Kong, which, codified in the Basic Law, has consistently proclaimed the status of the Special Administrative Region as a customs territory that, further to Articles 2 and 12, enjoys 'a high degree of autonomy'.

> On 21 December 2022, the Panel finally issued its report. '8.1. … [T]he Panel concludes as follows:
>
> a. Article XXI(b) is not entirely self-judging insofar as the unilateral determination granted to the invoking Member through the phrase "which it considers" in the *chapeau* of that provision does not extend to the subparagraphs. Instead, the subparagraphs are subject to review by a panel.
> b. The origin marking requirement is inconsistent with Article IX:1 of the GATT 1994 because it accords to products of Hong Kong, China treatment with regard to marking requirements that is less favourable than the treatment accorded to like products of any third country.
> c. The United States has not demonstrated that the situation at issue constitutes an emergency in international relations, and therefore the origin marking requirement is not justified under Article XXI(b)(iii).
>
> 8.2. The Panel exercises judicial economy on Hong Kong, China's claims that the origin marking requirement is inconsistent with Article I:1 of the GATT 1994, Articles 2(c) and 2(d) of the ARO, and Article 2.1 of the TBT Agreement.
>
> 8.3. Under Article 3.8 of the DSU, in cases where there is an infringement of the obligations assumed under a covered agreement, the action is considered *prima facie* to constitute a case of nullification or impairment. We conclude that, to the extent that the measure at issue is inconsistent with Article IX:1 of the GATT 1994, it has nullified or impaired benefits accruing to Hong Kong, China under that agreement.
>
> 8.4. Pursuant to Article 19.1 of the DSU, we recommend that the United States bring its measure into conformity with its obligations under the GATT 1994.'

World Trade Organization, *United States: Origin Marking Requirement – Report of the Panel* (21 December 2022) WT/DS597/R [8].

Plurilateral Initiatives

Under the auspices of the WTO, Hong Kong is a signatory of the plurilateral Agreement on Government Procurement (GPA) for the open, fair and transparent procurement of goods and services by public authorities and the Information Technology Agreement (ITA) including its expansion agreement for the removal of tariffs on information technology products. The Region is in negotiations for

87 World Trade Organization, *United States: Origin Marking Requirement – Communication from the Panel* (23 June 2022) WT/DS597/8.

the Environmental Goods Agreement (EGA), which would remove tariffs on environment-related products.

Outside the WTO, Hong Kong has been in negotiations – now in suspension – for the Trade in Services Agreement (TiSA),[88] which builds on the GATS with the aim to further liberalise trade in services and provide fairer access for that market. Also at the plurilateral level, Hong Kong is a member of the Asia–Pacific Economic Cooperation (APEC) forum; in fact, approximately 80 per cent of its exports and imports involve other APEC members.[89] The Region chairs APEC's Economic Committee. And it actively participates in APEC's Committee on Trade and Investment, which works, under the Aotearoa Plan of Action, to implement the Putrajaya Vision 2040 'to deliver, a free, open, fair, non-discriminatory, transparent and predictable trade and investment environment' for the Asia-Pacific as 'the world's most dynamic and interconnected regional economy'.[90] In these respects, APEC calls for the formation of a Free Trade Area of the Asia-Pacific (FTAA), a prospect which, despite the recommendations of the Lima Declaration on FTAAP of November 2016, seems, for now, uncertain. Moreover, with the advice and coordination of the Hong Kong Committee for Pacific Economic Cooperation, the Region is a member of the Pacific Economic Cooperation Council,[91] which, as its name implies, works 'to promote economic cooperation and the idea of a Pacific Community'[92] in close association with APEC. The Region is also an observer at the non-confidential parts of meetings of the Organisation of Economic Co-operation and Development's (OECD) Trade Committee and its Working Party.[93] These are all important diplomatic initiatives that Hong Kong pursues for the promotion of rules-based, non-discriminatory free trade.

Bilateral Trade Relations

In parallel with the WTO, Hong Kong regulates its external trade relations through agreements and arrangements (FTAs) with a number of select partners –

88 World Trade Organization, *Trade Policy Review Report by the Secretariat: Hong Kong, China (Revision)* (30 January 2019) WT/TPR/S/380/Rev.1 [2.39].
89 World Trade Organization, *Trade Policy Review Report by the Secretariat: Hong Kong, China (Revision)* (30 January 2019) WT/TPR/S/380/Rev.1 [2.38]. See also Merit E Janow, 'Assessing APEC's Role in Economic Integration in the Asia–Pacific Region' (1996–1997) 17 *Northwestern Journal of International Law & Business* 947–1013; Trade and Industry Department of the Hong Kong Special Administrative Region, International Trade Organisations, Asia-Pacific Economic Cooperation (APEC), APEC and Hong Kong, https://www.tid.gov.hk/english/ito/apec/apec_hk.html, accessed 1 July 2022.
90 APEC Putrajaya Vision 2040, the 27th APEC Economic Leaders' Meeting (Kuala Lumpur, 20 November 2020).
91 Trade and Industry Department of the Hong Kong Special Administrative Region, International Trade Organisations, Pacific Economic Cooperation Council (PECC), https://www.tid.gov.hk/english/ito/pecc/index.html, accessed 1 July 2022.
92 Article 2.1, The Pacific Economic Cooperation Council Charter (as amended 11 May 2009, Washington DC).
93 Trade and Industry Department of the Hong Kong Special Administrative Region, International Trade Organisations, Organisation for Economic Co-operation and Development (OECD), https://www.tid.gov.hk/english/ito/oecd/index.html, accessed 1 July 2022.

first of which, of course, is mainland China – at bilateral, plurilateral and regional levels.[94] The Region – the model free port – has long maintained a genuinely receptive attitude to such instruments. It remains actively open[95] to the negotiation of such further free trade initiatives if they serve the market access interests of its goods and services and, more generally, if they comply with the law and policy of the WTO and, thereby, further advance the liberalisation of multilateral trade.[96] Since Hong Kong is already free of customs duties, in true free trade spirit, its FTAs show a particular concern for the liberalisation of trade in services, which still remains an area sensitive to protectionist measures for most other WTO members. In these instruments, the Region applies its duty-free regime to trade in goods[97] and, what is more, it commits to the liberalisation of a substantial cross-section of trade in services sectors, mostly on the basis of a negative-list approach.[98] Keen on the promotion of good-quality agreements, the Region does not avoid difficult topic areas in its FTAs, such as market access to government procurement, trade in intellectual property rights, trade facilitation and the mutual recognition of qualifications.[99] Notably, Hong Kong's applied WTO regime is in alignment with the commitments under the FTAs to which it is a party, without prejudice.[100]

As of June 2022, the Region has entered into eight FTAs,[101] respectively with mainland China (June 2003), New Zealand (March 2010), the European Free Trade Association (EFTA) (June 2011), Chile (September 2012), Macao, China (October 2017), the Association of Southeast Asian Nations (ASEAN) (November 2017), Georgia (June 2018) and Australia (March 2019).[102] The Region is due to commence FTA negotiations with Peru in January 2023.

94 World Trade Organization, *Trade Policy Review Report by the Secretariat: Hong Kong, China (Revision)* (28 January 2015) WT/TPR/S/306/Rev.1 [7]. See generally Wai Ting, 'The External Relations and International Status of Hong Kong' (1997) 2 *Occasional Papers/Reprints Series in Contemporary Asian Studies* 1–72; Lung Wan Pun, 'Application and Conclusion of Treaties in the Hong Kong Special Administrative Region of the People's Republic of China: Sixteen Years of Practice' (2013) 12(3) *Chinese Journal of International Law* 589–612.

95 World Trade Organization, *Trade Policy Review Report by the Secretariat: Hong Kong, China (Revision)* (30 January 2019) WT/TPR/S/380/Rev.1 [2.15].

96 World Trade Organization, *Trade Policy Review Report by the Secretariat: Hong Kong, China (Revision)* (28 January 2015) WT/TPR/S/306/Rev.1 [2.15].

97 World Trade Organization, *Trade Policy Review Report by the Secretariat: Hong Kong, China (Revision)* (28 January 2015) WT/TPR/S/306/Rev.1 [2.17].

98 World Trade Organization, *Trade Policy Review Report by the Secretariat: Hong Kong, China (Revision)* (28 January 2015) WT/TPR/S/306/Rev.1 [2.17].

99 World Trade Organization, *Trade Policy Review Report by the Secretariat: Hong Kong, China (Revision)* (28 January 2015) WT/TPR/S/306/Rev.1 [2.17]; World Trade Organization, *Trade Policy Review Report by the Secretariat: Hong Kong, China (Revision)* (30 January 2019) WT/TPR/S/380/Rev.1 [2.16].

100 World Trade Organization, *Trade Policy Review Report by the Secretariat: Hong Kong, China (Revision)* (30 January 2019) WT/TPR/S/380/Rev.1 [2.15].

101 See, generally, Jo-Ann Crawford and CL Lim, 'Cast Light and Evil Will Go Away: The First Transparency Mechanism for Regulating Regional Trade Agreements Three Years After' (2011) 45(2) *Journal of World Trade* 375–400.

102 Trade and Industry Department of the Hong Kong Special Administrative Region, Trade and Investment Agreements, Hong Kong's Free Trade Agreements (FTAs), https://www.tid.gov.hk/english/ita/fta/index.html, accessed 1 July 2021.

Hong Kong–Mainland China Closer Economic Partnership Arrangement

Understandably, the Region's first trade deal is with mainland China; the mainland is Hong Kong's largest trading partner, accounting for over 50 per cent of Hong Kong's trade. Signed in June 2003, the Closer Economic Partnership Arrangement (CEPA) is more than a trade deal. Rather, CEPA is a kind of complementary economic constitution for the Region because it establishes a near complete economic union with mainland China.[103] Through that economic union, CEPA preserves and promotes Hong Kong's comparative advantage[104] in the global economy as *the* services entrepôt between Greater China and the rest of the world, and leverages it 'as key intermediary for mainland China's external trade'.[105]

Further to the Preamble, which calls the two sides '[t]o promote the joint economic prosperity and development' and also 'to facilitate the further development of economic links', CEPA states as its objectives in Article 1:

103 See, generally, Liang Zhang, 'Unprecedented RTA Practices between the Customs Territories of China' (2011) 4(1) *Journal of East Asia and International Law* 81–104; Martin Rudner, 'Institutional Approaches to Regional Trade and Cooperation in the Asia Pacific Area' (1994) 4(1) *Transnational Law & Contemporary Problems* 159–186; Kenneth W Abbott and Gregory W Bowman, 'Economic Integration for the Asian Century: An Early Look at New Approaches' (1994) 4(1) *Transnational Law & Contemporary Problems* 187–226; Ying Zhao, 'Economic Integration in Eastern Asia: On the View of GVC' (2015) 5(3) *Journal of WTO and China* 113–129; Dan Wei, 'China's Regional Trade Agreements: Implications and Comments' (2009) 6(1) *Manchester Journal of International Economic Law* 81–118; Chien-Huei Wu, 'One Country, Two Systems, and Three Memberships: Legal and Economic Integration between China and its Two SARs' (2007) 7(3) *Global Jurist* [i]–33; Carsten Fink and Martin Molinuevo, 'East Asian Preferential Trade Agreements in Services: Liberalization Content and WTO Rules' (2008) 7(4) *World Trade Review* 641–674; Carsten Fink and Martin Molinuevo, 'East Asian Free Trade Agreements in Services: Key Architectural Elements' (2008) 11(2) *Journal of International Economic Law* 263–311; Zeng Huaqun, 'One China, Four WTO Memberships: Legal Grounds, Relations and Significance' (2007) 8(5) *Journal of World Investment & Trade* 671–690; Jiangyu Wang, 'China's Regional Trade Agreements: The Law, Geopolitics, and Impact on the Multilateral Trading System' (2004) 8 *Singapore Year Book of International Law* 119–148; Gonzalo Villalta Puig, 'A Quasi-Adjudicative Dispute Settlement Mechanism for CEPA: The Rule of Law in Trade Relations between Mainland China and Hong Kong' (2013) 12(2) *Chinese Journal of International Law* 281–320; Douglas W Arner, Paul Lejot and Wei Wang, 'Assessing East Asian Financial Cooperation and Integration' (2008) 12 *Singapore Year Book of International Law* 1–42; Claude Barfield, 'The Dragon Stirs: China's Trade Policy for Asia – and the World' (2007) 24(1) *Arizona Journal of International and Comparative Law* 93–120; Timothy Webster, 'East Asia Institutionalises: China, Japan and the Vogue for Free Trade' (2008) 77(3) *Nordic Journal of International Law* 301–318; Guiguo Wang, 'The China–Hong Kong Closer Economic Partnership Arrangement Revisited' (2004) 5(1) *Journal of World Investment & Trade* 177–186; Francis Snyder, 'China, Regional Trade Agreements and WTO Law' (2009) 43(1) *Journal of World Trade* 1–57; Henry S Gao, 'Legal Issues under WTO Rules on the Closer Economic Partnership Arrangement (CEPA) between Mainland China and Hong Kong' (2003) 2(2) *Chinese Journal of International Law* 629–648.

104 World Trade Organization, *Trade Policy Review Report by the Secretariat: Hong Kong, China (Revision)* (25 January 2011) WT/TPR/S/241/Rev.1 vii [5].

105 World Trade Organization, *Trade Policy Review Report by the Secretariat: Hong Kong, China (Revision)* (28 January 2015) WT/TPR/S/306/Rev.1 [3], [14].

> To strengthen trade and investment cooperation between the Mainland and the Hong Kong Special Administrative Region … and promote joint development of the two sides, through the implementation of the following measures:
>
> 1. progressively reducing or eliminating tariff and non-tariff barriers on substantially all the trade in goods between the two sides;
> 2. progressively achieving liberalization of trade in services through reduction or elimination of substantially all discriminatory measures;
> 3. promoting trade and investment facilitation.[106]

Article 2 develops the principles of the arrangement:

> The conclusion, implementation and amendment of the 'CEPA' shall adhere to the following principles:
>
> 1. to abide by the 'one country, two systems' principle;
> 2. to be consistent with the rules of the World Trade Organisation … ;
> 3. to accord with the needs of both sides to adjust and upgrade their industries and enterprises and to promote steady and sustained development;
> 4. to achieve reciprocity and mutual benefits, complementarity with each other's advantages and joint prosperity;
> 5. to take progressive action, dealing with the easier subjects before the more difficult ones.[107]

CEPA liberalises and facilitates trade and investment between Hong Kong and mainland China.[108] It does so progressively and expansively, through 'a building block approach',[109] with a series of supplements (10 to date) and side agreements, including the all-important Agreement Concerning Amendment to the CEPA Agreement on Trade in Services of November 2019. In sum, CEPA can be regarded as a charter of and for free trade; liberalisation and cooperation characterise its integrative mission.[110]

106 Courtesy Translation, Mainland and Hong Kong Closer Economic Partnership Arrangement, Trade and Industry Department, The Government of the Hong Kong Special Administrative Region of the People's Republic of China, https://www.tid.gov.hk/english/cepa/files/main_e.pdf, accessed 25 January 2022.

107 Courtesy Translation, Mainland and Hong Kong Closer Economic Partnership Arrangement, Trade and Industry Department, The Government of the Hong Kong Special Administrative Region of the People's Republic of China, https://www.tid.gov.hk/english/cepa/files/main_e.pdf, accessed 25 January 2022.

108 World Trade Organization, *Trade Policy Review Report by the Secretariat: Hong Kong, China (Revision)* (28 January 2015) WT/TPR/S/306/Rev.1 [2.30].

109 World Trade Organization, *Trade Policy Review Report by the Secretariat: Hong Kong, China (Revision)* (25 January 2011) WT/TPR/S/241/Rev.1 16 [12].

110 World Trade Organization, *Trade Policy Review Report by the Secretariat: Hong Kong, China (Revision)* (25 January 2011) WT/TPR/S/241/Rev.1 16 [12].

Trade in Goods

Under CEPA, all trade in all goods between the two sides is free, subject, that is, to otherwise necessary rules of origin requirements.[111] CEPA rules of origin – open for consultations between the two sides twice yearly[112] – generally require a good to have a minimum of 30 per cent of Hong Kong value content[113] for it to have Hong Kong origin (under a Certificate of Hong Kong Origin for CEPA (CO-CEPA)) and, therefore, obtain duty-free (zero-tariff)[114] market access to mainland China. More than 20 per cent of mainland China's tariff lines come under CEPA rules of origin[115] and these, in turn, amount to almost 70 per cent of the Region's goods exports to mainland China,[116] especially pharmaceuticals, plastics and plastic products, food and beverages, and textiles.[117]

Trade in Services

While the benefits that CEPA entails for Hong Kong's goods exporters are very significant, the benefits that it extends to Hong Kong's service suppliers are even more so.[118] CEPA takes a negative-list approach to the liberalisation of trade in services for supply Mode 3 (Commercial Presence) and so, in principle, it does not exclude any service sectors, 62 of which receive national treatment from mainland China.[119] For supply Mode 1 (Cross-border Trade), Mode 2 (Consumption Abroad) and Mode 4 (Presence of Natural Persons) as well as in telecommunications and cultural services,

111 World Trade Organization, *Trade Policy Review Report by the Secretariat: Hong Kong, China (Revision)* (25 January 2011) WT/TPR/S/241/Rev.1 17 [16].
112 World Trade Organization, *Trade Policy Review Report by the Secretariat: Hong Kong, China (Revision)* (28 January 2015) WT/TPR/S/306/Rev.1 [2.31].
113 World Trade Organization, *Trade Policy Review Report by the Secretariat: Hong Kong, China (Revision)* (28 January 2015) WT/TPR/S/306/Rev.1 [2.32].
114 World Trade Organization, *Trade Policy Review Report by the Secretariat: Hong Kong, China (Revision)* (30 January 2019) WT/TPR/S/380/Rev.1 [2.23].
115 World Trade Organization, *Trade Policy Review Report by the Secretariat: Hong Kong, China (Revision)* (28 January 2015) WT/TPR/S/306/Rev.1 [2.31]; World Trade Organization, *Trade Policy Review Report by the Secretariat: Hong Kong, China (Revision)* (30 January 2019) WT/TPR/S/380/Rev.1 [2.23].
116 World Trade Organization, *Trade Policy Review Report by the Secretariat: Hong Kong, China (Revision)* (28 January 2015) WT/TPR/S/306/Rev.1 [2.31]; World Trade Organization, *Trade Policy Review Report by the Secretariat: Hong Kong, China (Revision)* (25 January 2011) WT/TPR/S/241/Rev.1 17 [16]; World Trade Organization, *Trade Policy Review Report by the Secretariat: Hong Kong, China (Revision)* (30 January 2019) WT/TPR/S/380/Rev.1 [2.23].
117 World Trade Organization, *Trade Policy Review Report by the Secretariat: Hong Kong, China (Revision)* (28 January 2015) WT/TPR/S/306/Rev.1 [2.33]; World Trade Organization, *Trade Policy Review Report by the Secretariat: Hong Kong, China (Revision)* (30 January 2019) WT/TPR/S/380/Rev.1 [2.24].
118 World Trade Organization, *Trade Policy Review Report by the Secretariat: Hong Kong, China (Revision)* (25 January 2011) WT/TPR/S/241/Rev.1 17[17]. See Adrian Emch, 'Services Regionalism in the WTO: China's Trade Agreements with Hong Kong and Macao in the Light of Article V(6) GATS' (2006) 33(4) *Legal Issues of Economic Integration* 351–378.
119 World Trade Organization, *Trade Policy Review Report by the Secretariat: Hong Kong, China (Revision)* (30 January 2019) WT/TPR/S/380/Rev.1 [2.26].

CEPA takes a positive-list approach.[120] Indeed, with every supplement and revision, CEPA has widened and deepened its preferential treatment for services and service suppliers – mainland China opens up as many as 153 out of 160 possible services trade sectors to Hong Kong service suppliers[121] – especially in those sectors of traditional, competitive significance to the Region's economy, including financial services, tourism services, trading and logistics services, and professional services.[122] In these respects, CEPA provides for the mutual recognition of professional qualifications,[123] most notably, in the areas of securities and futures and accounting and construction such as estate, quantity, and building surveyors, architects, structural engineers and planners.[124] Over and above WTO commitments, pursuant to CEPA, mainland China permits service suppliers from the Region to enter the market as wholly owned companies, not just as joint ventures.[125] Hong Kong, in return, undertakes not to place any new discriminatory measures on services and service suppliers from mainland China.[126]

In economic terms, CEPA is an intensely efficacious deal for Hong Kong. After all, Hong Kong's economic growth largely depends on that of mainland China:[127] the Region's comparative advantage as a financial centre in the world market benefits enormously from its access to mainland China's capital account and the ever greater international reserve use of the RMB,[128] the currency of mainland China. In support of the Region's role as the commercial window of the world into and out of mainland China, service suppliers from other WTO members with a substantive business

120 World Trade Organization, *Trade Policy Review Report by the Secretariat: Hong Kong, China (Revision)* (30 January 2019) WT/TPR/S/380/Rev.1 [2.26].
121 World Trade Organization, *Trade Policy Review Report by the Secretariat: Hong Kong, China (Revision)* (30 January 2019) WT/TPR/S/380/Rev.1 [2.26].
122 World Trade Organization, *Trade Policy Review Report by the Secretariat: Hong Kong, China (Revision)* (25 January 2011) WT/TPR/S/241/Rev.1 17 [19]. See Yun Zhao, 'Liberalization of Legal Services Under the CEPA Framework between Mainland China and Hong Kong' (2011) 38(4) *Legal Issues of Economic Integration* 321–339.
123 World Trade Organization, *Trade Policy Review Report by the Secretariat: Hong Kong, China (Revision)* (25 January 2011) WT/TPR/S/241/Rev.1 16 [12].
124 World Trade Organization, *Trade Policy Review Report by the Secretariat: Hong Kong, China (Revision)* (25 January 2011) WT/TPR/S/241/Rev.1 16 [14].
125 World Trade Organization, *Trade Policy Review Report by the Secretariat: Hong Kong, China (Revision)* (25 January 2011) WT/TPR/S/241/Rev.1 17 [18].
126 World Trade Organization, *Trade Policy Review Report by the Secretariat: Hong Kong, China (Revision)* (25 January 2011) WT/TPR/S/241/Rev.1 17 [18].
127 World Trade Organization, *Trade Policy Review Report by the Secretariat: Hong Kong, China (Revision)* (28 January 2015) WT/TPR/S/306/Rev.1 [1.4].
128 World Trade Organization, *Trade Policy Review Report by the Secretariat: Hong Kong, China (Revision)* (28 January 2015) WT/TPR/S/306/Rev.1 [1.4]. See Chi Kuen Simon Wu, 'Mainland–Hong Kong Closer Economic Partnership Arrangement and its impact on the Consolidation of Stock Markets in the People's Republic of China and Hong Kong' (2008) 16(1) *Asia Pacific Law Review* 47–72; YY Kueh and Raymond CW Ng, 'The Interplay of the China Factor and US Dollar Peg in the Hong Kong Economy' (2002) 170 *The China Quarterly* 387–412; Chris Brummer, 'The Renminbi and Systemic Risk' (2017) 20(3) *Journal of International Economic Law* 447–507. 'Hong Kong's share of RMB SWIFT payments globally' is over 70 per cent, the world's largest: Hong Kong Monetary Authority, *2020 Annual Report* (Hong Kong: Hong Kong Monetary Authority 2021) 11.

operation[129] in Hong Kong are – subject to Trade and Industry Department certification – eligible to qualify as Hong Kong Service Suppliers (HKSS) and, therefore, obtain preferential market access to mainland China,[130] even if they are of majority foreign ownership.[131] In that respect, CEPA is 'nationality blind';[132] it is neutral, in other words. This arrangement is, of course, reciprocal in application, but has, to date, been most relevant to foreign transport and logistics services suppliers with a base in the Region.[133]

Trade Facilitation

CEPA aims not only to liberalise trade but also to facilitate it.[134] To that aim, the arrangement requires the sides to cooperate on a number of select policy areas.[135] What is more, the side Agreement on Economic and Technical Cooperation directly manages the various bilateral cooperation activities in such novel areas as legal and dispute resolution services, financial and accounting services, innovation and technology, electronic commerce,[136] intellectual property, sub-regional integration and the participation of Hong Kong in the Belt and Road Initiative.[137]

Trade Integration

In relation to sub-regional integration,[138] apart from the side agreement on cooperation, CEPA sustains three other subsidiary agreements, namely, the Agreement

129 The criteria are as follows: five years of operation in Hong Kong; payment of profit tax in Hong Kong; rental or ownership of business premises in Hong Kong; and employment of 50 per cent of Hong Kong staff.

130 World Trade Organization, *Trade Policy Review Report by the Secretariat: Hong Kong, China (Revision)* (25 January 2011) WT/TPR/S/241/Rev.1 18 [21]; World Trade Organization, *Trade Policy Review Report by the Secretariat: Hong Kong, China (Revision)* (30 January 2019) WT/TPR/S/380/Rev.1 [2.25].

131 World Trade Organization, *Trade Policy Review Report by the Secretariat: Hong Kong, China (Revision)* (25 January 2011) WT/TPR/S/241/Rev.1 18 [22].

132 World Trade Organization, *Trade Policy Review Report by the Secretariat: Hong Kong, China (Revision)* (25 January 2011) WT/TPR/S/241/Rev.1 18 [22].

133 World Trade Organization, *Trade Policy Review Report by the Secretariat: Hong Kong, China (Revision)* (28 January 2015) WT/TPR/S/306/Rev.1 [2.34].

134 World Trade Organization, *Trade Policy Review Report by the Secretariat: Hong Kong, China (Revision)* (25 January 2011) WT/TPR/S/241/Rev.1 16 [13].

135 See trade and investment promotion; customs clearance facilitation; commodity inspection and quarantine; food safety and quality and standardisation; electronic business; transparency in laws and regulations; cooperation of small and medium enterprises; cooperation in industries; protection of intellectual property; cooperation on branding; and cooperation on education: World Trade Organization, *Trade Policy Review Report by the Secretariat: Hong Kong, China (Revision)* (28 January 2015) WT/TPR/S/306/Rev.1 [2.37].

136 See, generally, Yun Zhao, 'Liberalization of Electronic Commerce in Mainland China and Hong Kong Under the WTO–CEPA Regime' (2005) 19(2) *International Review of Law, Computers & Technology* 183–198.

137 World Trade Organization, *Trade Policy Review Report by the Secretariat: Hong Kong, China (Revision)* (30 January 2019) WT/TPR/S/380/Rev.1 [2.30].

138 World Trade Organization, *Trade Policy Review Report by the Secretariat: Hong Kong, China (Revision)* (30 January 2019) WT/TPR/S/380/Rev.1 [1.5]. See Robert F Ash and YY Kueh, 'Economic Integration within Greater China: Trade and Investment Flows

on Trade in Services, the Agreement on Trade in Goods, and the Investment Agreement.[139] The Agreement on Trade in Services is particularly significant because it builds on an earlier Agreement between the Mainland and Hong Kong on Achieving Basic Liberalisation of Trade in Services in Guangdong.[140] The consolidated version of the Agreement on Trade in Services pledges, in the Preamble, 'to progressively reduce or eliminate substantially all discriminatory measures on trade in services between the two sides, as well as to further enhance the level of bilateral economic and trade exchanges and cooperation'.[141]

Also of significance to sub-regional integration is the Investment Agreement, which provides measures to liberalise, facilitate and protect investment between the two sides.[142] The agreement takes a negative-list approach, which allows Hong Kong Investors to enjoy preferential treatment in all non-services sectors of the mainland China market.[143] It establishes investment dispute settlement mechanisms and optimises investment procedures with both easier availability of information and greater transparency of regulation.[144] Numerous, too, are the separate initiatives by Hong Kong Exchanges and Clearing and the Hong Kong Monetary Authority to promote the integration of the financial markets of mainland China and the Region – northbound and southbound – such as Stock Connect, Bond Connect and the Cross-boundary Wealth Management Connect Scheme in the Guangdong–Hong Kong–Macao Greater Bay Area.

between China, Hong Kong and Taiwan' (1993) 136 *The China Quarterly* 711–745; Kevin Tze-Wai Wong, Victor Zheng and Po-San Wan, 'The Impact of Cross-Border Integration with Mainland China on Hong Kong's Local Politics: The Individual Visit Scheme as a Double-Edged Sword for Political Trust in Hong Kong' (2016) 228 *The China Quarterly* 1081–1104; David Shambaugh, 'Introduction: The Emergence of Greater China' (1993) 136 *The China Quarterly* 653–659; Harry Harding, 'The Concept of Greater China: Themes, Variations and Reservations' (1993) 136 *The China Quarterly* 660–686; Michael Yahuda, 'The Foreign Relations of Greater China' (1993) 136 *The China Quarterly* 687–710; John Mo, 'The Greater China Free Trade Zone within the WTO – A Solution to Ease Tension across the Taiwan Strait' (2001) 2(1) *Journal of World Investment* 87–122; Guiguo Wang, 'The Across-the-Strait Relations against the Background of Globalization' (2006) 7(1) *Journal of World Investment & Trade* 5–24.

139 World Trade Organization, *Trade Policy Review Report by the Secretariat: Hong Kong, China (Revision)* (30 January 2019) WT/TPR/S/380/Rev.1 [2.22].

140 World Trade Organization, *Trade Policy Review Report by the Secretariat: Hong Kong, China (Revision)* (30 January 2019) WT/TPR/S/380/Rev.1 [2.25].

141 Courtesy Translation, Mainland and Hong Kong Closer Economic Partnership Arrangement: Agreement on Trade in Services (Consolidated Version), Trade and Industry Department, The Government of the Hong Kong Special Administrative Region of the People's Republic of China, https://www.tid.gov.hk/english/cepa/legaltext/files/sa27–11–2015_main_e.pdf, accessed 25 January 2022.

142 See, generally, Shu Shang, 'Responding to the ISDS Legitimacy Crisis by Way of Mediation: Implications from CEPA's Dispute Resolution Mechanism' (2019) 18(2) *Journal of International Business and Law* 217–236.

143 World Trade Organization, *Trade Policy Review Report by the Secretariat: Hong Kong, China (Revision)* (30 January 2019) WT/TPR/S/380/Rev.1 [2.28].

144 World Trade Organization, *Trade Policy Review Report by the Secretariat: Hong Kong, China (Revision)* (30 January 2019) WT/TPR/S/380/Rev.1 [2.29].

Thanks to its unique character as an inter-territorial arrangement with both an economically integrative mission and an economically liberal agenda, CEPA introduces, from time to time, pilot measures[145] to more widely and deeply integrate the economy of the Region into the Pearl River Delta Economic Zone[146] as part of the Guangdong–Hong Kong–Macao Greater Bay Area (Greater Bay Area) initiative.[147] These economic integration and development initiatives accord with the Outline of the 14th Five-Year Plan for National Economic and Social Development of the People's Republic of China and the Long-Range Objectives Through the Year 2035[148] and are a policy priority for the Government of the Region, as its Chief Executive's Policy Addresses in recent years demonstrate.[149] This framework supports Hong Kong's role in the country's dual circulation development model, both as a participant in domestic circulation and as a facilitator of international circulation.

Greater Bay Area Initiative

The Greater Bay Area initiative results from a July 2017 framework cooperation agreement between Hong Kong and the National Development and Reform

145 World Trade Organization, *Trade Policy Review Report by the Secretariat: Hong Kong, China (Revision)* (30 January 2019) WT/TPR/S/380/Rev.1 [2.36].

146 See, generally, Susan Tiefenbrun, 'US Foreign Trade Zones and Chinese Free Trade Zones: A Comparative Analysis' (2015) 14(2) *Journal of International Business and Law* 189–232; Yang Feng, 'Examining Legislation in China's Special Economic Zones: Framework, Practice and Prospects' (2017) 47(2) *Hong Kong Law Journal* 585–614; Shen Wei, 'A Tale of Three Zones – Promises and Pitfalls of Three Financial Experimental Zones in China' (2014) 131(5) *Banking Law Journal* 399–435.

147 World Trade Organization, *Trade Policy Review Report by the Secretariat: Hong Kong, China (Revision)* (25 January 2011) WT/TPR/S/241/Rev.1 18 [20]. On the Pearl River Delta Economic Zone, see Teresa Cheng, 'Special Economic Zones: A Catalyst for International Trade and Investment in Unsettling Times?' (2019) 20(1) *Journal of World Investment & Trade* 32–67; Xin He, 'Enforcing Commercial Judgments in the Pearl River Delta of China' (2009) 57(2) *American Journal of Comparative Law* 419–456; Thomas So, 'Great Bay Area' (2018) *Hong Kong Lawyer* 132; Ines Yang, 'Reposition and Reimagine' (2018) *Asian Legal Business* 16–25; Pearl Liu, 'Seeking a Reboot' (2017) *Asian Legal Business* 34–37.

148 Research Office, Legislative Council Secretariat, Hong Kong Special Administrative Region of the People's Republic of China, Fact Sheet: National 14th Five-Year Plan (FS06/20–21), https://www.legco.gov.hk/research-publications/english/2021fs06-national-14th-five-year-plan-20210610-e.pdf, accessed 25 January 2022 (see Chapters 61 and 31).

149 Carrie Lam, *The Chief Executive's 2021 Policy Address* (Hong Kong: Government of the Hong Kong Special Administrative Region 2021), Section IV: New Impetus to the Economy: Integration into the National Development (Leveraging Our Country and Engaging Ourselves) [40] ('The 14th Five-Year Plan, the Outline Development Plan for the Guangdong-Hong Kong-Macao Greater Bay Area, the Plan for Comprehensive Deepening Reform and Opening Up of the Qianhai Shenzhen-Hong Kong Modern Service Industry Co-operation Zone, the economic development pattern of not only greater domestic circulation but also domestic and international dual circulation, as well as the Belt and Road Initiative, have brought unlimited opportunities for enterprises and professional services providers in Hong Kong, thereby allowing Hong Kong to benefit from its proximity to the Mainland.').

Commission of mainland China with the People's Government of Guangdong Province and the Government of the Macao Special Administrative Region, both to promote infrastructural – gateway – connectivity (for example, the Hong Kong–Zhuhai–Macao Bridge (HZMB)[150] and the Guangzhou–Shenzhen–Hong Kong Express Rail Link (XRL)) and the establishment of a global innovation and technology hub[151] within the geographical area that consists of the Hong Kong Special Administrative Region, the Macao Special Administrative Region and the municipalities of Guangzhou, Shenzhen, Zhuhai, Foshan, Huizhou, Dongguan, Zhongshan, Jiangmen and Zhaoqing in Guangdong Province, thus taking forward this area's socioeconomic development.

The Framework Agreement on Deepening Guangdong–Hong Kong–Macao Cooperation in the Development of the Greater Bay Area[152] (Framework Agreement) states, in its first paragraph, that it is '[t]o fully leverage the integrated advantages of the Guangdong, Hong Kong and Macao region'. By way of general principles, the Framework Agreement states as follows:

> (1) Objectives of Cooperation. To implement the principle of 'one country, two systems' fully and accurately, improve and innovate the cooperation mechanism, establish a mutually complementary cooperation relationship, and jointly take forward the development of the Guangdong–Hong Kong–Macao Greater Bay Area.
> (2) Goals of Cooperation. For Guangdong, to reinforce its roles as the nation's pilot zone for reform and opening up, as well as a main propeller of economic growth, and develop technology and industrial innovation centres, as well as an advanced manufacturing and modern service industries base; for Hong Kong, to consolidate and enhance its status as international financial, transportation and trade centres, strengthen its status as a global offshore Renminbi business hub and an international asset management centre, promote the development of its professional services and innovation and technology industries, and establish a centre for international legal and dispute resolution services in the Asia–Pacific Region; for Macao, to take forward its development as a global tourism and leisure centre, establish an economic and trade cooperation platform between China and Portuguese-speaking countries, establish an exchange and cooperation base with Chinese culture as its

150 World Trade Organization, *Trade Policy Review Report by the Secretariat: Hong Kong, China (Revision)* (25 January 2011) WT/TPR/S/241/Rev.1 ix [19]. See also Jiang Xu and Anthony GO Yeh, 'Interjurisdictional Cooperation through Bargaining: The Case of the Guangzhou–Zhuhai Railway in the Pearl River Delta, China' (2013) 213 *The China Quarterly* 130–151.

151 World Trade Organization, *Trade Policy Review Report by the Secretariat: Hong Kong, China (Revision)* (30 January 2019) WT/TPR/S/380/Rev.1 [1.6].

152 Courtesy Translation, Constitutional and Mainland Affairs Bureau, The Government of the Hong Kong Special Administrative Region of the People's Republic of China, https://www.bayarea.gov.hk/filemanager/en/share/pdf/Framework_Agreement.pdf, accessed 25 January 2022.

> mainstream and the co-existence of different cultures, and foster the appropriately diversified and sustainable development of the economy of Macao. To strive to develop the Guangdong–Hong Kong–Macao Greater Bay Area into a more dynamic economic region, a quality living circle which is an ideal place for living, working and travelling and a showcase for in-depth cooperation between the Mainland and Hong Kong and Macao, and join hands in building a first-class bay area and world-class city cluster.

For Hong Kong, the emphasis is on the further consolidation of its status as an international centre for finance, trade, transportation and dispute resolution. The Outline Development Plan for the Guangdong–Hong Kong–Macao Greater Bay Area[153] (Outline Development Plan) of February 2019 (which, in the long term, extends to 2035) more specifically sets out, in the Preamble, the function of the Greater Bay Area initiative, thus:

> The Outline Development Plan ('the Plan') has been formulated to fully put the spirit of the 19th National Congress of the Communist Party of China into practice; fully and accurately implement the principle of 'one country, two systems'; fully leverage the composite advantages of Guangdong, Hong Kong and Macao; deepen cooperation among the Mainland, Hong Kong and Macao; further enhance the Greater Bay Area's supporting and leading role in the country's economic development and opening up; support the integration of Hong Kong and Macao into the development of the country; enhance the well-being of Hong Kong and Macao compatriots; maintain the long-term prosperity and stability of Hong Kong and Macao; and enable compatriots in Hong Kong and Macao to share with the people in the motherland both the historic responsibility of national rejuvenation and the pride of a strong and prosperous motherland.

The Outline Development Plan states the significance of the Greater Bay Area initiative in Section 3 of Chapter 1, which 'will facilitate the enrichment of the implementation of "one country, two systems" and foster closer cooperation between the Mainland and the two SARs, thereby creating more opportunities for the socio-economic development of the two SARs and for Hong Kong and Macao compatriots wishing to develop careers on the Mainland, as well as maintaining the long-term prosperity and stability of Hong Kong and Macao'. Current plans in support of the Greater Bay Area initiative include the Plan for Comprehensive Deepening Reform and Opening Up of the Qianhai Shenzhen–Hong Kong Modern Service Industry Cooperation Zone (Qianhai Plan) and the Plan for

153 Courtesy Translation, Constitutional and Mainland Affairs Bureau, The Government of the Hong Kong Special Administrative Region of the People's Republic of China, https://www.bayarea.gov.hk/filemanager/en/share/pdf/Outline_Development_Plan.pdf, accessed 25 January 2022.

the Development of the Guangdong–Macao Intensive Cooperation Zone in Hengqin (Hengqin Plan). Both appear in the policy agenda of the Government of the Region.[154]

Belt and Road Initiative

On the Belt and Road Initiative,[155] Hong Kong formalised its full participation in this project through the signature, in December 2017, of an arrangement with the National Development and Reform Commission. By way of principles and objectives, the Arrangement between the National Development and Reform Commission and the Government of the Hong Kong Special Administrative Region for Advancing Hong Kong's Full Participation in and Contribution to the Belt and Road Initiative (Arrangement) states:

> To fully and accurately implement the principle of 'One Country, Two Systems' under the framework of the Constitution and the Basic Law, the Parties are willing to act on the *Vision and Actions on Jointly Building Silk Road Economic Belt and 21st Century Maritime Silk Road*, following the principle of 'market operation under government guidance' and exercising the government's role as a 'facilitator' and a 'promoter', to strengthen communication and consultation for realising the 'five areas of connectivity' and make suitable arrangements for fully leveraging the unique advantages of Hong Kong in commerce and trade, finance and professional services for participating in and contributing to the Belt and Road Initiative, with a view to achieving mutually complimentary and co-ordinated development between the Mainland and Hong Kong.[156]

The Arrangement identifies areas for bilateral action, all with the aim to boost the Region's legal and other professional services sector and further secure its position as a global and regional finance, trading and logistics platform. The areas are six in

154 The Government of the Hong Kong Special Administrative Region of the People's Republic of China, Press Release: CE Welcomes Promulgation of Qianhai Plan and Hengqin Plan (6 September 2021), https://www.info.gov.hk/gia/general/202109/06/P2021090600594.htm, accessed 25 January 2022.

155 Gonzalo Villalta Puig, 'Free Trade Areas for China's Belt and Road' (2020) 24(1) *Currents: Journal of International Economic Law* 3–12; Gonzalo Villalta Puig, 'Unimpeded Trade? The Significance of Free Trade Areas to the Belt and Road Initiative of the People's Republic of China' in Lutz-Christian Wolff and Chao Xi (eds), *Legal Dimensions of China's Belt and Road Initiative* (Hong Kong: Wolters Kluwer Law & Business 2016) 103–138; Liu Weili, 'New Trends in International Trade and Investment Rules and China's FTA Strategy' (2017) 7(4) *Journal of WTO and China* 70–95.

156 Courtesy Translation, Arrangement between the National Development and Reform Commission and the Government of the Hong Kong Special Administrative Region for Advancing Hong Kong's Full Participation in and Contribution to the Belt and Road Initiative, The Government of the Hong Kong Special Administrative Region of the People's Republic of China, https://gia.info.gov.hk/general/201712/14/P2017121400551_274123_1_1513241987560.pdf, accessed 25 January 2022.

number. They are: finance and investment; infrastructure and maritime services; economic and trade facilitation; people-to-people bonds; taking forward the Greater Bay Area development; and, enhancing collaboration in project interfacing and dispute resolution services.[157] A Joint Conference mechanism under the Arrangement and a Mainland and Hong Kong Belt and Road Task Group with China's Ministry of Commerce jointly guide the Region's participation in the Belt and Road Initiative.

Other Provisions

Despite its expansive scope, CEPA does not cover government procurement. It does not cover competition policy either.[158] CEPA does, however, cover unfair trade practices through provisions on anti-dumping, subsidies and countervailing measures.[159] Moreover, the two sides commit not to apply such measures on each other's goods, appropriately so.[160] CEPA, however, does allow the application of safeguard measures on goods imports, but, to date, neither side has, sensibly, done so.[161]

Hong Kong–New Zealand Closer Economic Partnership Agreement

In 2010, almost seven years after the signature of CEPA, Hong Kong partnered with New Zealand to sign its first FTA with a foreign customs territory. The similarly titled Closer Economic Partnership Agreement (CEP Agreement) has gradually phased out tariffs on all[162] goods from Hong Kong to New Zealand[163] and, correspondingly, from New Zealand to Hong Kong.[164] With regard to trade in services, the CEP Agreement takes a negative-list approach for services in Modes 1 to 3 and a positive-list approach for services in Mode 4. More specifically, New Zealand liberalises its business services, communication services, financial services

157 World Trade Organization, *Trade Policy Review Report by the Secretariat: Hong Kong, China (Revision)* (30 January 2019) WT/TPR/S/380/Rev.1.
158 World Trade Organization, *Trade Policy Review Report by the Secretariat: Hong Kong, China (Revision)* (30 January 2019) WT/TPR/S/380/Rev.1 [2.27]; World Trade Organization, *Trade Policy Review Report by the Secretariat: Hong Kong, China (Revision)* (28 January 2015) WT/TPR/S/306/Rev.1 [2.38].
159 World Trade Organization, *Trade Policy Review Report by the Secretariat: Hong Kong, China (Revision)* (25 January 2011) WT/TPR/S/241/Rev.1 16 [13].
160 World Trade Organization, *Trade Policy Review Report by the Secretariat: Hong Kong, China (Revision)* (25 January 2011) WT/TPR/S/241/Rev.1 16 [13].
161 World Trade Organization, *Trade Policy Review Report by the Secretariat: Hong Kong, China (Revision)* (25 January 2011) WT/TPR/S/241/Rev.1 16 [13].
162 World Trade Organization, *Trade Policy Review Report by the Secretariat: Hong Kong, China (Revision)* (25 January 2011) WT/TPR/S/241/Rev.1 16 [10]; World Trade Organization, *Trade Policy Review Report by the Secretariat: Hong Kong, China (Revision)* (30 January 2019) WT/TPR/S/380/Rev.1 [2.15].
163 World Trade Organization, *Trade Policy Review Report by the Secretariat: Hong Kong, China (Revision)* (30 January 2019) WT/TPR/S/380/Rev.1 [2.18].
164 World Trade Organization, *Trade Policy Review Report by the Secretariat: Hong Kong, China (Revision)* (28 January 2015) WT/TPR/S/306/Rev.1 [2.19].

and transport services while the Region liberalises its financial services and most sub-sectors in communication services, construction services, transport services and tourism services.[165] Both parties, however, use a 'GATS-floor' reservation.[166] Additionally, the CEP Agreement covers a rather broad selection of related matters of mutual concern,[167] such as government procurement,[168] competition, e-commerce, intellectual property, sanitary and phytosanitary and technical barriers to trade measures, conformity assessment and customs procedures and cooperation.[169]

Hong Kong–European Free Trade Area (Member States) Free Trade Agreement

Only a year later, Hong Kong entered into its second FTA with a foreign trading partner, this time with a collection of customs territories around a common free trade area: the Member States of EFTA, namely, Iceland, Norway and Switzerland/Liechtenstein.[170] The EFTA Agreement regulates trade and such related aspects as government procurement, intellectual property rights, and investment.[171] Side agreements – severally between the various customs territories – specifically regulate trade in agriculture.[172] Under the EFTA Agreement, the Region removes tariffs on all goods imports from EFTA,[173] including agricultural goods.[174] Correspondingly, EFTA gives tariff-free market access to Hong Kong industrial goods and, subject to some exceptions, fish and marine products.[175] However, under the side agreements, EFTA retains tariffs on a majority of the Region's agricultural goods.[176]

165 World Trade Organization, *Trade Policy Review Report by the Secretariat: Hong Kong, China (Revision)* (28 January 2015) WT/TPR/S/306/Rev.1 [2.20].
166 World Trade Organization, *Trade Policy Review Report by the Secretariat: Hong Kong, China (Revision)* (28 January 2015) WT/TPR/S/306/Rev.1 [2.20].
167 World Trade Organization, *Trade Policy Review Report by the Secretariat: Hong Kong, China (Revision)* (25 January 2011) WT/TPR/S/241/Rev.1 16 [10].
168 World Trade Organization, *Trade Policy Review Report by the Secretariat: Hong Kong, China (Revision)* (28 January 2015) WT/TPR/S/306/Rev.1 [2.21].
169 World Trade Organization, *Trade Policy Review Report by the Secretariat: Hong Kong, China (Revision)* (28 January 2015) WT/TPR/S/306/Rev.1 [2.22].
170 See, generally, Brian Hook and Miguel Santos Neves, 'The Role of Hong Kong and Macau in China's Relations with Europe' (2002) 169 *The China Quarterly* 108–135.
171 World Trade Organization, *Trade Policy Review Report by the Secretariat: Hong Kong, China (Revision)* (28 January 2015) WT/TPR/S/306/Rev.1 [2.23].
172 World Trade Organization, *Trade Policy Review Report by the Secretariat: Hong Kong, China (Revision)* (28 January 2015) WT/TPR/S/306/Rev.1 [2.23].
173 World Trade Organization, *Trade Policy Review Report by the Secretariat: Hong Kong, China (Revision)* (28 January 2015) WT/TPR/S/306/Rev.1 [2.24].
174 World Trade Organization, *Trade Policy Review Report by the Secretariat: Hong Kong, China (Revision)* (28 January 2015) WT/TPR/S/306/Rev.1 [2.25].
175 World Trade Organization, *Trade Policy Review Report by the Secretariat: Hong Kong, China (Revision)* (28 January 2015) WT/TPR/S/306/Rev.1 [2.24].
176 World Trade Organization, *Trade Policy Review Report by the Secretariat: Hong Kong, China (Revision)* (28 January 2015) WT/TPR/S/306/Rev.1 [2.25].

The EFTA Agreement is relatively liberal in its regulation of trade in services. For one, it takes a negative-list approach.[177] Notably, it gives Hong Kong access to EFTA markets in telecommunications services, financial services, business services, education services, environmental services and testing and certification services while it gives EFTA access to the Region's markets in financial services, telecommunications services, logistics services, business services, energy services, tourism and travel-related services and construction and related engineering services.[178] These bilateral commitments largely build on individual GATS commitments,[179] although EFTA does maintain certain most-favoured-nation reservations and horizontal limitations.[180] The parties have subsequently adopted procedures and disciplines for an easier and more effective implementation of the agreement.[181]

Hong Kong–Chile Free Trade Agreement

An FTA with Chile was next for Hong Kong. Signed in 2012, it provides reciprocal duty-free market access with as high a coverage as 98 per cent of Chile's tariff lines on Hong Kong goods.[182] Ironically, the balance of the Chilean schedule continues to apply on goods for which the Region has no significant industrial base such as cereals, sugar and iron and steel exports.[183]

In contrast to Hong Kong's other FTAs, the Chile FTA takes a positive-list approach to the liberalisation of trade in services.[184] Nevertheless, its provisions are over and above GATS.[185] Thus, the Chile FTA gives Hong Kong access to Chilean markets in financial services, telecommunications services, tourism services, environmental services and certain business services[186] while it gives Chile access to the Region's markets in architectural services, engineering services, audio-visual

177 World Trade Organization, *Trade Policy Review Report by the Secretariat: Hong Kong, China (Revision)* (28 January 2015) WT/TPR/S/306/Rev.1 [2.26].
178 World Trade Organization, *Trade Policy Review Report by the Secretariat: Hong Kong, China (Revision)* (28 January 2015) WT/TPR/S/306/Rev.1 [2.26].
179 World Trade Organization, *Trade Policy Review Report by the Secretariat: Hong Kong, China (Revision)* (28 January 2015) WT/TPR/S/306/Rev.1 [2.26].
180 World Trade Organization, *Trade Policy Review Report by the Secretariat: Hong Kong, China (Revision)* (28 January 2015) WT/TPR/S/306/Rev.1 [2.26].
181 World Trade Organization, *Trade Policy Review Report by the Secretariat: Hong Kong, China (Revision)* (30 January 2019) WT/TPR/S/380/Rev.1 [2.19].
182 World Trade Organization, *Trade Policy Review Report by the Secretariat: Hong Kong, China (Revision)* (30 January 2019) WT/TPR/S/380/Rev.1 [2.20].
183 World Trade Organization, *Trade Policy Review Report by the Secretariat: Hong Kong, China (Revision)* (28 January 2015) WT/TPR/S/306/Rev.1 [2.27].
184 World Trade Organization, *Trade Policy Review Report by the Secretariat: Hong Kong, China (Revision)* (28 January 2015) WT/TPR/S/306/Rev.1 [2.28].
185 World Trade Organization, *Trade Policy Review Report by the Secretariat: Hong Kong, China (Revision)* (30 January 2019) WT/TPR/S/380/Rev.1 [2.20].
186 World Trade Organization, *Trade Policy Review Report by the Secretariat: Hong Kong, China (Revision)* (28 January 2015) WT/TPR/S/306/Rev.1 [2.28].

services and construction services,[187] with specific provision for government procurement market access in alignment with Hong Kong's GPA commitments.[188] Both parties have subsequently entered into a complementary investment protection and facilitation agreement.[189]

Hong Kong–Macao Closer Economic Partnership Arrangement

Five years after the Chile FTA came a deal with Macao, which – as an instrument between the two Special Administrative Regions of the People's Republic of China – is appropriately referred to as a Closer Economic Partnership Arrangement. The text of the instrument holds much similarity with CEPA and the objectives and principles contained in both arrangements closely overlap with one another. The Preamble calls on the arrangement '[t]o promote the joint economic prosperity and development of the Hong Kong Special Administrative Region and the Macao Special Administrative Region ..., and to facilitate the further development of economic links between the two sides and the Mainland'.[190] Not surprisingly, as neighbouring free ports, the Hong Kong–Macao CEPA is outstandingly liberal in its treatment of trade in goods. Both parties bind their respective tariffs on reciprocal goods imports at zero.[191] Moreover, they commit against tariff rate quotas as well as non-tariff barriers to trade, if inconsistent with the WTO.[192]

In relation to trade in services, both parties make WTO-plus commitments albeit on a positive-list approach.[193] Specifically, the arrangement gives Hong Kong access to Macao markets in business services, communication services, educational services, environmental services, recreational services, cultural and sporting services and transport services[194] while it gives Macao access to Hong Kong markets in environmental services, health-related and social services, and certain

187 World Trade Organization, *Trade Policy Review Report by the Secretariat: Hong Kong, China (Revision)* (28 January 2015) WT/TPR/S/306/Rev.1 [2.28].

188 World Trade Organization, *Trade Policy Review Report by the Secretariat: Hong Kong, China (Revision)* (28 January 2015) WT/TPR/S/306/Rev.1 [2.29].

189 World Trade Organization, *Trade Policy Review Report by the Secretariat: Hong Kong, China (Revision)* (30 January 2019) WT/TPR/S/380/Rev.1 [2.21].

190 Courtesy Translation, Hong Kong Special Administrative Region and Macao Special Administrative Region Closer Economic Partnership Arrangement, Trade and Industry Department, The Government of the Hong Kong Special Administrative Region of the People's Republic of China, https://www.tid.gov.hk/english/ita/fta/hkmacao/files/full_text_of_the_agreement.pdf, accessed 25 January 2022.

191 World Trade Organization, *Trade Policy Review Report by the Secretariat: Hong Kong, China (Revision)* (30 January 2019) WT/TPR/S/380/Rev.1 [2.31].

192 World Trade Organization, *Trade Policy Review Report by the Secretariat: Hong Kong, China (Revision)* (30 January 2019) WT/TPR/S/380/Rev.1 [2.31].

193 World Trade Organization, *Trade Policy Review Report by the Secretariat: Hong Kong, China (Revision)* (30 January 2019) WT/TPR/S/380/Rev.1 [2.32].

194 World Trade Organization, *Trade Policy Review Report by the Secretariat: Hong Kong, China (Revision)* (30 January 2019) WT/TPR/S/380/Rev.1 [2.32].

business services.[195] The Hong Kong–Macao CEPA does not cover government procurement,[196] neither does it cover competition policy.[197]

Hong Kong–Association of Southeast Asian Nations Free Trade Agreement

Hong Kong's next FTA, with ASEAN, was, like the Hong Kong–Macao CEPA, also signed in 2017. ASEAN Member States collectively constitute Hong Kong's second largest trading partner. On trade in goods, the Region formalises its zero tariffs on ASEAN imports[198] while individual ASEAN Member States only pledge tariff reductions.[199] Again like the Hong Kong–Macao CEPA, the ASEAN FTA takes a positive-list approach to the liberalisation of trade in services.[200] Subject to different commitments by individual ASEAN Member States, it gives Hong Kong access to ASEAN markets in professional services, business services, telecommunications services, construction and related engineering services, educational services, financial services, tourism and travel-related services, transport and arbitration services.[201] In return, the agreement gives ASEAN Member States access to the Region's markets in an array of sectors as diverse as architectural services, engineering services, urban planning and landscape architectural services, audio-visual services, distribution services, educational services, environmental services, tourism and travel-related services, recreational services, cultural and sporting services and transport services.[202] As with the Hong Kong–Macao CEPA, the ASEAN FTA covers neither government procurement nor competition policy.[203] It does, however, include a complementary investment protection and facilitation agreement.[204] Notably, Hong Kong seeks to accede ASEAN's Regional Comprehensive Economic Partnership agreement.

195 World Trade Organization, *Trade Policy Review Report by the Secretariat: Hong Kong, China (Revision)* (30 January 2019) WT/TPR/S/380/Rev.1 [2.32].
196 World Trade Organization, *Trade Policy Review Report by the Secretariat: Hong Kong, China (Revision)* (30 January 2019) WT/TPR/S/380/Rev.1 [2.33].
197 World Trade Organization, *Trade Policy Review Report by the Secretariat: Hong Kong, China (Revision)* (30 January 2019) WT/TPR/S/380/Rev.1 [2.33].
198 World Trade Organization, *Trade Policy Review Report by the Secretariat: Hong Kong, China (Revision)* (30 January 2019) WT/TPR/S/380/Rev.1 [2.34].
199 World Trade Organization, *Trade Policy Review Report by the Secretariat: Hong Kong, China (Revision)* (30 January 2019) WT/TPR/S/380/Rev.1 [2.34].
200 World Trade Organization, *Trade Policy Review Report by the Secretariat: Hong Kong, China (Revision)* (30 January 2019) WT/TPR/S/380/Rev.1 [2.35].
201 World Trade Organization, *Trade Policy Review Report by the Secretariat: Hong Kong, China (Revision)* (30 January 2019) WT/TPR/S/380/Rev.1 [2.35].
202 World Trade Organization, *Trade Policy Review Report by the Secretariat: Hong Kong, China (Revision)* (30 January 2019) WT/TPR/S/380/Rev.1 [2.35].
203 World Trade Organization, *Trade Policy Review Report by the Secretariat: Hong Kong, China (Revision)* (30 January 2019) WT/TPR/S/380/Rev.1 [2.37].
204 World Trade Organization, *Trade Policy Review Report by the Secretariat: Hong Kong, China (Revision)* (30 January 2019) WT/TPR/S/380/Rev.1 [2.36].

Hong Kong–Georgia Free Trade Agreement

In more recent years, Hong Kong has, in its choice of FTA partners, shown strong support for the Belt and Road Initiative, as evidenced by its signature in 2018 of an FTA with Georgia. With its location in the Caucasus and as the gateway to the wider Eurasia region, Georgia serves as an ideal trans-Asian corridor. This agreement is fairly comprehensive in scope.[205] On trade in goods, Georgia removes tariffs on almost 97 per cent of its lines for Hong Kong imports,[206] with only agricultural goods – always sensitive – and beverages and spirits out of free trade.[207] In return, the Region agrees to allow duty free market access for all Georgian goods imports.[208] With regard to trade in services, the agreement gives Hong Kong access to Georgian markets in financial services, telecommunications services, certain business services, wholesale and retailing services, arbitration services, audio-visual services, construction and related engineering services, environmental services, certain transport services and printing and publishing services,[209] all sectors in which Hong Kong has a core strength. Correspondingly, the agreement gives Georgia access to the Region's markets in architectural services, engineering services, distribution services, tourism and travel-related services and maritime transport services.[210] Specifically, in support of the Belt and Road Initiative, the agreement assures non-discriminatory access to and use of ports for vessels of either party.[211] The agreement covers investment protection and facilitation, intellectual property rights and competition policy.[212]

205 Trade and Industry Department, The Government of the Hong Kong Special Administrative Region of the People's Republic of China (Press Release: Hong Kong and Georgia sign Free Trade Agreement, 28 June 2018), https://www.tid.gov.hk/english/aboutus/presspeech/press/2018/20180628.html, accessed 1 July 2021.

206 Trade and Industry Department, The Government of the Hong Kong Special Administrative Region of the People's Republic of China (Press Release: Hong Kong and Georgia sign Free Trade Agreement, 28 June 2018), https://www.tid.gov.hk/english/aboutus/presspeech/press/2018/20180628.html, accessed 1 July 2021.

207 Trade and Industry Department, The Government of the Hong Kong Special Administrative Region of the People's Republic of China (Trade and Investment Agreements, Free Trade Agreement between Hong Kong, China and Georgia, 17 May 2021), https://www.tid.gov.hk/english/ita/fta/hkgefta/index.html, accessed 1 July 2021.

208 Trade and Industry Department, The Government of the Hong Kong Special Administrative Region of the People's Republic of China (Trade and Investment Agreements, Free Trade Agreement between Hong Kong, China and Georgia, 17 May 2021), https://www.tid.gov.hk/english/ita/fta/hkgefta/index.html, accessed 1 July 2021.

209 Trade and Industry Department, The Government of the Hong Kong Special Administrative Region of the People's Republic of China (Press Release: Hong Kong and Georgia sign Free Trade Agreement, 28 June 2018), https://www.tid.gov.hk/english/aboutus/presspeech/press/2018/20180628.html, accessed 1 July 2021.

210 Trade and Industry Department, The Government of the Hong Kong Special Administrative Region of the People's Republic of China (Trade and Investment Agreements, Free Trade Agreement between Hong Kong, China and Georgia, 17 May 2021), https://www.tid.gov.hk/english/ita/fta/hkgefta/index.html, accessed 1 July 2021.

211 Trade and Industry Department, The Government of the Hong Kong Special Administrative Region of the People's Republic of China (Trade and Investment Agreements, Free Trade Agreement between Hong Kong, China and Georgia, 17 May 2021), https://www.tid.gov.hk/english/ita/fta/hkgefta/index.html, accessed 1 July 2021.

212 Trade and Industry Department, The Government of the Hong Kong Special Administrative Region of the People's Republic of China (Press Release: Hong Kong

Hong Kong–Australia Free Trade Agreement

With the Belt and Road Initiative in its sight, Hong Kong partnered with Australia in 2019 with the signature of a high-quality Free Trade and Investment Agreement. Not surprisingly for two like champions of free trade, this agreement is well in excess of the respective WTO commitments of the parties.[213] The agreement is the Region's as well as Australia's most ambitious to date, indeed their best deal,[214] so much so that it commits each party to the removal of all customs duties on all goods imports from either party. In acknowledgement of the importance of electronic commerce, it extends that commitment to electronic transmissions. What is more, the agreement significantly simplifies customs procedures for more transparent and predictable trade.[215] With respect to trade in services, the agreement takes a negative-list approach. It gives Hong Kong access to Australian markets in some 140 sectors, including professional services (such as arbitration, conciliation and mediation services), business services, transport services (even rail transport services), financial services and telecommunications services. Importantly, Australia also commits to extend to the Region any additional liberalisation measures that it grants to other partners in its future FTAs.[216] Hong Kong, in return, makes comparable services trade commitments.[217] The agreement incorporates investment protection and facilitation and, more particularly, it raises monetary thresholds for foreign investment screening.[218] It

and Georgia Sign Free Trade Agreement, 28 June 2018), https://www.tid.gov.hk/english/aboutus/presspeech/press/2018/20180628.html, accessed 1 July 2021.

213 Trade and Industry Department of the Hong Kong Special Administrative Region of the People's Republic of China (Press Release: Free Trade Agreement and Investment Agreement between Hong Kong and Australia Enter into Force, 18 December 2019), https://www.info.gov.hk/gia/general/202001/17/P2020011700365.htm?fontSize=1, accessed 1 July 2021.

214 Trade and Industry Department, The Government of the Hong Kong Special Administrative Region of the People's Republic of China (Press Release: Hong Kong and Australia Sign Free Trade Agreement and Investment Agreement, 26 March 2019), https://www.info.gov.hk/gia/general/201903/26/P2019032600160.htm, accessed 1 July 2021.

215 Trade and Industry Department, The Government of the Hong Kong Special Administrative Region of the People's Republic of China (Press Release: Free Trade Agreement and Investment Agreement between Hong Kong and Australia Enter into Force, 18 December 2019), https://www.info.gov.hk/gia/general/202001/17/P2020011700365.htm?fontSize=1, accessed 1 July 2021.

216 Trade and Industry Department, The Government of the Hong Kong Special Administrative Region of the People's Republic of China (Free Trade Agreement (FTA) and Investment Agreement between Hong Kong (HK) and Australia: Frequently Asked Questions), https://www.tid.gov.hk/english/ita/fta/hkaufta/files/faq_e.pdf, accessed 1 July 2021.

217 Trade and Industry Department, The Government of the Hong Kong Special Administrative Region of the People's Republic of China (Free Trade Agreement (FTA) and Investment Agreement between Hong Kong (HK) and Australia: Frequently Asked Questions), https://www.tid.gov.hk/english/ita/fta/hkaufta/files/faq_e.pdf, accessed 1 July 2021.

218 Trade and Industry Department, The Government of the Hong Kong Special Administrative Region of the People's Republic of China (Press Release: Free Trade Agreement and Investment Agreement between Hong Kong and Australia Enter into

facilitates business travel and access to government procurement markets, protects intellectual property rights, and promotes competition.[219]

Free Trade Agreement Negotiations

To further shore up the Belt and Road Initiative, Hong Kong began FTA negotiations with Maldives but an agreement was never signed. Hong Kong is now due to commence negotiations for an FTA with Peru in January 2023. Both parties have jointly stated their intention to cover in negotiations such areas as trade in goods, services, investment, electronic commerce, government procurement, intellectual property, competition, and small and medium sized enterprises.

In the meantime, the Region actively seeks accession to the Regional Comprehensive Economic Partnership (RCEP) agreement between ASEAN's Brunei, Cambodia, Indonesia, Laos, Malaysia, Myanmar, the Philippines, Singapore, Thailand, and Vietnam together with Australia, China, Japan, New Zealand and South Korea. The Region, moreover, has expressed interest in exploratory trade talks with the Pacific Alliance of Chile, Colombia, Mexico and Peru.

Investment Promotion and Protection Agreements

Hong Kong has entered into numerous bilateral agreements[220] to manage foreign investment relations. Formally known as Investment Promotion and Protection Agreements (IPPAs), these instruments aim to promote and protect investments by investors of one contracting party in the jurisdiction of the other contracting party.[221] Under the principles of most-favoured-nation treatment and national treatment, they specifically extend to direct investments from either side both fair and equitable regulation as well as

Force, 18 December 2019), https://www.info.gov.hk/gia/general/202001/17/P2020011700365.htm?fontSize=1, accessed 1 July 2021.

219 Trade and Industry Department, The Government of the Hong Kong Special Administrative Region of the People's Republic of China (Press Release: Free Trade Agreement and Investment Agreement between Hong Kong and Australia Enter into Force, 18 December 2019), https://www.info.gov.hk/gia/general/202001/17/P2020011700365.htm?fontSize=1, accessed 1 July 2021.

220 See also Zeng Huaqun, 'Initiative and Implications of Hong Kong's Bilateral Investment Treaties' (2010) 11(5) *Journal of World Investment & Trade* 669–696; Derek Zhaoke Zhu, 'International Investment Agreements among China, Japan, and Korea: From Bilateral to Trilateral – The Way toward a Better Protection for Foreign Investors' (2015) 12(1) *Manchester Journal of International Economic Law* 80–107; An Chen, 'Queries to the Recent ICSID Decision on Jurisdiction upon the Case of *Tza Yap Shum v. Republic of Peru*: Should China–Peru BIT 1994 Be Applied to Hong Kong SAR Under the One Country Two Systems Policy' (2009) 10(6) *Journal of World Investment & Trade* 829–864.

221 Interestingly, the suggestion is that mainland China's Investment Promotion and Protection Agreements protect Hong Kong investments abroad: Chin Leng Lim, 'Fragrant Harbour and Oyster Mirror: Beijing's Investment Treaty Policy toward Hong Kong and Macao' in Lisa E Sachs and Lise Johnson (eds), *Yearbook on International Investment Law & Policy 2015–2016* (Oxford: Oxford University Press 2018) 375–411; see *Sanum Investments Ltd v Government of the Lao People's Democratic Republic* [2016] SGCA 57.

full security and protection against expropriation. They establish investor-to-government dispute settlement mechanisms as well.[222] The Region has signed 22 IPPAs, but not all are in force. Those in force are, in alphabetical order, with ASEAN, Australia, Austria, the Belgo-Luxembourg Economic Union, Canada, Chile, Denmark, Finland, France, Germany, Italy, Japan, Mexico, South Korea, Kuwait, the Netherlands, New Zealand, Sweden, Switzerland, Thailand, the United Arab Emirates and the United Kingdom. Among these, the agreements with ASEAN, Australia, Mexico and the UAE are the most recent. Besides, Hong Kong has negotiated – but not yet signed – IPPAs with Bahrain, Maldives and Myanmar and is in negotiations with Iran, Russia and Turkey. Noticeably, some of these jurisdictions are participants in the Belt and Road Initiative.

Conclusion

Trade liberalisation or, more commonly, free trade,[223] is an economic idea – a policy – that, although not entirely without contest, commands almost universal acceptance. It developed out of the rapid expansion of the capitalist – often mercantilist – free market economy during the late eighteenth and nineteenth centuries.[224] And, fundamentally, it revolves around the liberty to transact that inheres in the ability of the individual citizen to act as an economic agent, what we define to be economic liberty.[225] In constitutional terms, free trade is a norm that conceives the sale and purchase of goods and services – products – among or within customs territories as a movement and exchange without protectionist discrimination in market access.[226] As such, the norm of non-discrimination in trade constitutionalises the political economy of jurisdictions. The establishment of the WTO suggests that global systems of political economy have the constitutional norm of non-discrimination in trade at their foundation.[227] It is an implicit assumption that local systems have that normative foundation, too.

222 See, generally, Micah Burch and Luke Nottage, 'Novel Treaty-Based Approaches to Resolving International Investment and Tax Disputes in the Asia–Pacific Region' (2011) 18 *Australian International Law Journal* 127–140.

223 Gonzalo Villalta Puig, 'Freedom of Trade and Commerce' in Rainer Grote, Frauke Lachenmann and Rüdiger Wolfrum (eds), *Max Planck Encyclopedia of Comparative Constitutional Law* (Oxford: Oxford University Press 2017), https://oxcon.ouplaw.com/view/10.1093/law-mpeccol/law-mpeccol-e227?rskey=GkuSQK&result=45&prd=OXCON, accessed 4 May 2022. See also Gonzalo Villalta Puig, 'Free Trade as an Australian Constitutional Value: A Functionalist Approach to the Interpretation of the Economic Constitution of Australia' in Rosalind Dixon (ed.), *Australian Constitutional Values* (Oxford: Hart Publishing 2018) 287–304.

224 Gordon Bannerman, 'The Free Trade Idea' in Lisa L Martin, *The Oxford Handbook of the Political Economy of International Trade* (Oxford: Oxford University Press 2015) 37–56, 52–53.

225 Razeen Sally, *New Frontiers in Free Trade: Globalization's Future and Asia's Rising Role* (Washington DC: Cato Institute 2008) 127.

226 *Canada – Certain Measures Affecting the Automotive Industry* (Appellate Body Report) (WTO Docs WT/DS139/AB/R and WT/DS142/AB/R, AB-2000-2, 31 May 2000) [84].

227 Has the era of free markets and globalisation that began in the 1990s come to an end with the development of a multipolar world order and a low-growth – high-debt

The value of free trade responds to the call of prosperity. Thus, on application of the Heckscher–Ohlin model of international trade and later Ricardian theories, free trade facilitates economic efficiency.[228] More particularly, it facilitates the optimal allocation of resources through the twin principles of comparative advantage and geographical specialisation, which, together, lead to trade creation and, with it, greater wealth and lesser poverty in a near perfect state of polity interdependency. The greater overall production that results from free trade is an outcome of the freedom of each producer to specialise in what he or she has a natural advantage. Free trade, the theory explains, empowers the individual citizen as economic agent to export his or her labour to import goods, for it is of a lower cost to obtain goods than to produce them directly, with minimum state interference.[229] Deviations from free trade – such as restrictions on the entry of foreign goods into the domestic market – impose costs onto the market as a whole that are not dissimilar to those that monopoly and other restraints on competition[230] impose. Conversely, as Friedrich Hayek observed, respect for free trade tends to enable territories and their governments to benefit from 'the increased information and larger population that resulted'.[231]

Hong Kong is an open market economy under the Basic Law. Its constitutionalisation of the 'free trade' idea under Article 115 has enabled the Region to become – as a 'separate customs territory' further to Article 116 – a reliable member of the WTO and a collaborative facilitator of the multilateral trading system. The Region's regime of trade in services largely follows the liberal[232] approach that it takes to the regulation of trade in goods subject, as it is, to a standstill negative-list practice, with almost no reservations.[233] Such a model commitment to trade liberalisation has meant, unsurprisingly, that the Region has never been a respondent in a WTO dispute. Instead, it regulates its external trade relations through agreements and arrangements with select partners at bilateral, regional and plurilateral levels that complement the WTO's rules.[234]

economic model? See Michael O'Sullivan, *The Levelling: What's Next After Globalization* (New York: PublicAffairs 2019).

228 See Paul R Krugman, Maurice Obstfeld and Marc J Melitz, *International Economics: Theory & Policy* (12th edn) (London: Pearson 2022).

229 Jim Cox, *The Concise Guide to Economics* (3rd edn) (Auburn: Ludwig von Mises Institute 2007) 59.

230 Agnar Sandmo, *Economics Evolving: A History of Economic Thought* (Princeton: Princeton University Press 2011) 54.

231 FA Hayek, *The Fatal Conceit* (London: Routledge 1988) 44.

232 World Trade Organization, *Trade Policy Review Report by the Secretariat: Hong Kong, China (Revision)* (28 January 2015) WT/TPR/S/306/Rev.1 [16].

233 World Trade Organization, *Trade Policy Review Report by the Secretariat: Hong Kong, China (Revision)* (28 January 2015) WT/TPR/S/306/Rev.1 [16].

234 World Trade Organization, *Trade Policy Review Report by the Secretariat: Hong Kong, China (Revision)* (28 January 2015) WT/TPR/S/306/Rev.1 [7]. See generally Wai Ting, 'The External Relations and International Status of Hong Kong' (1997) 2 *Occasional Papers/Reprints Series in Contemporary Asian Studies* 1–[xx]; Wan Pun Lung, 'Application and Conclusion of Treaties in the Hong Kong Special Administrative Region of the People's Republic of China: Sixteen Years of Practice' (2013) 12(3) *Chinese Journal of International Law* 589–612.

Since the Region is a free port and already free of customs duties, Hong Kong's FTAs show a particular concern for trade in services liberalisation. In these instruments, the Region binds its duty-free regime for trade in goods,[235] while, for trade in services, it strives for the liberalisation of a substantial cross-section of sectors, mostly on a negative-list approach.[236] Keen to strike good-quality deals, the Region's FTAs typically address difficult, cutting-edge topics such as market access to government procurement, trade in intellectual property rights, trade facilitation and the mutual recognition of qualifications.[237] As regards investment, Hong Kong has entered into multiple bilateral IPPAs. Specifically, under CEPA, trade in goods between the Region and mainland China is free, subject to rules of origin requirements.[238] On services, CEPA takes a negative-list approach to the liberalisation of supply through commercial presence mode. For supply through cross-border trade, consumption abroad and presence of natural persons modes as well as in telecommunications and cultural services, it takes a positive-list approach.[239] Notably, CEPA not only liberalises trade but also facilitates it. Thus, CEPA sustains three subsidiary agreements (Trade in Goods, Trade in Services, Investment, Economic and Technical Cooperation); strategies such as the Greater Bay Area initiative;[240] and, at a more global level, the Belt and Road Initiative.[241]

To conclude, further to the Basic Law, the Region's external economic policy showcases an enthusiastic and dependable champion of free trade. The external dimensions of Hong Kong's free market constitutionalism have operated efficiently, admirably so. And Hong Kong remains the model free port, the world's free port.

235 World Trade Organization, *Trade Policy Review Report by the Secretariat: Hong Kong, China (Revision)* (28 January 2015) WT/TPR/S/306/Rev.1 [2.17].

236 World Trade Organization, *Trade Policy Review Report by the Secretariat: Hong Kong, China (Revision)* (28 January 2015) WT/TPR/S/306/Rev.1 [2.17].

237 World Trade Organization, *Trade Policy Review Report by the Secretariat: Hong Kong, China (Revision)* (28 January 2015) WT/TPR/S/306/Rev.1 [2.17]; World Trade Organization, *Trade Policy Review Report by the Secretariat: Hong Kong, China (Revision)* (30 January 2019) WT/TPR/S/380/Rev.1 [2.16].

238 World Trade Organization, *Trade Policy Review Report by the Secretariat: Hong Kong, China (Revision)* (25 January 2011) WT/TPR/S/241/Rev.1 17 [16].

239 World Trade Organization, Trade Policy Review Report by the Secretariat: Hong Kong, China (Revision) (30January 2019) WT/TPR/S/380/Rev.1 [2.26].

240 World Trade Organization, *Trade Policy Review Report by the Secretariat: Hong Kong, China (Revision)* (25 January 2011) WT/TPR/S/241/Rev.1 18[20]. On the Pearl River Delta Economic Zone, see Teresa Cheng, 'Special Economic Zones: A Catalyst for International Trade and Investment in Unsettling Times?' (2019) 20(1) *Journal of World Investment & Trade* 32–67; Xin He, 'Enforcing Commercial Judgments in the Pearl River Delta of China' (2009) 57(2) *American Journal of Comparative Law* 419–456.

241 See Liu Weili, 'New Trends in International Trade and Investment Rules and China's FTA Strategy' (2017) 7(4) *Journal of WTO and China* 70–95.

7

THE FUTURE OF FREE MARKET CONSTITUTIONALISM IN HONG KONG

Introduction

A central insight of constitutional economics, the research programme to which we, in this book, subscribe, is that constitutions produce economic outcomes.[1] And different constitutions produce different economic outcomes. Some point towards economic liberty, others point away from it.[2] An efficient constitution – evolved and codified along Hayekian lines – can help to secure a good yield of public – non-rivalrous, non-excludable – goods of the kind that private interests can only undersupply, such as public infrastructure, and security and defence.[3] It can, that is, if it forestalls private interests that seek to capture the state for themselves and if it channels political and personal conflicts away from violence to electoral processes and judicial institutions[4] as the state's resolution mechanisms. Long-term domestic and foreign investments are then encouraged by constitutional safeguards of property rights[5] that disseminate, through the free flow of information, third-party judgements about whom to trust in business.[6] In their development of mutual decision-making processes, the distribution of political power and the establishment

1 Stefan Voigt, *Constitutional Economics: A Primer* (Cambridge: Cambridge University Press 2020) 20.
2 John A Dove and Andrew T Young, 'What Is a Classical Liberal Constitution?' (2021) 26(3) *The Independent Review* 385–405, 385.
3 Tom Ginsburg and Aziz Z Huq, *How to Save a Constitutional Democracy* (Chicago: University of Chicago Press 2018) 22.
4 Tom Ginsburg and Aziz Z Huq, *How to Save a Constitutional Democracy* (Chicago: University of Chicago Press 2018) 23.
5 Jon Elster, 'The Impact of Constitutions on Economic Performance' (1994) 8(1) *The World Bank Economic Review* 209–226, 216.
6 Kam Hon Chu, 'Financial Development in Hong Kong and China: A Hayekian Perspective' (2021) 41(1) *Cato Journal* 25–44, 33.

DOI: 10.4324/9780429341229-7

of limits to political conflict,[7] constitutional rules could not be more relevant to markets, the structure of which is, in many ways, 'a consequence of political decisions, a stake of political struggles, and a source of political interests and conflicts'.[8]

Over the course of little more than 180 years, Hong Kong transformed from 'a trading port to a manufacturing hub, then to a foremost financial centre of the world'.[9] We argue in previous chapters that the territory initially owed its success to the *free market constitutionalism* that naturally sprang from the limited government norms and common law traditions of the Victorian era under British colonial rule. Hong Kong ditched manufacturing for financing, not because of some top-down ingenious plan; rather, the transition emerged bottom-up, almost spontaneously, from the territory's favourable geographical location, its status as a forum for East and West, and its conventions of 'positive non-interventionism'.[10]

The trailblazing principle of 'one country, two systems' was made possible by a unique combination of historical contingencies such as the rise of a 'pragmatic, open-minded' leadership in China under Deng Xiaoping, the 'strong leadership' of the United Kingdom's Margaret Thatcher throughout the 1980s that prevented Sino-British negotiations from being derailed by any change of government in Whitehall and the implementation of Mikhail Gorbachev's *glasnost* and *perestroika* reform polices prior to the dissolution of the Soviet Union.[11] Through its adoption of a large part of the constitutional outfit of the defunct British enclave, the Hong Kong Basic Law enabled the conservation of a legal culture dependent on the traditional common law principles of contract and property. It has, consequently, travelled far in the protection of 'freedoms, … our liberty from cruel or arbitrary legal procedures, and the security of our homes, papers, effects, and other properties',[12] and in judicial independence and the rule of law, all on which the Region's free market constitutionalism rests.[13] Thus, in continuity with a long line of economic jurisprudence, the High Court recently affirmed in *Tam Sze Leung v Commissioner of*

7 See Tom Ginsburg, Mark D Rosen and Georg Vanberg 'Introduction: Liberal Constitutions During Financial Crises' in Tom Ginsburg, Mark D Rosen and Georg Vanberg (eds) *Constitutions in Times of Financial Crisis* (New York: Cambridge University Press 2019) 3–17.

8 Gerald F Davis, 'Politics and Financial Markets' in Karin Knorr Cetina and Alex Preda (eds) *The Oxford Handbook of the Sociology of Finance* (Oxford: Oxford University Press) 33–51, 36.

9 Henry Litton, *Reflections on Democracies, Autocracies and other Fallacies* (Hong Kong: Kin Kwok Printing Press 2022) 10.

10 Kam Hon Chu, 'Financial Development in Hong Kong and China: A Hayekian Perspective' (2021) 41(1) *Cato Journal* 25–44, 30.

11 Albert HY Chen and Michael Ng, 'The Making of the Constitutional Order of the Hong Kong SAR: The Role of Sino–British Diplomacy (1982–90)' in Kevin YL Tan and Michael Ng (eds), *Constitutional Foundings in Northeast Asia* (Oxford: Hart Publishing 2022) 70–71.

12 Tom W Bell, *Your Next Government: From the Nation State to Stateless Nations* (Cambridge: Cambridge University Press 2018) 115.

13 Hans H Tung, Ming-Jen Lin and Yi-Fan Lin, 'Anti-ELAB Movement, National Security Law, and Heterogeneous Institutional Trust in Hong Kong' (2021) 22 *Japanese Journal of Political Science* 287–311, 291.

Police[14] that 'access to property, or use of property' are 'constitutional rights' guaranteed by Articles 6 and 105 of the Basic Law and that 'the means by which the government may restrict those rights must be both clearly prescribed by law and proportionate'.[15] Savers of capital in Hong Kong have, accordingly, been disposed to fund enterprises, making for a vibrant financial hub given the rigorous enforcement of contractual obligations in a market free from arbitrary state interference, which can, to borrow Friedrich Hayek's words, reconcile 'different purposes for the mutual benefit' of its participants.[16] Investors in this market have been similarly disposed to improve their economic conditions through innovation and voluntary exchange given also the robust protection of private property rights.[17]

Hong Kong can distinguish itself as one of the few economies to grow out of the Third World and into the First World 'without exploiting petroleum or achieving independence from colonial rule'.[18] From China's resumption of the exercise of sovereignty over Hong Kong in 1997 until 2018 – the eve of the outbreak of 'violent public lawlessness'[19] in 2019 – the Region experienced a steady increase in gross domestic product (GDP) per capita and life expectancy in the teeth of the Asian financial crisis of 1997, the SARS outbreak of 2003, the Great Recession between 2007 and 2009 and its own Occupy Movement of 2014.[20] The Basic Law's express obligation to 'safeguard the free operation of financial business and financial markets'[21] has been and continues to be fulfilled. Drawn forth by the listing of companies from mainland China on its stock exchange, Hong Kong has emerged first in the world in raising capital for initial public offerings (IPOs), having floated US$33.5 billion worth by the fourth quarter of 2015.[22] By December 2018, its share of the global IPO market stood at 17.6 per cent, compared to 13.9 per cent for the New York Stock Exchange,[23] hence proudly establishing itself as China's window onto the world's money.[24] In

14 *Tam Sze Leung v Commissioner of Police* [2022] 1 HKLRD 480.
15 *Tam Sze Leung v Commissioner of Police* [2022] 1 HKLRD 480, 515 (Coleman J).
16 FA Hayek, 'The Principles of a Liberal Social Order' in Chiaki Nishiyama and Kurt R Leube (eds), *The Essence of Hayek* (Stanford: Hoover Institution Press 1984) 363–381, 366.
17 Robert D Cooter and Hans-Bernd Schäfer, *Solomon's Knot: How Law Can End the Poverty of Nations* (Princeton: Princeton University Press 2012).
18 Peter E Hamilton, *Made in Hong Kong: Transpacific Networks and a New History of Globalization* (New York: Columbia University Press 2021) 1.
19 *Kwok Wing Hang v Chief Executive in Council* (2020) 23 HKCFAR 518, 531 (Ma CJ, Ribeiro, Fok and Cheung PJJ and Lord Hoffmann NPJ).
20 Bernard Yeung, *Hong Kong's 2019–2020 Social Unrest: The Trigger, History and Lessons* (Singapore: World Scientific 2021) 50.
21 Basic Law of the Hong Kong Special Administrative Region of the People's Republic of China, Article 110(2).
22 Andrew Sheng, 'Financial Sector in Hong Kong, China' in Ulrich Volz, Peter J Morgan and Naoyuki Yoshino (eds), *Routledge Handbook of Banking and Finance in Asia* (New York: Routledge 2019) 39–53, 45.
23 Enoch Yiu, 'Hong Kong Regains Global IPO Crown from New York in 2018 Thanks to its Listing Reforms' *South China Morning Post* (24 December 2018).
24 David R Meyer, 'Hong Kong, Shanghai, and Beijing: China's Contenders for Global Financial Centre Leadership' in Youssef Cassis and Dariusz Wójcik (eds), *International*

2019, Hong Kong – the third most important international financial centre – was rivalling the Nasdaq Stock Market for the biggest-ever IPO of new shares.[25]

Challenges to the future of free market constitutionalism have emerged within the world's freest market economy, however. Each of the sections that follow explores how this formula has come under a different challenge in recent years. The chapter ends the book optimistically, with concluding remarks on how free market constitutionalism should still have a future in the Region.

Income Inequality

Hong Kong's legal framework mandates no universal social security, such as a pension system or a system of unemployment benefits, neither maximum working hours nor fine-tuning of economic motives by way of tax incentives.[26] Although this minimalism is, undoubtedly, a merit of Hong Kong's free market constitutionalism, it partly explains why its society is becoming ever more polarised.[27] Its Gini coefficient rose from 0.43 in 1971 to 0.539 in 2016, attesting a 'notoriously high level' of income inequality.[28] Two decades of wage stagnation[29] have disincentivised young people from saving up for the long term.[30] Income inequality has been accompanied by unaffordable housing and living costs,[31] largely consequences of land hoarding by property developers;[32] permutations in rural planning;[33] and surging real estate prices

Financial Centres after the Global Financial Crisis and Brexit (New York: Oxford University Press) 126–153.

25 Adam Tooze, *Shutdown: How Covid Shook the World's Economy* (New York: Viking 2021) 198.

26 Stephen Phua and Andrew Halkyard, 'The Impact of Tax Incentives on Economic Development in Singapore and Hong Kong' in Nolan C Sharkey (ed.), *Taxation in ASEAN and China: Local Institutions, Regionalism, Global Systems and Economic Development* (New York: Routledge 2012) 191–213.

27 Andrew Sheng, 'Financial Sector in Hong Kong, China' in Ulrich Volz, Peter J Morgan and Naoyuki Yoshino (eds), *Routledge Handbook of Banking and Finance in Asia* (New York: Routledge 2019) 39–53, 47.

28 Mathew YH Wong and Stan HW Wong, 'Income Inequality and Political Participation: A District-Level Analysis of Hong Kong Elections' (2022) *Social Indicators Research*, https://doi.org/10.1007/s11205-021-02863-9, accessed 1 May 2022.

29 Regina Ip Lau, 'The Challenges Facing the Next Chief Executive of Hong Kong in 2022: Managing Growth, Conflict, Change and Continuity' (2021) 24(2) *Public Administration and Policy: An Asia-Pacific Journal* 117–124, 119.

30 Joseph Yu-shek Cheng, 'Overall Evaluation of the C. Y. Leung Administration' in Joseph Yu-shek Cheng (ed.), *Evaluation of the C. Y. Leung Administration* (Hong Kong: City University Press 2020) 1–30, 4.

31 Mathew YH Wong and Stan HW Wong, 'Income Inequality and Political Participation: A District-Level Analysis of Hong Kong Elections' (2022) *Social Indicators Research*, https://doi.org/10.1007/s11205-021-02863-9, accessed 1 May 2022.

32 Bernard Yeung, *Hong Kong's 2019–2020 Social Unrest: The Trigger, History and Lessons* (Singapore: World Scientific 2021) 51.

33 Mee Kam Ng, 'The Making of "Violent" Hong Kong: A Centennial Dream? A Fight for Democracy? A Challenge to Humanity?' (2020) 21(3) *Planning Theory & Practice* 483–494, 492.

driven by mainland Chinese demand.[34] Regina Ip, a Non–official Member of the Executive Council, has suggested that 'the inability of large numbers of decent Hong Kong people to own affordable homes' was 'the root cause of the anger of many in our society'.[35]

In her 2021 Policy Address, Chief Executive Carrie Lam revealed that, in just four years, social expenditure had increased 'significantly' (by 62 per cent) to HK $105.7 billion (US$13.49 billion), taking the largest slice of the Region's budget out of all of the policy domains and accounting for roughly 20 per cent of recurrent government expenditure.[36] Indeed, recurrent government expenditure on cash welfare increased by 56 per cent.[37] Notably, in 2021, against an ever higher spiral of real estate prices, Hong Kong's property developers released farmland for public housing, a development with obvious (in principle) repercussions on free markets, their undoubted benefits notwithstanding.[38]

That said, the role of Hong Kong residents as champions of free market constitutionalism warrants special mention. The prevalent ethos in Hong Kong society of individual commitment to work and loyalty to the employer – sometimes described as neo-Confucianism – in addition to the forces of the free market, are considered to be 'important factors' that help to explain the 'particular pattern of development' of the Region.[39] Despite some policy detachment in contemporary times from the tradition under British colonial rule of positive non-interventionism, orthodoxly understood, most residents continue, as of old, to live up to the ethos of self-reliance.[40] That the average Hong Kong household, even among the elderly, would rather live in poverty than depend on Comprehensive Social Security Assistance in the face of unemployment is no exaggeration.[41] The results of a leading survey of local attitudes on issues like income inequality found only slight variations among residents of different socioeconomic strata: there is an 'enduring adherence to capitalism and individualism' as witness a societal consensus 'that the market is a legitimate means of distributing income; that everyone should work hard to succeed in competition with others; that those who work hard

34 Adam Tooze, *Shutdown: How Covid Shook the World's Economy* (New York: Viking 2021) 198.

35 Regina Ip Lau, 'The Challenges Facing the Next Chief Executive of Hong Kong in 2022: Managing Growth, Conflict, Change and Continuity' (2021) 24(2) *Public Administration and Policy: An Asia-Pacific Journal* 117–124, 119.

36 Carrie Lam, *The Chief Executive's 2021 Policy Address* (Hong Kong: Government of the Hong Kong Special Administrative Region 2021) [120].

37 Carrie Lam, *The Chief Executive's 2021 Policy Address* (Hong Kong: Government of the Hong Kong Special Administrative Region 2021) [122].

38 *The Economist*, 'Hong Kong's Tycoons: Check Your Privilege' (22–28 May 2021).

39 Alvin Y So, 'The Economic Success of Hong Kong: Insights from a World-System Perspective' 29(2) *Sociological Perspectives* 241–258, 242 (1986).

40 See Eric C Ip, 'The Constitution of Economic Liberty in Hong Kong' (2015) 26(3) *Constitutional Political Economy* 307–327.

41 See Leo F Goodstadt, *Poverty in the Midst of Affluence: How Hong Kong Mismanaged its Prosperity* (Hong Kong: Hong Kong University Press 2013).

should be and would be rewarded; and that economic failure is mainly an individual's own problem'.[42] This ethic still informs the Region's welfare policy.

Financial Secretary Paul Chan, in an interview by prominent mainland Chinese political scientist Eric X Li, insisted that the country's socialist policies, such as the recent 'common prosperity' campaign,[43] were not influencing Hong Kong, 'a capitalist, open and small economy'; that the Government of the Region 'believed in active non-interference and a free market'; that it has been 'trying to alleviate poverty by cash initiatives, such as social security allowance'; and that it is committed to 'equality in opportunity', which is 'different from the concept of common prosperity'.[44] In a similar vein, former Chief Secretary John Lee, elected Chief Executive in May 2022 to succeed Lam, stated in his election manifesto that 'it is crucial that Hong Kong continues to maintain its status and image as a pluralistic, inclusive and open global metropolis', 'fostering a freer and more transparent business environment based on the rule of law, thereby strengthening its vibrancy and enhancing its overall competitiveness' in line with China's 14th Five-Year Plan, which affirms Hong Kong's status as the country's 'international financial centre, international transportation centre, international trade centre; as well as centre for international legal and dispute resolution services in the Asia-Pacific region'.[45]

Social Polarisation

It is no accident for a society to undergo an upheaval of polarisation amid persistently high rates of income inequality and unaffordable housing and living costs.[46] Data from a 2015 survey on evaluations of the Region's status quo exposed a wide gap between the older generation, who had thrived in old Hong Kong, and the younger.[47] Four years later, that generational gap merged into 'a turning point' for the Region and its implementation of the Basic Law.[48] In June 2019, demonstrations against the Fugitive

42 See Timothy KY Wong, Po-San Wan and Kenneth WK Law, 'Public Perceptions of Income Inequality in Hong Kong: Trends, Causes and Implications' (2009) 18(61) *Journal of Contemporary China* 657–673.

43 See Michael Dunford, 'The Chinese Path to Common Prosperity' (2022) 12(1) *International Critical Thought* 35–54.

44 Tony Cheung, 'Hong Kong will Take Different Approach to President Xi Jinping when it Comes to Alleviating Poverty, Finance Minister tells Mainland China Academic' *South China Morning Post* (3 September 2021).

45 John Lee, *Starting A New Chapter for Hong Kong Together: Election Manifesto of Chief Executive Election 2022* (Hong Kong: John Lee Ka-chiu Election Campaign Office 2022) 19.

46 See Xinhua, 'Behind Hong Kong's Chaos Lie Deep–seated Social Problems' *China Daily Hong Kong* (7 September 2019), https://www.chinadailyhk.com.articles/144/238/1567867358984.html, accessed 9 May 2022.

47 Man Yee Karen Lee and Yan Lam Lo, 'Contesting Visions of Hong Kong's Rule of Law and Young People's Political Discontent' (2020) 29(6) *Social & Legal Studies* 858–880, 875.

48 Richard Cullen, *Hong Kong Constitutionalism: The British Legacy and the Chinese Future* (New York: Routledge 2020) 220.

Offenders and Mutual Legal Assistance in Criminal Matters Legislation (Amendment) Bill, which sought to facilitate extradition between Hong Kong, Macao, Taiwan and mainland China, brought to the surface the 'political polarisation and socioeconomic problems of Hong Kong society'.[49] Within months, the demonstrations had morphed into an insurrection typified by mass law breaking.[50] In *Kwok Wing Hang v Chief Executive in Council*,[51] Chief Justice Geoffrey Ma, Justices Roberto Ribeiro, Joseph Fok and Andrew Cheung, with Lord Hoffmann sitting as the fifth judge on the Court of Final Appeal, offered a long list of 'public order events':

> [R]epeatedly charging police cordon lines with weapons whilst wearing body armour; blocking roads, including scattering nails on roads; vandalising public facilities (including pavements, roadside fences and barriers, signs, dust bins, lamp posts, traffic lights, street lights and CCTV cameras) and Government buildings (including the [Legislative Council] Complex, Police Headquarters, Cheung Sha Wan Government Offices); setting fires at and near police stations and other public places; damaging private shopping malls, shops and restaurants; looting some of the damaged shops; damaging residential premises and harassing residents; attacking members of the public and police officers with weapons including high-powered laser pointers, slingshots, sharpened objects, bricks and inflammable liquids; throwing petrol bombs at police vehicles and police stations; damaging and obstructing the operation of critical infrastructure including Hong Kong International Airport, the Mass Transit Railway and the Cross-Harbour Tunnel; stopping motorists and extorting mobile phones or money by threatening to damage their vehicles.[52]

This series of public order events had economic repercussions. The Director of the State Council's Hong Kong and Macao Affairs Office, reportedly, called a meeting in Shenzhen on 7 August 2019 to request the Hong Kong business community to help in the restoration of stability.[53] And, in September 2019, again reportedly, the State Council's State-owned Assets Supervision and Administration Commission encouraged its largest firms to take a more involved role in Hong Kong through increased participation in its finance sector.[54] Arguably, in terms of positive non-

49 Albert HY Chen, *The Changing Legal Orders in Hong Kong and Mainland China: Essays on 'One Country, Two Systems'* (Hong Kong: City University of Hong Kong Press 2021) 387.

50 Man Yee Karen Lee and Yan Lam Lo, 'Contesting Visions of Hong Kong's Rule of Law and Young People's Political Discontent' (2020) 29(6) *Social & Legal Studies* 858–880, 875.

51 *Kwok Wing Hang v Chief Executive in Council* (2020) 23 HKCFAR 518.

52 *Kwok Wing Hang v Chief Executive in Council* (2020) 23 HKCFAR 518, 556–557 (Ma CJ, Ribeiro, Fok and Cheung PJJ, Lord Hoffmann NPJ).

53 Keith Zhai, 'Exclusive: China Prods State Firms to Boost Investment in Crisis-Hit Hong Kong' Reuters, https://www.reuters.com/article/us-hongkong-protests-soe-exclusive/exclusive-china-prods-state-firms-to-boost-investment-in-crisis-hit-hong-kong-idUSKCN1VY08C, accessed 2 May 2022.

interventionism, participation in internal corporate governance could, in the long run, yield mixed economic results.

National Security Law

Demonstrations waned in 2020 with the outbreak of the COVID-19 pandemic,[55] which prompted the enactment of the Prevention and Control of Disease (Prohibition on Gathering) Regulation (Cap 599G) and a host of social distancing regulations.[56] On 22 May 2020, a Vice–Chairman of the Standing Committee of the National People's Congress hinted that a new law would be adopted to 'plug the loophole' in Hong Kong's existing laws, including the Legislative Council's failure to enact local legislation on national security in response to the social unrest of earlier years.[57] On 30 June 2020, the Standing Committee approved the hinted-at Law on Safeguarding National Security in the Hong Kong Special Administrative Region of the People's Republic of China, commonly referred to as the National Security Law (or NSL). A 'momentous development' in the recent constitutional history of Hong Kong,[58] it aligned with the Government of the Region's wishes to 'prevent, suppress and impose punishment for the offences of secession, subversion, organisation and perpetration of terrorist activities, and collusion with a foreign country or with external elements to endanger national security in relation to the Hong Kong Special Administrative Region'.[59] Financial institutions like HSBC, Jardine Matheson, Standard Chartered and Swire soon announced their support for the new Law.[60]

Article 1 states that the National Security Law is enacted in accordance with the Basic Law. Articles 4 and 5 expressly promise respect for human rights – including those featured in the International Covenant on Civil and Political Rights – as well as 'the principle of the rule of law', so that there is 'no question of irreconcilable inconsistency between these two provisions and other provisions of the [National Security Law]'.[61] These provisions, inter alia, exempt from judicial review the

54 Mee Kam Ng, 'The Making of "Violent" Hong Kong: A Centennial Dream? A Fight for Democracy? A Challenge to Humanity?' (2020) 21(3) *Planning Theory & Practice* 483–494, 491.
55 Cora Chan, 'Subnational Constitutionalism: Hong Kong' in David S Law (ed.), *Constitutionalism in Context* (New York: Cambridge University Press 2022) 377–402, 386.
56 John M Carroll, *The Hong Kong–China Nexus* (Cambridge: Cambridge University Press 2022) 72.
57 Albert HY Chen, *The Changing Legal Orders in Hong Kong and Mainland China: Essays on 'One Country, Two Systems'* (Hong Kong: City University of Hong Kong Press 2021) 389.
58 Cora Chan, 'Subnational Constitutionalism: Hong Kong' in David S Law (ed.), *Constitutionalism in Context* (New York: Cambridge University Press 2022) 377–402, 390.
59 The Law of the People's Republic of China on Safeguarding National Security in the Hong Kong Special Administrative Region (Adopted at the 20th session of the Standing Committee of the 13th National People's Congress on 30 June 2020), Article 1.
60 Adam Tooze, *Shutdown: How Covid Shook the World's Economy* (New York: Viking 2021) 200.

decisions of the statutory Committee for Safeguarding National Security, chaired by the Chief Executive,[62] and remove from the jurisdiction of the Region the acts and staff of the Office for Safeguarding National Security of the Central People's Government in the course of the performance of duty.[63] In the wake of the National Security Law, '[m]any anti-China and anti-Hong Kong organizations have disbanded, suspended activities, died down, or operated in a low-key manner', according to Lau Siu-kai, Vice-President of the State Council's Chinese Association of Hong Kong and Macao Studies, who also stated that '[t]he vast majority of opposition members in the Legislative Council have already left and can no longer interfere with the administration of the government by paralyzing the operation of the legislature'.[64]

The courts have, in their best endeavour, reconciled this statute with common law principles.[65] In *HKSAR v Lai Chee Ying*,[66] Chief Justice Andrew Cheung, Justices Roberto Ribeiro and Joseph Fok, with Non–Permanent Judges Patrick Chan and Frank Stock of the Court of Final Appeal, ruled that, although 'there is no [judicial] power to hold any provision of the NSL to be unconstitutional or invalid as incompatible with the Basic Law and Bill of Rights', it cannot be that 'human rights and freedoms and rule of law values are inapplicable'; but 'rights, freedoms and values are to be protected and adhered to in applying the NSL'.[67] In *Tong Ying Kit v Secretary for Justice*,[68] Chief Judge of the High Court Jeremy Poon, on behalf of the Court of Appeal, ruled that the 'well-established common law technique of purposive and contextual construction'[69] remains fully applicable to the construction of the National Security Law. What is more, any provision of the Law 'has to be read together with' the Hong Kong Bill of Rights, which domesticated the International Covenant on Civil and Political Rights, 'to ensure that the defendant's constitutional right to a fair trial as embodied in those provisions is not compromised'.[70]

61 Johannes Chan, 'Judicial Responses to the National Security Law: *HKSAR v Lai Chee Ying*' (2021) 51(1) *Hong Kong Law Journal* 1–13, 6.
62 The Law of the People's Republic of China on Safeguarding National Security in the Hong Kong Special Administrative Region (Adopted at the 20th session of the Standing Committee of the 13th National People's Congress on 30 June 2020), Article 14.
63 The Law of the People's Republic of China on Safeguarding National Security in the Hong Kong Special Administrative Region (Adopted at the 20th session of the Standing Committee of the 13th National People's Congress on 30 June 2020), Article 60.
64 Siu-kai Lau, 'The National Security Law: Political and Social Effects on the Governance of the Hong Kong Special Administrative Region' (2021) 24(3) *Public Administration and Policy: An Asia-Pacific Journal* 234–240, 235.
65 Hingchau Lam, 'The Ouster Clause in the Hong Kong National Security Law: Its Effectiveness in the Common Law and its Implications for the Rule of Law' (2021) 76 *Crime, Law and Social Change* 543–561, 559.
66 *HKSAR v Lai Chee Ying* (2021) 24 HKCFAR 33.
67 *HKSAR v Lai Chee Ying* (2021) 24 HKCFAR 33, 55 (Cheung CJ, Ribeiro and Fok PJJ, Chan and Stock NPJJ).
68 *Tong Ying Kit v Secretary for Justice* [2021] 3 HKLRD 350.
69 *Tong Ying Kit v Secretary for Justice* [2021] 3 HKLRD 350, 362 (Poon CJHC).
70 *Tong Ying Kit v Secretary for Justice* [2021] 3 HKLRD 350, 365 (Poon CJHC).

That the courts are able to and do indeed construe the National Security Law in accordance with common law principles and practices is a reaffirmation of the 'one country, two systems' principle.[71] Even so, Lord Reed and Lord Hodge, President and Deputy President of the Supreme Court of the United Kingdom, resigned, on 30 March 2022, as Non–Permanent Judges of the Hong Kong Court of Final Appeal, in response to their and the Government of the United Kingdom's perception of developments around the National Security Law, yet affirming that '[t]he courts in Hong Kong continue to be internationally respected for their commitment to the rule of law'.[72] Retired Justice of the Supreme Court of the United Kingdom, Lord Sumption, who decided to stay on the Hong Kong Court of Final Appeal, observed that '[i]t is not a proper function of judges to participate in political boycotts', for '[t]hey will serve the cause of justice better by participating in the work of Hong Kong's courts'.[73]

Overhaul of the Electoral System

The enactment of the National Security Law was not the sole milestone in Hong Kong's recent constitutional history.[74] On 11 March 2021, the National People's Congress resolved that only 'patriots' can govern the Region under a 'democracy with Hong Kong characteristics'.[75] On 30 March 2021, in what turned out to be an overhaul of the Region's electoral system, the Standing Committee amended Annex I of the Basic Law to expand the Election Committee,[76] which elects the Chief Executive, to consist thereafter of 1,500 members from five 'sectors': (1) the industrial, commercial and financial sectors; (2) the professions; (3) grassroots, labour, religious and other sectors; (4) Members of the Legislative Council, representatives of district organisations and other organisations; and, (5), Hong Kong deputies to the National People's Congress, Hong Kong members of the National Committee of the Chinese People's Political Consultative Conference and representatives of Hong Kong members of relevant national organisations.[77] On the

71 Hingchau Lam, 'The Ouster Clause in the Hong Kong National Security Law: Its Effectiveness in the Common Law and its Implications for the Rule of Law' (2021) 76 *Crime, Law and Social Change* 543–561, 547.

72 Lord Reed, 'Role of UK Supreme Court judges on the Hong Kong Court of Final Appeal – Update' (30 March 2022), https://www.supremecourt.uk/news/role-of-uk-judges-on-the-hong-kong-court-of-final-appeal-update-march-2022.html, accessed 1 May 2022.

73 Lord Sumption, 'Britain should Avoid Undermining the Hong Kong Judiciary' *The Times* (18 March 2021).

74 John D Wong, 'Constructing the Legitimacy of Governance in Hong Kong: "Prosperity and Stability" Meets "Democracy and Freedom"' (2022) 81(1) *The Journal of Asian Studies* 43–61, 58.

75 John M Carroll, *The Hong Kong–China Nexus* (Cambridge: Cambridge University Press 2022) 73.

76 Basic Law of the Hong Kong Special Administrative Region of the People's Republic of China, Article 45(1).

same day, the Standing Committee adopted an amendment to Annex II empowering the Election Committee to nominate candidates for Legislative Council seats as well as to elect 40 of its 90 members. The other 50 seats fell to 20 members popularly elected in geographical constituencies and 30 from functional constituencies. One observable effect of this electoral system overhaul is that business influence over the selection of the Chief Executive and members of the Legislative Council has been moderated by the inclusion of a more political class on the Election Committee and the Legislative Council;[78] the consequences of this development for free market constitutionalism are yet to be known. The State Council Information Office explained, in a 2021 white paper, that these changes were 'to ensure that … those who seek to overturn Hong Kong's constitutional order and destabilize Hong Kong are disbarred from participation in Hong Kong's government system'.[79] In the same document, the State Council Information Office signalled that the Central People's Government 'will work with all social groups, sectors and stakeholders towards the ultimate goal of election by universal suffrage of the Chief Executive and all members of the Legislative Council'.[80]

COVID–19 Pandemic

Everywhere in the world, COVID–19 has become the catalyst for state intervention, even by self-professed libertarian leaders such as former Prime Minister of the United Kingdom, Boris Johnson, thrusting the economy into 'hopeless calculational chaos'.[81] Non-pharmaceutical interventions – such as social distancing measures and mass quarantines – impose sometimes economically inviable limits on the public accessibility and operational practice of businesses.[82]

That is the principle. The practice, it seems, follows also. The public health crisis that COVID-19 has brought to Hong Kong has affected the local economy, which has suffered the largest decline on record. High Court Judge Russell Coleman, in *Law Yee Mei v Chief Executive of Hong Kong SAR*,[83] spoke about the Region's COVID–19 emergency measures, thus:

77 Decision of the National People's Congress on Improving the Electoral System of the Hong Kong Special Administrative Region (Adopted at the Fourth Session of the Thirteenth National People's Congress on 11 March 2021).

78 *The Economist*, 'Hong Kong's Tycoons: Check Your Privilege' (22–28 May 2021) 52–53.

79 State Council Information Office of the People's Republic of China, *Hong Kong Democratic Progress Under the Framework of One Country, Two Systems* (Beijing: Foreign Language Press 2021) 41.

80 State Council Information Office of the People's Republic of China, *Hong Kong Democratic Progress Under the Framework of One Country, Two Systems* (Beijing: Foreign Language Press 2021) 55.

81 Murray Rothbard, *For a New Liberty* (Auburn: Mises Institute Press 2020) 248.

82 Vincent Geloso, Kelly Hyde and Ilia Murtazashvili, 'Pandemics, Economic Freedom, and Institutional Trade–offs' (2021) *European Journal of Law and Economics* 1–25, https://doi.org/10.1007/s10657-021-09704-7, accessed 2 May 2022.

83 *Law Yee Mei v Chief Executive of Hong Kong SAR* [2022] HKCFI 688.

> There may well be room for people to say that a number of decisions and announcements made by the HKSAR Government relating to the Covid–19 pandemic have seemed to be: lacking in logic or common sense; riddled with inconsistencies; short on empathy and human understanding; detached from local personal and business realities; focused on distractions, hence being reactive to what seems urgent at the expense of being proactive to what is important; blind to the need for a coherent longer-term strategy and contingency planning and the clear public communication of it; and sometimes even apparently contrary to the very 'science' which is invoked to justify them.[84]

To bail out the economy, the Government of the Region rolled out three rounds of first-ever relief measures, involving some HK$191.5 billion. These measures are over and above the HK$120 billion relief package in the 2020–2021 budget.[85] And to specifically deal with the outbreak of the Omicron variant, Financial Secretary Chan pledged to hand out cash vouchers worth HK$10,000 (US$1,280) to each of Hong Kong's 6.6 million adult residents, in spite of the estimated consolidated deficit in 2022–2023 climbing to HK$56 billion.[86]

Hong Kong's 'zero-COVID' restrictions[87] have coincided with an exit of business talent.[88] A mid-2021 survey of members of The American Chamber of Commerce in Hong Kong found that 42 per cent of 325 respondents were either considering or planning to leave.[89] The departure from Hong Kong of regional headquarters or offices of dozens of international companies in recent years is, reportedly, contributing to the highest rate of commercial real estate vacancies in 15 years.[90] An survey in early 2022 found that nearly half of European businesses in

84 *Law Yee Mei v Chief Executive of Hong Kong SAR* [2022] HKCFI 688, [2] (Coleman J).

85 Ho-him Chan, 'Hong Kong to Give Out Spending Vouchers as Covid Cases Hit Record Level' Financial Times (23 February 2022), https://www.ft.com/content/196eee9a-d8c1-434d-971a-42745b7f33f9, accessed 2 May 2022.

86 Ho-him Chan, 'Hong Kong to Give Out Spending Vouchers as Covid Cases Hit Record Level' Financial Times (23 February 2022), https://www.ft.com/content/196eee9a-d8c1-434d-971a-42745b7f33f9, accessed 2 May 2022.

87 Lilian Cheng and Gigi Choy, 'Coronavirus: Hong Kong Leader Concedes Anti-pandemic Measures Contributed to Brain Drain, "Fully Understands" Anxiety of Diplomats, Business Delegates' *South China Morning Post* (30 March 2022).

88 Lilian Cheng and Gigi Choy, 'Coronavirus: Hong Kong Leader Concedes Anti-pandemic Measures Contributed to Brain Drain, "Fully Understands" Anxiety of Diplomats, Business Delegates' *South China Morning Post* (30 March 2022).

89 John Lyons and Frances Yoon, '"Do We Need to Be in Hong Kong?" Global Companies Are Eying the Exits; Buffeted by Political Upheaval, A Crackdown by Mainland China and the Pandemic, Global Companies are Heading for Rival Cities such as Singapore and Shanghai' *The Wall Street Journal (Online)* (7 June 2021), https://www.wsj.com/articles/hong-kong-global-companies-leaving-protests-china-crackdown-11622998192, accessed 2 May 2022.

90 John Lyons and Frances Yoon, '"Do We Need to Be in Hong Kong?" Global Companies Are Eying the Exits; Buffeted by Political Upheaval, A Crackdown by Mainland China and the Pandemic, Global Companies are Heading for Rival Cities such as Singapore and

the Region were contemplating relocating elsewhere within a year.[91] Chief Executive Lam's response was that, in spite of their 'temporary' impact on foreign confidence, strict public health measures were necessary to prevent the Region from 'serving as a loophole for imported cases that will affect Hong Kong and the mainland'.[92]

Hong Kong's Economic Relations with Mainland China

The China–United States (US) trade war[93] has, in recent years, spilled over into Hong Kong, perhaps inevitably so, given the Region's traditionally 'significant role' in balancing bilateral trade[94] between the world's two largest economies. The US – Hong Kong's third largest trading partner – responded to the introduction of the National Security Law on 14 July 2020 when President Donald Trump signed into law the Hong Kong Autonomy Act under which he issued an Executive Order on Hong Kong Normalization, determining that the Region is 'no longer sufficiently autonomous to justify differential treatment'[95] for the purposes of export control regulations. In spite of the presumably disruptive impact[96] of this measure on the operation of Hong Kong's autonomy as a customs territory under the Basic Law, relative to other parts of China, the Region continues to occupy a position of great importance in the global economy[97] thanks to its geopolitical location and its constitutional right to negotiate and conclude trade and investment agreements and arrangements with other customs territories.[98]

Shanghai' *The Wall Street Journal (Online)* (7 June 2021), https://www.wsj.com/articles/hong-kong-global-companies-leaving-protests-china-crackdown-11622998192, accessed 2 May 2022.

91 Lilian Cheng and Gigi Choy, 'Coronavirus: Hong Kong Leader Concedes Anti-pandemic Measures Contributed to Brain Drain, "Fully Understands" Anxiety of Diplomats, Business Delegates' *South China Morning Post* (30 March 2022).

92 Lilian Cheng and Gigi Choy, 'Coronavirus: Hong Kong Leader Concedes Anti-pandemic Measures Contributed to Brain Drain, "Fully Understands" Anxiety of Diplomats, Business Delegates' *South China Morning Post* (30 March 2022).

93 Richard Cullen, *Hong Kong Constitutionalism: The British Legacy and the Chinese Future* (New York: Routledge 2020) 222.

94 Bruce VonCannon, *Status Anxiety: Hong Kong's Crisis of Identity* (Singapore: Palgrave Macmillan 2021) 40.

95 Executive Order 13936, The President's Executive Order on Hong Kong Normalization, 85 Fed Reg 43413 (14 July 2020). See Elizabeth Peters, 'Targeted Economic Sanctions in Light of the Hong Kong Autonomy Act and US –China Tensions' (2020) 25 *North Carolina Banking Institute* 529–564.

96 Kerry Liu, 'Hong Kong: Inevitably Irrelevant to China?' (2020) 40(1) *Economic Affairs* 2–23, 17.

97 Jie Liu and Congyan Cai, 'From Hong Kong Policy Act of 1992 to Hong Kong Human Rights and Democracy Act of 2019: The Evolution of the US's Hong Kong Policy in the Context of the Rise of China' (2020) 13(1) *Journal of East Asia and International Law* 7–20, 19.

98 Mee Kam Ng, 'The Making of "Violent" Hong Kong: A Centennial Dream? A Fight for Democracy? A Challenge to Humanity?' (2020) 21(3) *Planning Theory & Practice* 483–494, 490.

Hong Kong is well known for being mainland China's 'all-purpose window' onto the world's capital markets, its financial sector offering the gamut of intermediary services to the global economy: asset management, corporate finance, dealing and brokering, investment advice, and mergers and acquisitions skills.[99] Chinese companies are still keen on being listed on the Hong Kong Stock Exchange because of its advanced market regulatory structures, legal and accounting services, and world class communications and logistics facilities. By connecting with the Region, they are able to absorb best practices in accounting, management, and compliance. Not surprisingly, in the year following the enactment of the National Security Law, capital raised through IPOs on the Hong Kong Stock Exchange, mostly by mainland Chinese companies, exceeded HK$500 billion (US $63.8 billion), a more than 50 per cent increase year over year.[100]

Mainland China needs access to US dollars and gets it from Hong Kong's currency peg.[101] China's capital controls make the use of the RMB in international transactions lag behind its economic strength.[102] Hong Kong's free currency and capital markets furnish to Beijing an offshore laboratory to experiment with monetary innovations that it would otherwise be cautious to introject 'onshore', kept under strict embargo as by restrictions on convertibility.[103] The Region's financial freedom allows China's monetary agencies to keep financial instability on the mainland at bay, while availing themselves of RMB liquidity for offshore operations.[104] Indeed, as at 2016, up to 70 per cent of the trade settled in RMB moves between Hong Kong and mainland China, which, in reality, is naught but a shuttling of cash between Chinese enterprises and their offshore subsidiaries.[105] A set of agreements between the People's Bank of China and the Hong Kong Monetary Authority has made Hong Kong into the global hub of offshore RMB business.

In August 2019, the Central Committee of the Communist Party of China and the State Council released a document titled 'Opinions on Supporting Shenzhen in

99 David R Meyer, 'Hong Kong, Shanghai, and Beijing: China's Contenders for Global Financial Centre Leadership' in Youssef Cassis and Dariusz Wójcik (eds), *International Financial Centres after the Global Financial Crisis and Brexit* (New York: Oxford University Press) 126–153.

100 Government of the Hong Kong Special Administrative Region, *Report on Hong Kong's Business Environment: A Place with Unique Advantages and Unlimited Opportunities* (Hong Kong: Government of the Hong Kong Special Administrative Region 2021) 28.

101 See Bob Tricker and Gregg Li, *Understanding Corporate Governance in China* (Hong Kong: Hong Kong University Press 2019).

102 Yun-Wing Sung, 'Becoming Part of One National Economy: Maintaining Two Systems in the Midst of the Rise of China' in Tai-lok Lui, Stephen WK Chiu and Ray Yep (eds), *Routledge Handbook of Contemporary Hong Kong* (New York: Routledge 2018) 66–86, 79.

103 Benjamin J Cohen, *Currency Statecraft: Monetary Rivalry and Geopolitical Ambition* (Chicago: The University of Chicago Press 2019) 79.

104 See Paola Subacchi, *The People's Money: How China is Building a Global Currency* (New York: Columbia University Press 2017).

105 See Ho-fung Hung, 'Chinese State Capitalism in Hong Kong' in Tai-lok Lui, Stephen WK Chiu and Ray Yep (eds), *Routledge Handbook of Contemporary Hong Kong* (New York: Routledge 2018) 430–447.

Building a Pioneering Demonstration Zone for Socialism with Chinese Characteristics', exciting speculation that it was 'a policy direction of boosting Shenzhen and dumping Hong Kong'.[106] In December 2019, Beijing announced a policy suite for turning the neighbouring Macao Special Administrative Region into a financial centre for the purpose of expanding RMB businesses, among other things.[107] And in June 2020, the Central Committee of the Communist Party of China and the State Council released a master plan to transform Hainan into the country's largest free trade port by 2035, including the liberalisation of its finance and capital mobility.[108] Neither Macao nor Hainan could compete with Hong Kong's sophisticated financial markets, at least not immediately, but these initiatives[109] certainly encourage the Region and its residents to consider the development of the Hong Kong brand as Asia's world city – its comparative advantage – into the future.[110]

More optimistically, the fundamental issue is not the decreasing size of the Hong Kong economy relative to that of mainland China or even that of Guangdong Province but the relevance of its comparative advantage, that is, 'the ability to do things in Hong Kong which cannot be done in the rest of China'.[111] Hong Kong's most formidable competitors on the mainland – Shanghai and Shenzhen – are not likely to supersede the Region anytime soon. Their ability, in particular, to supply the full range of financial products is held back by state-imposed capital controls[112] and the lack of a fully convertible currency.[113] Neither is Beijing likely to cede to Shanghai and Shenzhen a business culture predisposed to prudent financial control. Ultimately, the Chinese state is unlikely to relinquish tight regulation of cross-border monetary flows or forgo provision of finance to the economy by state-owned banks in the near future[114] since, under 'the guidance of Marxism–Leninism',[115] the Constitution in Article 7 proclaims '[t]he state sector of the economy, that is, the sector of the socialist

106 Tin-yai Ko, 'What Does the New Shenzhen Reform Plan Mean for Hong Kong?' *Hong Kong Economic Journal* (21 August 2019), https://www.ejinsight.com/eji/article/id/2226150/20190821-What-does-the-new-Shenzhen-reform-plan-mean-for-Hong-Kong, accessed 2 May 2022.

107 See Yu-wai Vic Li, 'The Irreplaceable Outpost? Whither Hong Kong in China's Financial Future' (2020) 20(3) *China Review* 261–278.

108 Kam Hon Chu, 'Financial Development in Hong Kong and China: A Hayekian Perspective' (2021) 41(1) *Cato Journal* 25–44, 28.

109 Kerry Liu, 'Hong Kong: Inevitably Irrelevant to China?' (2020) 40(1) *Economic Affairs* 2–23, 17.

110 Hualing Fu, 'One Country, Two Systems: A Critical Analysis of Benny Tai's Account' (2020) 29(1) *Social & Legal Studies* 128–133, 133.

111 Tim Summers, *China's Hong Kong* (Newcastle upon Tyne: Agenda Publishing 2019) 136.

112 Jiangyuan Fu and Bryan Mercurio, 'Do Beijing's Capital Controls Bind Hong Kong? Reality or Illusion' (2021) 9(1) *The Chinese Journal of Comparative Law* 109-122.

113 See Damian Tobin and Ulwich Volz, 'The Development and Transformation of the Financial System in the People's Republic of China' in Volz U, Morgan PJ, Yoshino N (eds), *Routledge Handbook of Banking and Financial Asia* (New York: Routledge 2019) 15–38.

114 Bob Tricker and Gregg Li, *Understanding Corporate Governance in China* (Hong Kong: Hong Kong University Press 2019).

115 Constitution of the People's Republic of China (Adopted at the Fifth Session of the Fifth National People's Congress and promulgated by the Announcement of the

economy under ownership by the whole people … [as] the leading force in the economy'.[116] If constitutionally protected openness to foreign investment, entrenched internationalisation of capital markets, advanced financial services and infrastructure[117] and free convertibility of currency[118] were forthcoming in Shanghai and Shenzhen, then, Hong Kong would, in all probability, lose (and quickly so) its top ranking as the country's financial centre, but, even then, the ideals and institutions of free market constitutionalism that it has modelled for almost two centuries would remain endlessly influential.

Conclusion

Whether Hong Kong stays relevant to China depends, in large part, on the continuity of its free market constitutionalism, which, in turn, depends on the commitment of China's central authorities and those of the Region's to this ideal. And this ideal is about institutions, not resources, '[t]he people, not the place, are responsible for the success' of Hong Kong's free market economy.[119] The invisible hand of positive non-interventionism turned the territory into an international financial centre without state planning at any level of sophistication.[120] Thanks to its constitution of economic liberty, codified in the Basic Law, Hong Kong continues to be 'the quintessential free trade port on the planet', having a role to play in mustering capital and furthering trade.[121] The raft of challenges that this chapter outlines notwithstanding, Hong Kong's economic importance cannot disappear overnight or be displaced by competitors like Shanghai, Shenzhen or even Singapore, due to its geographical proximity to South China where it should 'remain significant and as a facilitator between East and West'.[122] Companies should continue to be drawn to the Region to tap into the myriad international and Chinese networks of capital that congregate there.[123] Hong Kong truly remains Asia's world city, offering a world of opportunities for trade and commerce.

National People's Congress on 4 December 1982; last amendment adopted at the First Session of the Thirteenth National People's Congress on 11 March 2018), Preamble.

116 Constitution of the People's Republic of China, Article 7.

117 See Michael Siam Heng and Mu Yang, *Global Financial Crisis and Challenges for China* (Singapore: World Scientific 2012).

118 See Tim Summers, *China's Hong Kong* (Newcastle upon Tyne: Agenda Publishing 2019).

119 See Martin Purbrick, 'A Report of the 2019 Hong Kong' (2019) 50(4) *Asian Affairs* 465–487, 483.

120 Kam Hon Chu, 'Financial Development in Hong Kong and China: A Hayekian Perspective' (2021) 41(1) *Cato Journal* 25–44, 30.

121 Bruce VonCannon, *Status Anxiety: Hong Kong's Crisis of Identity* (Singapore: Palgrave Macmillan 2021) 100.

122 Bruce VonCannon, *Status Anxiety: Hong Kong's Crisis of Identity* (Singapore: Palgrave Macmillan 2021) 100.

123 David R Meyer, 'Hong Kong, Shanghai, and Beijing: China's Contenders for Global Financial Centre Leadership' in Youssef Cassis and Dariusz Wójcik (eds), *International Financial Centres after the Global Financial Crisis and Brexit* (New York: Oxford University Press) 126–153, 132.

James M Buchanan once argued that some form of 'mythology' is necessary for a constitution to be perennially enforceable.[124] A sustainable Basic Law embodying a classically liberal economic constitution needs to show credible evidence to all major stakeholders that property rights and contractual obligations will never be without enforcement; that the Government of the Region, backed by Beijing, holds itself self-interested in maintaining Hong Kong's standing as an international financial centre nonpareil, having a firm commitment to the principles of the free market and the rule of law; and that China has such a strong interest in upholding the Basic Law that it cannot rationally forgo to invest in a place where investor interests are honoured by the political authorities[125] and by competent, impartial judges. Whether Hong Kong's free market constitutionalism will continue in the decades to come – the key question for the Region's place in the global economy – depends on whether its constitutional self-fulfilling prophecy will indeed continue to be fulfilled.[126]

China's resumption of the exercise of sovereignty over Hong Kong on 1 July 1997 did not change Hong Kong's capitalist system and way of life.[127] The Basic Law assured the continuity of the constitutional foundations of economic liberty, serving to undergird the markets for foreign exchange, gold, securities, futures and so forth, and to maintain the free flow of capital within, into, and out of the new Special Administrative Region, in continuity, that is, with the Victorian uncodified constitution under British colonial rule. One of the paradoxes of the economic constitution of Hong Kong is that its free capital markets have empowered mainland China to keep its economy partially, appropriately, closed even while reaping the benefits of connection with global markets, avoiding a fundamental overhaul of its socioeconomic – socialist – fabric.[128] A no less significant paradox is the increasing importance of preserving Hong Kong's economic liberty for the sake of the mainland's own financial sustainability while it strengthens its Marxist–Leninist political institutions. Were China to model the legal and economic systems of its other municipalities on Hong Kong, the Region's strategic importance would decline. But this prospect is unlikely in the near future and so the Region, in principle, remains 'disproportionately useful'[129] and 'the territory's value as a gateway remains'.[130]

124 James M Buchanan, *Explorations into Constitutional Economics* (College Station: Texas A&M University Press 1989) 146–147.

125 See Kelvin Hiu Fai Kwok, 'Antitrust Enforcement and State Restraints at the Mainland China–Hong Kong Interface: The Importance of Bilateral Antitrust Co-operation' (2017) 12(2) *Asian Journal of Comparative Law* 335, 338.

126 See Eric C Ip, 'Constitutional Finance: The Role of the Hong Kong Basic Law During the Global Financial Crisis' (2019) 49(1) *Hong Kong Law Journal* 295–314.

127 Basic Law of the Hong Kong Special Administrative Region of the People's Republic of China, Article 5.

128 Matthias Vanhullebusch, 'Finance, Rule of Law and Human Rights in China' in Jiaxing Hu, Matthias Vanhullebusch and Andrew Harding (eds), *Finance, Rule of Law and Development in Asia: Perspectives from Singapore, Hong Kong and Mainland China* (Leiden: Brill 2016) 168–194.

129 *The Economist*, 'Hong Kong's Tycoons: Check Your Privilege' (10–16 August 2019).

130 *The Economist*, 'A Tale of Three Cities' (2–8 July 2022).

In an address delivered in Hong Kong on 1 July 2022 to celebrate the 25th anniversary of Hong Kong's return to China and the inaugural ceremony of the sixth-term government of the Hong Kong Special Administrative Region, President Xi Jinping said that, '[s]ince its return', Hong Kong 'has been breaking new ground, functioning as an important bridge between the Chinese mainland and the rest of the world' and '[a]s a result, it has made irreplaceable contributions to our country's economic miracle'.[131] Hong Kong, he said, has maintained 'its status as an international financial, shipping, and trading center'[132] and 'has remained one of the most liberal and open economies in the world'.[133] These advancements, Xi explained, are attributable to 'the success of "one country, two systems"'[134] to which he referred in these words:

> Today, I would like to stress again that 'one country, two systems' has been tested repeatedly in practice. It serves the fundamental interests of not only Hong Kong and Macao, but also the whole country and the nation. It has gained wide support from the 1.4 billion-plus Chinese people including the residents of Hong Kong and Macao. It is also widely accepted by the international community. There is no reason for us to change such a good policy, and we must adhere to it in the long run.[135]

Xi expressed the full support of the Central Government for the Region 'in its effort to maintain its distinctive status and edges, to improve its presence as an international financial, shipping, and trading center, to keep its business environment free, open, and regulated, and to maintain the common law, so as to expand and facilitate its exchanges with the world'.[136]

131 Xi Jinping, Address at the Meeting Celebrating the 25th Anniversary of Hong Kong's Return to the Motherland and the Inaugural Ceremony of the Sixth-Term Government of the Hong Kong Special Administrative Region (Hong Kong: Joint Publishing 2022) 2–3.
132 Xi Jinping, Address at the Meeting Celebrating the 25th Anniversary of Hong Kong's Return to the Motherland and the Inaugural Ceremony of the Sixth-Term Government of the Hong Kong Special Administrative Region (Hong Kong: Joint Publishing 2022) 3.
133 Xi Jinping, Address at the Meeting Celebrating the 25th Anniversary of Hong Kong's Return to the Motherland and the Inaugural Ceremony of the Sixth-Term Government of the Hong Kong Special Administrative Region (Hong Kong: Joint Publishing 2022) 3–4.
134 Xi Jinping, Address at the Meeting Celebrating the 25th Anniversary of Hong Kong's Return to the Motherland and the Inaugural Ceremony of the Sixth-Term Government of the Hong Kong Special Administrative Region (Hong Kong: Joint Publishing 2022) 2.
135 Xi Jinping, Address at the Meeting Celebrating the 25th Anniversary of Hong Kong's Return to the Motherland and the Inaugural Ceremony of the Sixth-Term Government of the Hong Kong Special Administrative Region (Hong Kong: Joint Publishing 2022) 5–6.
136 Xi Jinping, Address at the Meeting Celebrating the 25th Anniversary of Hong Kong's Return to the Motherland and the Inaugural Ceremony of the Sixth-Term

Beijing has, in fact, been cautiously yet heavily relying on Hong Kong's free market constitutionalism to cement its position in the global economy, while multinationals in emerging markets without convenient access to China have found in Hong Kong a viable alternative, unlike New York or London. No Chinese city since 1949 could have facilitated China's insertion into the world's currency markets as 'smoothly and safely' as Hong Kong.[137] In the final analysis, the free market constitutionalism of the Hong Kong Special Administrative Region of the People's Republic of China stands or falls on the mainland's perception of its utility. The Region has its work cut out to reinforce just that perception.

We believe that there is cause for hope.

Government of the Hong Kong Special Administrative Region (Hong Kong: Joint Publishing 2022) 9.

137 Leo F Goodstadt, *A City Mismanaged: Hong Kong's Struggle for Survival* (Hong Kong: Hong Kong University Press 2018) 161.

INDEX

For Product Safety Concerns and Information please contact our EU
representative GPSR@taylorandfrancis.com
Taylor & Francis Verlag GmbH, Kaufingerstraße 24, 80331 München, Germany

www.ingramcontent.com/pod-product-compliance
Ingram Content Group UK Ltd.
Pitfield, Milton Keynes, MK11 3LW, UK
UKHW020139200926
475702UK00005B/827
* 9 7 8 0 3 6 7 3 5 7 0 7 8 *